Frances Owen

Mrs. Owen's cook book, and useful hints for the household

Frances Owen

Mrs. Owen's cook book, and useful hints for the household

ISBN/EAN: 9783744785914

Printed in Europe, USA, Canada, Australia, Japan

Cover: Foto ©Lupo / pixelio.de

More available books at **www.hansebooks.com**

MRS. OWENS'

COOK BOOK,

AND

USEFUL HINTS

FOR THE

HOUSEHOLD.

By MRS. FRANCES E. OWENS.

CHICAGO, ILL.:
Household Publishing Society,
530 FULTON STREET.
J. D. SMILEY, PUBLISHER.
1882.

TO THOSE
UNTIRING WORKERS,
WHO ARE COMPELLED TO ADD TO THE
RESPONSIBLE POSITIONS OF WIVES AND MOTHERS
THE CARES AND PERPLEXITIES
OF HOUSEKEEPERS, WHOSE ANXIOUS LABORS
I HAVE SHARED,
I RESPECTFULLY DEDICATE
THIS BOOK,
WITH THE FOND HOPE THAT IT WILL HELP
LIGHTEN THEIR BURDENS.

PREFACE.

Every housewife has a notably good way of doing certain things. The province of this book is to present a large number of these successes in a cheap and convenient form for daily reference.

Since it became known that I had undertaken to publish this little book, letters have come to me from friends living in all sections, containing choice cooking recipes and hints for the household, culled from practical every day experience. In many cases the writers had collected from their immediate friends, thus adding to the number.

The different departments will be found sufficiently elaborate for almost any occasion in an ordinary domestic life.

But the special object of this work is to help those of our sisterhood who unite the qualities of wives, mothers and house maids. And the easiest way has been selected whenever a choice could be made with that end in view.

The housewife whose means are unrestricted need not study the little harrowing details of trying to make one dollar do duty for five in providing for her table. But the masses, from sheer necessity, must count their pennies and tighten their purse strings when tempted to indulge the appetite beyond a prescribed limit.

There are suggestions in these pages which, if carried out, will vary a bill of fare and make it pleasing to the eye and appetizing to the palate at the smallest possible outlay of money.

In the section devoted to "HASH" there are directions for using up remnants of food that will go very far towards furnishing the bulk of one meal per day to a family. These dishes are palatable, too, and very distinct from the cheap boarding-house commodity know by that name.

"THE LAUNDRY" hints, if acted upon, will add years to the lives of our women who toil. I know whereof I speak. A woman with a house full of little ones, having but two hands to do the work which would give employment to six, must husband her strength if she would be spared to her children. It is worse than folly to devote ten hours to a task which may be accomplished in five. These aids will make that difference. Give them one month's trial, and the old ways will belong to the dead past, never to be revived.

Mrs. Owens' Cook Book.

SOUPS.

Soup bones or soup meat should be put to cook in plenty of cold water and simmer, not boil. As soon as the scum rises, take it off.

Beef is considered the best meat for a stand by, but we subjoin recipes that include other kinds, all of which will be found palatable. It is well to keep a stock pot of meat broth on hand for soups. Any bits of bones or trimmings, the bones from roasts, the tough ends from porter-house steaks, or the cold bits of cooked meats, or fowls, should be put into it, and when cooked done the broth should be strained through a colander, and into an earthern vessel, for future use. This may then be made the basis of almost any kind of soup; maccaroni, vermicelli, different vegetables, rice, or noodle. Keep it in a cool place; take off the fat that rises.

Force meat balls for soup are made of cooked meat or fowl, minced fine, and seasoned well, and bound together with egg. Roll in cracker or bread crumbs, and fry in hot lard in balls the size of the yolk of an egg.

CROUTONS.

Cut bread free from crusts, half an inch square. Fry in smoking hot fat. Keep on a plate, unless served immediately. Serve in pea soup.

GERMAN SOUP BALLS.

Mix together butter and cracker crumbs into a firm round ball. Drop into the soup a very short time before serving. Very nice with chicken broth.

[Catsups and different sauces are added to soups, according to the tastes of families.]

NOODLES.

Take one egg, a pinch of salt, half an egg-shell full of water. Stir in all the flour it will take; roll as thin as you possibly can; hang over a chair-back on a napkin to dry. Then roll up like jelly-cake and slice off as thin as a wafer.

SUGGESTIONS.

If soup is over salted add a teaspoon of sugar and a tablespoon of vinegar, and it will help modify it.

If soups or sauces, or beef tea, have an excess of

fat, dip in a piece of coarse brown wrapping paper, and it will absorb the fat, and the liquid will run off. Two or three papers will free it sufficiently.

GUMBO SOUP.
Olive H.

Boil a spring chicken, though one a year old is just as good if sufficiently boiled; when almost done add a quart of fresh-picked okra, seasoning with salt, pepper, spice; for variety add chopped onions and cabbage (though they are not an ingredient proper of Gumbo) and parsley. Just before serving break in a half dozen butter crackers, and add a large lump of butter. This is *bona fide* Gumbo soup, and is for three quarts of soup.

RICE SOUP.
Mrs. J. W. S.

Boil a beef bone till the meat is well cooked. Half an hour before dinner, put in half a cup of rice. Season well. (Excellent.)

WHITE SOUP.

Six potatoes, four onions, three tomatoes if desired, four tablespoons of crushed tapioca, one and-a-half pints milk; butter, pepper and salt. Boil the vegetables in two quarts of water till soft, rub through a sieve, return the paste to the water, add the tapioca and boil fifteen minutes; season, add the 'milk, and as soon as hot, serve.

ECONOMICAL SOUP.
A. C. P., in Household.

In cool weather, save up all the bones and trimmings from roasts and steaks for two or three days. Put into a kettle with four or five quarts of water early in the day; add half a cup of beans and a large ripe tomato. Keep it boiling gently till an hour before dinner, then strain through a colander. Return soup to the boiler, slice in three or four potatoes, a grated carrot, salt, pepper, and pot-herbs, cut fine. Then beat up an egg, and lightly mix with a cup of flour. Stir this mixture into the soup in crumbs, let boil ten minutes, and serve.

TOMATO SOUP.

Take eight ripe tomatoes, or half a can, and put to boil in two quarts of soup stock, with a bunch of herbs. When well done, thicken with a little flour made smooth with water. Then strain, season with butter, pepper and salt, and serve.

TOMATO SOUP.
Mrs. Rice, Sioux Falls, Dak.

Six tomatoes skinned. Boil in a pint of water till

done; season with butter, pepper and salt, and add a quart of milk. Remove from the fire as soon as it comes to a boil, to prevent curdling.

POTATO SOUP.

Peel and slice thin, three or four large potatoes, and boil in enough water to cover them until done. Then season and add a quart of milk.

ONION SOUP.

Put a quarter of a pound of butter in a stewpan, with six large white onions cut in slices; let them fry a nice brown, then add six crackers rolled, pepper to taste, and a quart of boiling milk and water; let it simmer for fifteen minutes and serve.

PEA HULL SOUP.

W. T. W.

After hulling the peas from the pods, tie the pods in a bag made of some coarse cotton or linen cloth; place the bag in cold water over a moderate fire; boil until the sweetness is extracted from the pods; remove the bag; then squeeze it so that all the juice will be left in the water; after that is done season as any other soup, and depend on it you will have as fine and highly flavored a plate of soup as ever graced a table or tempted an appetite. Don't throw away the pods of the peas when a soup can be had for so small a cost.

BEAN SOUP.

A pint of beans put into two quarts of water. Simmer slowly on the back of the stove several hours. A very delicious soup. No seasoning but salt and pepper.

OX TAIL SOUP.

Chop the ox tails into small pieces. Brown over the fire in a spoonful of butter; then put it in water and cook slowly until done. Season with pepper and salt. A little turnip, onion, carrot, tomatoes and parsley, (all minced fine,) may be added fifteen minutes before serving.

CHICKEN SOUP.

Cut a chicken up small; cook until tender; take out and use for salads or pressing. Season the broth for soup with a little taste of onion, celery, tomato, or anything preferred. Before sending to the table, add a well-beaten egg and cook slightly.

LOUISIANA PLANTATION SOUP.

THE GENUINE GUMBO SOUP.

Take one squirrel, or if not to be had, take chicken or veal, instead. One ham bone; the leaves of okra, and young corn and tomatoes. The quantities may be estimated from other recipes in the book.

CONFEDERATE ARMY SOUP,

AS MADE AT GENERAL PICKETTS' HEAD QUARTERS.

One ham bone, one beef bone, one pod red pepper, black-eyed peas. Boil in a mess kettle. Splendid soup for a wet day.

CHESTNUT SOUP.

Boil a quart of chestnuts and rub the meats through a fine sieve with a potato masher. Take a tablespoon of flour and a tablespoon of butter, mix smooth in a saucepan over the fire, add gradually, a quart of milk. When scalding hot, season with a saltspoon of salt, a pinch of pepper and pinch of nutmeg, and add the sifted chestnuts.

GIBLET SOUP.

Take a turnip, carrot and onion, and slice them, and fry in hot butter; add a little flour and the giblets. Let them brown and then add the amount of water required. Simmer four or five hours. Season with salt and pepper and thicken with a spoonful of browned flour. Take yolks of hard boiled eggs and put one in each soup plate when it is served. The giblets of one chicken will make but little more than a quart of good soup.

MOCK TURTLE SOUP.

N. A. D.

Take a calf's head and feet, boil them until the meat separates from the bones; pick the bones out and cut the meat into inch pieces; put back and boil two hours more; chop the brains fine; add eight or ten onions and a little parsley; mix mace, cloves, pepper and salt with this, and put it in the soup an hour or more before it is done; roll six or eight crackers with half a pound of butter, and when nearly done, drop it in; brown a little flour and put in; make force meat balls of veal, fry them and put in the bottom of the tureen.

[The following soup recipes were procured direct from Miss JULIET CORSON, by the writer, while in attendance at her course of Demonstrative Lessons in Cookery. They are published with the full consent of Miss Corson. The writer has tested them, and finds them excellent.]

TO CLARIFY SOUP.

Skim off the cold fat that is at the top. Put in the bottom of a sauce pan for each quart of soup stock the white and shell of one egg and one tablespoon of water; mix, and then pour the soup on. Set the saucepan on the fire, and let boil very slowly.

As the soup heats, the white will harden, and the egg will rise to the surface together with the blood and cloudiness that remain in the soup. Let boil slowly until the under portion is very clear; then strain through a towel laid in a colander.

SOUP STOCK, OR BROTH.

For clear soup leave the vegetables whole, simply peeling them. This gives all the flavor, without the cloudiness arising from the vegetables cut up. Use the neck of beef, one pound of meat or bone for each quart of soup. Have the meat cut from the bone in a solid piece, to serve afterwards; crack the bone and put in the bottom of the soup kettle, the meat on the bone, then add cold water. Place over the fire to heat gradually; as it boils, the blood and albumen will rise. For clear soup, this must be skimmed off. It is never necessary to wash meat if it comes from a clean market; it detracts from its flavor and nutriment. Add a carrot, turnip, and an onion for three or four quarts. Stick six or eight cloves in the onion; salt and pepper lightly; add a bouquet or fagot of herbs; a small bunch of parsley, (two tablespoons,) take the roots if you wish the green for a garnish; the green stalk of celery is nice to add. A sprig of any kind of dried sweet herb, except sage, and one bay leaf. A single leek may be used instead of the onion. If wished for the gelatinous property, a knuckle of veal may be added to the soup stock. Cook slowly two hours after adding the vegetables; that time will secure the flavor. If cooked longer, it will assume a jellied consistency. Strain through a sieve, or through a folded towel laid in a colander into an earthern vessel, not in metal. When cold, remove the fat that rises. This soup is perfectly clear.

VERY CHEAP SOUP.
COSTING LESS THAN TEN CENTS A GALLON.

Take a cup full of little cut pieces of meat either cooked or raw. Take a cup each of carrots and turnips, half cup onions, all cut small; one cup rice, salt and pepper to taste; five quarts cold water; cook slowly two hours. A cup of tomatoes, when in season. If mutton is used, substitute barley for rice.

BRUNOISE, OR BROWN SOUP.

One cup of vegetables cut up into half inch pieces, any kind you like, for four quarts of soup. Brown them over the fire in a tablespoon each of sugar and butter, in the kettle in which the soup is to be made. When browned, pour on the soup broth; cook slowly till tender.

PEA SOUP.

A pint of dried peas or beans, will make six quarts of soup. Use split yellow peas. If put on to cook in cold water, add half a cup of cold water every fifteen minutes. Let them get soft before salting. When tender, rub them through a fine colander with a potato masher. Take the empty saucepan and set over the fire. Rub together in it a tablespoon each of butter and flour. When made perfectly smooth, add the strained soup. The meal of the peas will be held in suspension by the addition of the butter and flour, and the result will be a creamy, even soup. Meat bones may be used if desired, but should not be put in till after the peas commence boiling. If an onion is used, fry it in a saucepan before the peas are put over.

POTAGE A LA REINE.

Take bits of cold chicken, same quantity of rice, boil together till very tender. Rub through a sieve; then make of the consistency of cream, with boiling milk. Season to taste, with salt, pepper, and a little nutmeg. One pound of chicken and one pound of rice will make four quarts of soup.

OX-TAIL SOUP.

Have the ox-tail cut up small, wash thoroughly. Put on the stove in a kettle of cold water and let come to a boil; then take out and dry on a towel. Fry brown in a tablespoon of butter or drippings in a saucepan over the fire. Add a tablespoon of flour and stir amongst it. Cover with water, cut a carrot, a turnip, and a potato in dice; stick six or eight cloves in a whole onion. Put all of these vegetables together with a bouquet of herbs into the soup. Season palatably, and cook slowly two hours; take out the onion and bouquet, then serve.

PUREE OF GAME.

For this soup, potted, or canned, game may be used, or cold roast game. If the latter, boil the skin and bones for a half hour in water, and use that water, strained, for the soup. Rub the flesh of the game through a fine colander with a potato masher. For each quart wanted, take a tablespoon of flour and a tablespoon of butter, put in a saucepan over the fire, and stir till they are brown, then add the water or broth, spoken of above, and the sifted flesh. Season with salt and pepper.

PUREE OF FISH,

OR CREAM SOUP OF FISH.

A pound of cold boiled fish will make about two quarts of soup. It must be rubbed through a fine sieve. For each quart take a tablespoon of butter, same of flour, mix smooth in a saucepan over the fire and add a quart of milk, or milk and water; then add the puree of fish. Any game or vegetable soup may be made the same way.

WREXHAM SOUP.

One pound of lean meat cut in small pieces, either beef or mutton. Peel and slice one large or two small carrots, one large turnip, half a dozen medium sized onions, a pint of tomatoes, a green stalk of celery, if in season, and a small bunch of parsley. Tie up the parsley, celery, a dozen cloves, same of pepper, a sprig of any sweet herb, except sage. Put in a saucer a tablespoon of salt, a teaspoon of sugar and a salt spoon of pepper; mix, and put all these ingredients in layers in a jar, and two quarts of cold water. Paste the cover on, and bake slowly five hours.

CREAM OF SPINACH—SOUP.

Wash very carefully. Take the leaves for the soup. Half a peck will make about two quarts of leaves. One quart of leaves will answer for four quarts of soup. Throw the leaves into two quarts of boiling salted water. Cook only till tender. Frequently it will take but three minutes, and never over ten. When done, put them into cold water to set the color. For each quart of soup take one tablespoon of butter, the same of flour, mix in a saucepan over the fire; when melted smoothly, begin to pour in milk, stirring all the while half a cup at a time, until a quart has been used. Season with a teaspoon of salt and a pinch of nutmeg and pepper. This soup may be made of all milk, or half milk and half water, all water, or of cream. Rub the cooked spinach through a fine colander with a potato masher, and add to the cream, and the soup is ready to serve.

JULIENNE SOUP.

Use vegetables of at least three colors, carrots, turnips, and either lettuce, celery, cabbage or string beans. Cut the vegetables into strips an inch and a half long, and these strips into match-like pieces, very, very thin. Keep in cold water till wanted. The proportion of vegetables is a cup full all together for a gallon of soup. Put each kind separately into boiling salted water. When tender, drain and lay in cold water. This way retains the flavor and color perfectly. Then dish up in the hot soup. Foreigners add a tablespoon of vinegar to a quart of Julienne soup.

BROWN FISH SOUP.

Any kind of fish will answer; cut in small pieces; roll in flour and brown in some olive oil or butter in a saucepan; cover with hot water. Season with salt and pepper, and boil slowly for about fifteen minutes. See that there is plenty of water. One pound will make a quart of soup. A clove of garlic may be added. (Excellent.)

FISH.

Notice that the body of the fish is firm and the eyes full, and the gills red.

Do not allow fish to remain but a short time in water. It makes them soft and flabby.

To thaw out frozen fish, lay them in cold water till the ice cleaves from the body.

Large fish are usually boiled or baked. Small ones fried or broiled.

A fish is scaled more easily by plunging for an instant in hot water.

FISH CHOWDER.

Fresh cod or haddock are regarded as best for chowder, although our common lake fish may be used. Cut into two inch pieces. Fry some slices of salt pork in an iron pot crisp. Take out and chop fine, leaving the fat. Put a layer of fish in this fat, then a layer of split crackers, then some bits of the pork, some thick slices of peeled potatoes and some chopped onion and pepper. Then another layer of fish, with a repetition of the other articles. Cover with boiling water and cook half an hour.

Skim it out in the dish in which it is to be served, thicken the gravy with flour, add a little catsup, boil up and pour over the chowder. Remove the bones if convenient, when dishing up.

EELS.

Skin them. Take off head and tail, cut up into frying pieces, throw into boiling water for five minutes, then drain, roll in flour or corn meal peppered and salted, and fry in very hot lard.

FROGS.

Cook the same way as eels. The hind legs only are used.

BOILED FISH.

Wrap a large fish in a cloth. Secure it with a string. Put it on in cold water, salt well, and it will generally cook in half an hour. Remove the cloth and serve with drawn butter.

FRIED FISH.

Clean the fish well. Cut up into pieces about two by four inches. Lay around in a colander skin down, and sprinkle with salt. Let stand an hour, or half a day if need be. Have the fat hot in a frying pan. Roll in flour or corn meal, fry slowly and cook a long time, till thoroughly done through. It is nice dipped in beaten egg and rolled cracker after the flour, but is not essential.

BAKED FISH.

Clean well, sprinkle with salt for an hour before cooking. Tie it with a string, sprinkle flour over it, baste with butter, place on a wire gridiron across a dripping pan. Allow one and one-half hours.

STUFFING FOR FISH.
Mrs. E. B. B.

One-half cup of fat pork chopped fine. One large spoon butter. Parsley, thyme, sweet marjoram, salt and pepper, a few oysters, two beaten eggs. All mixed with bread crumbs.

A much simpler dressing is good, when the above ingredients are not at hand. Bread crumbs are usually on hand, and with a little seasoning and mincing, serve very well.

CODFISH STEW.

Cut up into inch pieces, allowing half a teacup full to a pint of milk. Put on the stove in a stew pan or spider, well covered with cold water. When it comes to a boil drain, and pour in a pint or quart of milk, according to size of family. When hot, thicken with a spoonful of flour made smooth with cold milk or water. An egg broken in and stirred rapidly at the last is an improvement. Season with a teaspoon of butter. Serve with baked potatoes.

CODFISH BALLS.
Larra Lemland.

One pint salt codfish picked very fine but not freshened, two pints whole, raw, peeled potatoes, boil together in (cold) water till potatoes are well cooked, remove from the fire and drain off all the water, mash and beat well, add butter size of an egg, two well-beaten eggs, and a little pepper. Mix thoroughly with a wooden spoon. Into a frying pan of boiling lard or drippings drop a spoonful of the mixture and fry brown. Do not mold cakes, but drop them from spoon. These fish balls are not only fashionable but good.

CLAM CHOWDER.
Creusa.

Butter a deep tin basin, put in a layer of grated bread crumbs or cracker crumbs. Sprinkle in pepper and bits of butter, then put in a double layer of clams, and season with pepper and butter, another layer of crumbs, then of clams, and finish with bread crumbs or a layer of soaked crackers. Add a cup of milk or water, turn a plate over the basin, and bake three-fourths of an hour. To fifty clams, one-half pound soda biscuit and one-fourth pound butter is the right proportion.

CLAM FRITTERS.

Take twenty-five clams and stew them in their own liquor, salt and pepper them slightly, cook for fifteen minutes slowly, drain the clams, chopping them as fine as possible, removing all the hard portions first. Make a batter of four eggs, with a half pint of sifted flour and a pint of milk, get it as smooth as possible, mix the clams with it, use butter for frying. A small addition of parsley is excellent.

FRESH MACKEREL.

This is one of the most delicate and dainty dishes to be found. It is best broiled. Rub over it melted butter or drippings, or olive oil if preferred. Grease the bars of the gridiron. Butter it and garnish with chopped parsley.

SALT MACKEREL.

They may be cooked in several different ways. The one most in vogue is boiling. To freshen, put in a large pan of water, skin side up, early in the evening. Before bedtime change the water, and in the morning rinse in clear water. Boil about five minutes in a frying pan. Take up carefully on a platter. Have ready in a basin a cup of cream or rich milk with a spoon of butter, heated, and pour over.

SALT MACKEREL.

Put half a cup of vinegar in the spider with a little water. Boil the mackerel in it. Serve with slices of lemon.

SALT MACKEREL.
Mrs. L. S. H.

After freshening, hang up for a day or two, or until perfectly dry. Then put in a dry tin and set in the oven for ten minutes. It will be found cooked through. Serve with drawn butter.

LOBSTER SALAD.
Mrs. M. A. S.

Chop lobster up fine. Chop some lettuce fine, mix, season with pepper, salt, mustard and vinegar. If lettuce is not to be had, use fine white cabbage.

PICKLED FISH.
Stella.

Spice the vinegar as for cucumbers, put your fish in, and let them boil slowly for a few minutes, until done, without breaking, then set them away for several weeks, and the bones will be entirely destroyed.

[The following very nice recipes for cooking fish were procured from Miss Juliet Corson at her cooking lessons, and are published by her consent. They may be safely relied upon:]

BOILED PIKE WITH EGG SAUCE.

Any fish will do. After it is dressed, tie it in the form of a circle by putting its tail into its mouth, and take a stitch with a trussing needle in its head and tail to hold it in place. To two quarts of water put half a cup of vinegar, a teaspoon of whole cloves, same of whole peppers, a bay leaf. Half a lemon sliced is a nice addition, and a tablespoon of salt. Put over in cold water and boil till the fins pull off easily. The skin may be easily removed if desired. Serve with egg sauce, made by adding hard boiled eggs cut up in small pieces to a white sauce. Pour the sauce inside the circle of fish. Lay a sprig of parsley on top of one side of the fish, and a few slices of lemon at the side on the platter.

HALIBUT—CREOLE STYLE.

Get a thick, square piece of halibut, or other fish if preferred. Wash it and lay it on a baking dish. Season with salt and pepper. Chop a clove of white garlic about the size of a bean, and strew over the fish, then put on a cup of canned or fresh tomatoes.

Bake until the flakes separate. Dish up without breaking. The combination of garlic and tomatoes gives the name Creole to a dish.

BAKED FISH WITH CREAM SAUCE.

Take a tablespoon of butter and a tablespoon of flour, mix in a saucepan over the fire, add either milk or water till a pint has been used. Season with salt and pepper. Take any kind of baked fish, remove the bones and skin, put in a baking dish, cover with the sauce, and dust with cracker dust. Bake a delicate brown.

TO FRY SMELTS.

Dry on a towel. Dip in milk, then in cracker dust, then in beaten egg, then in cracker dust again, and the dust will all stay on. Fry in hot fat.

SHAD ROE WITH OYSTERS.

Fish spawn, especially the shad, is a delicacy greatly prized by epicures. Wash and wipe, fry in hot fat in a frying pan on both sides. Season. It takes fifteen or twenty minutes to cook. Dish up on a platter and place around it a row or double row of plain fried oysters. Put a bunch of parsley in the center, and half a lemon with the peel cut in saw teeth, and the effect is very pretty.

BOILED FISH WITH HOLLANDAISE SAUCE.

A thin, long fish like a pike is best for boiling. Do not have it split open, but draw it at the gills. A large fish should be put over in cold water, but a small one in boiling water, for the reason that a fish cooks so quickly that almost as soon as it touches the boiling water it is done; and if a large one were put on in boiling water the outside would be done and the inside raw. If you have no fish kettle, wrap in a cloth. Sew the fish very securely in the shape of a letter S, by drawing cord through it and fastening tightly. When cooked, and strings loosened, it will retain its shape, and is exceedingly pretty to look at. Pour the sauce around it on the platter, and put a sprig of parsley at the side.

HOLLANDAISE SAUCE.

For each pint use one tablespoon each of butter and flour, mix in a saucepan over the fire, and gradually add boiling water. Stir into this the yolks of three eggs, a tablespoon of lemon juice or vinegar, three tablespoons salad oil, and a little mustard, if liked.

FISH CROQUETTES.

Stir together in a saucepan over the fire a tablespoon each of flour and butter. Add either water or milk, making a thick sauce. This quantity is for a pint of cold flakes of fish. Let the sauce boil up, season with salt and pepper, put in the cold fish and scald up, then remove and stir into it the yolks of two or three eggs. Rub a deep plate with salad oil, and pour the mixture in and let get thoroughly cold. Then make up into cork-shaped rolls. Wet the hands to prevent sticking. Roll in sifted bread crumbs, dip in beaten egg, then again in bread crumbs, and fry in smoking hot fat, like doughnuts, until a delicate brown. Take out of the fat with a skimmer, and lay on a brown paper an instant to absorb the fat. A teaspoon of onion chopped fine and fried in the butter before the sauce is made, imparts a nice flavor to the croquettes. A perfect croquette is semi-liquid in the center. Melted butter is not so good as oil for greasing the dish, as it will not prevent sticking. The finer the cracker dust the more easily the croquettes are prepared, and the nicer they will fry. They should be rolled and sifted.

TURBANS OF FISH.

Flounders are best. Cut down the middle of the fish till the bone is reached, then cut the fillet or strip out from the side, avoiding the bone. Lay the fillet on the board, remove from the skin by turning the blade of the knife between the flesh and skin, and keeping it perfectly parallel with the board, and thus cutting and separating the skin and flesh. After cutting the entire fish into fillets, roll each one up and fasten with a broom straw. These little rolls are called Turbans. They are nice stuffed with highly seasoned soaked bread. If they are not stuffed, spread some butter on the bottom of the pan, but no water. Cook in the oven only long enough for the flakes to separate. They are to be lifted out and placed on tartar sauce. For Tartar Sauce, see "Sauces and Catsups."

POTTED FISH.

Remove the fins and head of the fish, clean well, cut in slices an inch thick, pack it in a little jar having a cover, in layers, and between the layers put whole cloves, whole peppers, salt, some blades of mace, using about a teaspoon each of cloves and pepper, two blades of mace, a bay leaf, tablespoon of salt. When all is used, cover with vinegar and water, half and half. Put over it a buttered paper, or else fasten the jar cover on with paste. Put in a hot oven and bake four or five hours. The bones will have entirely disappeared. Eat cold or hot.

BROILED FISH.

To broil a shad or any other fish, grease the bars of the broiler well. Put the inside to the fire first. The back bone is easily removed by running a knife along under it, and the long bones can be loosened and taken out, one or more at a time, with a little knife. after the back bone is cut away from them. Let brown without burning, till the flakes separate. Turn the skin part to the fire just long enough to brown. Season either before or after cooking.

OYSTERS.

Use the very largest for frying, the medium for scallops and broiling, small for soup, and very small for raw. Every oyster should be looked at that no bit of shell remain attached to it. This is a very important matter, and should not be neglected.

A very pretty center piece for a table at an entertainment or gathering of any kind, is a large block of ice on a handsome platter, with a center melted out and filled with raw oysters. Garnish the edge with slices of lemon, and green sprigs may decorate the sides if desired.

OYSTER FRICASSEE.
Juliet Corson.

A tablespoon each of butter and flour mixed in a saucepan over the fire till a smooth paste is formed, then add the oyster liquor strained. A little water may be added if necessary. Season with salt and pepper, a very little nutmeg, boil up, add the oysters and cook till the edges curl. Remove from the fire and stir in the yolks of three raw eggs, three tablespoons salad oil, one tablespoon vinegar or lemon juice, and one tablespoon chopped parsley. Serve.

MOBILE ROAST OYSTERS.

Use deep oyster shells, place them in a tin in the oven, and heat so hot that they begin to scale off. Put a half teaspoon of butter and a pinch of salt and pepper in each shell, drop an oyster in each, turn it over and serve in the shell. If not quite done, set in the oven for a minute.

OYSTER SOUP.

To the liquor of one quart of oysters add a quart of water. Let it boil. Skim, season with a pinch of cayenne pepper, good piece of butter, add the oysters. Let boil up once, put in salt and serve.

VIRGINIA OYSTER STEW.

Take a quart of oysters, strain the liquor off, and put it over to boil. Take the yolks of three hard boiled eggs and one-half teaspoon mustard, make into a smooth paste with one tablespoon or more of salad oil. Add one cup of the boiling liquor, stir well and keep warm. To the remaining liquor add the oysters and cook till the edges curl. Pour part of the liquor in the oysters over toast, let the remainder be with the oysters, and add to it the egg salad, and seasoning of salt, pepper or sauces to suit the taste. Serve the toast with the oysters. Much nicer than crackers.

OYSTER STEW.

Three pints of oysters. Put the liquor in a stew pan, let it boil up, skim carefully, put in a quart or more of milk, let it come to a boil, add the oysters, having looked them over and removed every bit of shell. The moment they curl up remove from the fire and salt to taste. Season well with butter. Serve in hot soup scallops.

FRIED OYSTERS.

Only the large selects are fit for frying. Dry them on a folded towel. Allow six eggs to a quart. Roll cracker very fine and put salt and pepper in it. Beat eggs very light, dip an oyster in the cracker, then in the egg, then in the cracker again, and fry in plenty of hot butter and lard mixed; or better still, in olive oil.

STEAMED OYSTERS IN THE SHELL.

Wash well and lay in a steamer. When they are cooked enough, the shell will open. They may be turned into hot dishes or served in the shells. To be seasoned by the consumer.

STEAMED OYSTERS.

Take select oysters, put in a round vegetable dish, season with salt, pepper and butter, set in a steamer over boiling water, and steam till they begin to curl. Very fine.

SCALLOPED OYSTERS.

A layer of rolled cracker in a buttered pudding dish, then a layer of oysters with seasoning of butter, pepper and salt. Repeat till the dish is full, with crumbs on top. Pour on the liquor mixed with a little milk. A beaten egg with milk is nice to put over the top. Cover and bake about half an hour. Remove cover and brown before sending to table.

OYSTER SAUCE WITH TURKEY.

A pint of oysters cut up small and boiled up in their own liquor, add a cup of cream, tablespoon of flour made smooth with part of the cream; salt, pepper and butter.

CREAM OYSTERS ON THE HALF SHELL.

Pour into your saucepan a cup of hot water, another of milk, and one of thick cream with a little salt. Set the saucepan into the kettle of hot water until it just boils, when stir in two tablespoons of butter, and two heaping tablespoons of rice flour, corn starch, or arrow root, wet up with a little cold milk. Have your oyster shells washed and buttered (clam shells are more roomy) and a fine large oyster laid in each one. Arrange them closely in a large baking pan, propping them up with pebbles or bits of shell, and fill up each shell with the prepared cream, having stirred and beaten it well first. Bake five or six minutes in a hot oven until brown, and serve in the shell.

STUFFED OYSTERS.

Chop fine a dozen oysters, mix with them the beaten yolk of one egg, and thicken with bread crumbs, a tablespoon of thick cream, salt and pepper to taste. Fill the shells, rounding them nicely on the top. Brown in a quick oven.

PICKLED OYSTERS.

Drain the liquor from the oysters and add to it whole pepper, allspice, a few sticks of mace, and salt. When the liquor boils drop in the oysters and boil them one minute. Then take them out quickly and cool them. Add half as much vinegar as liquor, boil a few minutes and pour over the oysters.

NEW WAY OF COOKING OYSTERS.

Take mashed potatoes, mix a can of oysters with the potatoes, and with a knife cut the mass up fine.

Add one-half pound of rolled crackers. Season with butter, pepper and salt, and moisten the whole with oyster juice. Take little pats of this, roll them in powdered cracker crumbs and fry till brown in butter, and the result when served warm is delicious.

STEWED OYSTERS WITH CELERY.

In a large stewpan put a pint of strong and clear broth, made of the cuts of beef. Instead of milk and water, or milk even, as the prevailing practice is, use only the richest and sweetest of cream. Of this cream add one pint to the same quantity of the best of beef broth. Also four ounces of the most excellent table butter, three teaspoons of salt, two of white pepper, as much more of ground mace, and a teaspoon of extract of celery. If the celery is to be had in stalk, chop up fine and throw in. No more delicate or healthy flavor can be added to any stew, soup or broth than this exquisite vegetable. Now set to cooking, and while on the fire dredge in finely powdered cracker dust and a little of the best corn starch flour, until thickened to your taste. Have ready, parboiled, not in water, but in their own juice, fifty of the same oysters in a hot tureen. Pour over these parboiled oysters the sauce compounded as above, and serve while still scalding hot.

SUGGESTIONS.

Peanut oil or cotton seed oil may be procured much more cheaply than olive oil, and answers every purpose.

In cases where butter is given to be used with oysters, many prefer olive oil. Use but half the quantity that you would butter.

OYSTER PIE.

Make a pie paste for the sides of a large baking dish. Take one quart large fresh oysters, season with pepper, salt and butter. Take the yolks of three hard boiled eggs, chop fine, and mix with grated bread crumbs. Sprinkle this over the oysters after putting them in the dish. Pour the liquor over, cover with pie crust, and bake quickly.

OYSTER OMELET.

One dozen large fresh oysters chopped into small pieces, half a teaspoon of salt sprinkled on them, and then let them stand in their own liquor half an hour. Beat six eggs, the yolks and whites apart, the former to a firm, smooth paste, the latter to a stiff froth. Add to the yolks a tablespoon of rich, sweet cream, pepper and salt in sufficient quantity, and then lightly stir the whites in. Put an ounce and a half of butter into a hot frying pan. When it is thoroughly melted and begins to fry, pour in your egg mixture, and add as quickly as possible the oysters. Do not stir, but with a broad-bladed omelet knife, lift, as the eggs set, the omelet from the bottom of the pan, to prevent its scorching. In five minutes it will be done. Place a hot dish bottom upward over the omelet, and dexterously turn the pan over with the brown side uppermost upon the dish. Eat without delay.

EGGS.

BOILED EGGS.

Use a wire egg-boiler for boiling eggs. Three minutes cooks the white about right for soft boiled eggs. If put into cold water and let remain to a boiling point, they are cooked more evenly than by plunging into hot water at first. And it is further recommended to pour boiling water on the eggs and set the vessel on the hearth for five minutes.

SCRAMBLED EGGS.

Put a tablespoon of butter in a frying pan. When hot put in the requisite number of eggs beaten lightly. Pepper and salt them, and add half a cup of milk to a dozen eggs. Stir constantly, and as soon as they begin to set, take off and pour out. They must not be hard.

FRIED HAM AND EGGS.

Freshen the ham, if it requires it, by putting it on the stove in cold water, and pouring off as soon as it comes to a scald. Fry the ham in its own fat, then fry the eggs afterwards in the same. Dish up on the same platter.

BROILED HAM AND EGGS.

Broil thin slices of ham. Put a bit of butter on each piece when done. Poach the eggs in water, and lay one neatly on each piece of ham.

PROPER WAY TO COOK EGGS.

Butter a tin plate and break in your eggs. Set in a steamer, place over a kettle of boiling water and steam till the whites are cooked. If broken into patty pans they look nicer, by keeping their forms better. Or still better, if broken into egg cups and steamed until done, they are very nice. Cooked in this way there is nothing of their flavor lost.

BAKED EGGS.

Take a large platter. Break on it as many eggs as you need for your meal, sprinkle over with salt, pepper and lumps of butter. Set in the oven, and in about five minutes the whites will be set and the eggs sufficiently cooked. A handy way on washing or ironing days, when the top of the stove is all in use. Try it.

EGG CHOWDER.

Fry the pork, cook onions, potatoes, etc., just the same as for a fish chowder. After everything is done, just before you take it off, break in as many eggs as there are persons to eat, and let it boil up sufficiently to cook them through. I think those who try it will like it, and no danger of choking children with bones.

POACHED EGGS.

Set some muffin rings in boiling water. Break each egg in a ring, and it will take the form of the ring, and be much more pleasing to the eye than the old way.

FRIED EGGS.

Butter some gem irons and break an egg in each one and set in the oven, after seasoning with salt and pepper. Very nice.

PANNED EGGS.

Make a minced meat of chopped ham, fine bread crumbs, pepper, salt, and some melted butter. Moisten with milk to a soft paste, and half fill some patty pans with the mixture. Break an egg carefully upon the top of each. Dust with pepper and salt, and sprinkle some finely powdered cracker over all. Set in the oven and bake about eight minutes. Eat hot.

SCALLOPED EGGS.

Prepare a cup of thick drawn butter gravy, and a dozen hard boiled egg. Butter a pudding dish and place in it a layer of ine bread crumbs moistened with milk or broth. Add two beaten eggs to the drawn butter. Cut the boiled eggs in slices, dip each slice in gravy and place in layers upon the bread crumbs. Sprinkle these with cold meat or fowl minced fine. Repeat the layers and put over all a covering of sifted bread crumbs. Heat well through in a moderate oven.

HOT EGG SALAD.
Juliet Corson.

A tablespoon salad oil made hot. Break three eggs into it, and stir a little. Season with salt and pepper. Turn out as soon as it hardens a trifle, sprinkle over the top a tablespoon chopped cucumber, same of grated lemon rind, a tablespoon lemon juice and three tablespoons salad oil.

OMELET.
Mrs. M. A. S.

For minced ham, veal, beef or tongue. To twelve eggs beaten to a froth put three ounces of minced meat (add little salt to veal), melt four ounces butter and put part with the eggs, the remainder put in a frying pan. When hot, turn in the mixture and stir till it begins to set. When brown on the under side it is cooked sufficiently. The pan should be small enough to have the omelet an inch thick. Place a flat dish over the top and turn the frying pan upside down when you wish to take it up.

EGG OMELET.

Six eggs, six tablespoons milk, one tablespoon melted butter, and one of flour. Beat well together. Turn into a well-buttered and hot frying pan, and when the edge begins to cook roll it over and over like a jelly roll, and turn out on a hot platter with as little handling as possible.

OMELET SOUFFLE.

Beat the yolks of six eggs light, add half a teaspoon of lemon juice, grated lemon, some nutmeg, and half a teaspoon of sugar. Beat well and add lightly five tablespoons of cream. Butter the omelet pan, heat, pour in the eggs and stir in lightly with a fork the well-beaten whites. Cook five or six minutes in a quick oven. Turn upside down on a hot plate and serve instantly.

NOTE.—If possible, keep one pan for omelets alone.

OMELET SACCHARINE.

To the yolks of six eggs add a tablespoon of powdered sugar, and a teaspoon or more of some essence.

Mix and add carefully to the well-beaten whites. Pour into a hot buttered frying pan. As it cooks at the edges, lift it with a fork and toss to the center. Take up on a hot dish and dust with powdered sugar.

OMELET CELESTINE.

Juliet Corson.

The same as the above, by adding a couple of spoons of currant jelly before taking up.

ORANGE OMELET.

Three eggs, a teaspoon of orange juice, and a teaspoon of grated rind of orange. Beat the yolks and whites separately, then add them carefully together and put in a buttered heated frying pan

PICKLED EGGS.

Boil eggs very hard and remove the shell. Take one teaspoon each of cinnamon, allspice and mace, put in a little muslin bag in cold water, boil well, and if it boils away add enough to make half a pint when the spices are taken out. Add one pint of strong vinegar, pour over the eggs. If you want them colored, put in some beet juice. Very good

TO KEEP EGGS.

Take a colander full at a time and pour a teakettle full of boiling water over them. I have known eggs to be used several months after being put up in this way, and they were equal to new laid eggs. They should be kept in a cool place. I kept eggs three months last winter in an egg case with no preparation whatever. The last I used were as good as the first. Close contact would have spoiled them.

TO COLOR EGGS FOR EASTER.

Wind strips of bright-colored calico around the eggs, and then boil in ashes lye; you will find them gayly colored. To color them yellow, boil with onion skins.

FOWLS.

To singe a fowl pour a few drops of alcohol on a plate and burn. Handier than burning a paper.

To draw a chicken for stuffing, cut a slit under one of the legs, so it may be hidden by sewing up. Take the crop out from a cut in the back of the neck.

Rub clear lard, or lay a piece of fat pork over a fowl when put to roast.

A peeled lemon laid inside of a wild fowl will absorb that strong fishy taste if left in for a few hours.

The giblets of poultry are the head, neck, wings, feet, gizzard, heart and liver.

ROAST POULTRY.

If prepared the day before, it will be all the better seasoned. Half an hour to the pound is a good general rule. Baste frequently.

FULL DIRECTIONS FOR CUTTING UP A CHICKEN.

As Demonstrated by Miss Corson in her Cooking Lessons.

After singeing the fowl, wipe with wet towel. Don't wash it, because if it is so dirty as to need washing, it is not fit for food; and, by washing a clean chicken, you draw out with the water more or less of the blood and, consequently, the nourishment which the chicken contains. In order to get as many pieces as possible, cut off the wings so that a little piece of the breast remains with the wing. Remove the crop by cutting the skin at the back of the neck. Cut off the neck close to the body. Next take off the wing side-bones. Having cut them loose from the backbone, bend them toward the front and they will part at the joint; loosen them with the knife. Take off the legs next. Instead of making a division between the second joint and drum-stick, cut midway the second joint, and then just below the joint, and trim off the lower end of the drum-stick. Next cut through the side just where the breast-bone joins the ribs. Then the breast-bone can be pulled free from the back, and the entrails can be taken out easily without breaking, which is decidedly a consideration, because if, in drawing a chicken, the entrails are broken, it becomes necessary to wash the chicken very thoroughly, and you thus destroy its flavor. Cut off the lower part of the breast-bone without splitting it, because, while that is a very nice piece, it is apt to be a very small one. If there are any pieces of ribs attached to the sides of the breast-bone trim them off. Cut the upper part into two pieces right down the middle, or into four — down the middle and then each piece in two — according to the size of the chicken. Having cut up the breast-bone, the entrails are to be taken away from the back, cutting around the vent being necessary in order to loosen them. The oil bag is of course to be removed; the liver also, without breaking the gall, which can be avoided by leaving a little piece of the liver attached to it. There are two or three ways of preparing the gizzard. Adopt the easiest. Instead of taking the trouble, to split the gizzard, and trying to take out the bag of stones within, I believe it best to cut from the outside just that portion of purplish flesh which is used. If there is on it any appearance of the contents wash it; not otherwise. Now separate the backbone and neck and notice the back side-bones, where are located the "oysters." If the back were split entirely down the "oysters" would be cut in two; but cutting off the end of the backbone they are preserved. To some, they are the choicest part of the chicken.

ROAST TURKEY.

A year old is considered best. After dressing, salt and pepper the inside. Take a loaf and a half of stale baker's bread for a good sized turkey. Rub fine with the hands; cut a large white onion and cook a few minutes in butter in a frying pan. Do not brown it. Then stir in your bread, one teaspoon salt, ditto of pepper, ditto of sage; mix the onion in, and use melted butter sufficient to bind it all together; stuff, tie the wings and thighs, to keep in place. Salt and pepper the outside. Put a cup and a half of water in the dripping pan with the turkey. Lay two or three pieces of fat pork on the top, or rub well with lard. Roast three hours in a moderate oven, with an even fire. If oysters are liked, a pint may be chopped with the dressing. Lay the giblets by the side of the turkey, and when done chop fine, and put in the gravy, thickened with a tablespoon of flour. Serve with cranberry sauce, celery, turnips, boiled onions, or any vegetable, fresh or canned.

CHICKEN STEW.

Cut a chicken up small. Boil till tender; make a thickening of flour and milk, using a pint of rich milk, or cream, if it is to be had. Season well with butter, pepper and salt. Have ready in a tureen, some fresh soda, or baking powder biscuits broken in halves. Pour some of the gravy over them, and reserve the remainder to serve with the fowl in a platter. Be sure and have plenty of gravy; it will all be wanted.

CHICKEN PIE.

Stew chicken till tender. Season well with butter, pepper and salt. Thicken the gravy with a tablespoon of flour. Have ready some peeled boiled potatoes. Line the sides of a deep dish with rich crust; put in a layer of chicken and a layer of potatoes in thick slices. Repeat, and pour over the gravy. Cover with the pie-crust. Serve hot.

CHICKEN POT PIE.

Cut up good sized chicken small. Put a small plate in the bottom of the kettle. Cover the chicken well with water. Season high, with butter, pepper and salt. A half hour before it is done, drop in small lumps of dough made like biscuit. A quart of flour is sufficient for one large chicken. Cover closely. Take out with skimmer carefully, and if gravy is not thick enough, thicken it with a small spoon of flour and water made smooth. Serve with mashed potatoes and any vegetables wished.

SMOTHERED CHICKEN.

Cut your chickens open at the back after dressing them. Sprinkle salt and pepper and little lumps of butter over. Put them in a baking pan with another over, and bake one hour. Baste often, with butter. (Delicious.)

FRICASEE CHICKEN.

Cut every joint separate, the back in two, and the breast in three or more. Stew in water enough to cover them at first, until the meat is very tender, and only about a teacup of water is left in the pot. Add a large cup of sweet milk, in which a teaspoon of flour is smoothly mixed; season with salt and pepper, and boil a few moments longer; if you add, about half an hour before serving up, a couple of slices of salt pork in fine strips, you will find it an improvement, and not fatty, unless the pork is boiled too long.

FRIED CHICKEN.

Cut young tender chickens at the joints. Season with salt and pepper, dip into flour and fry slowly in butter and lard until browned on both sides. When done, lay on a hot platter and turn in cream or milk, and thicken with a spoon of flour; pour over the chicken.

PRAIRIE CHICKEN.

Cut open; lay on them thin slices of salt pork and put in a dripping pan and cook in the oven. Serve with thickened gravy.

ROAST GOOSE.

Parboil for two hours, at least. Then stuff with seasoned mashed potatoes, and roast. Baste often.

GERMAN RELISH.

Take a nice fat goose, turkey or chicken, take off the loose fat of the goose, season with a little salt and pepper, boil till nearly tender, with just water enough to cook it, then put in one pint good cider vinegar, then boil till very tender, like pigs' feet; then pack in stone crock, leaving the bones in with the meat. It is a very dainty relish. To be sliced up cold.

ROAST DUCKS.

If parboiled for an hour, or even longer, the strong taste is lessened. Baste same as turkey.

STUFFING FOR DUCKS.
Mrs. E. B. B.

Half pound of fat pork chopped fine; eight rolled crackers; one egg; one onion; one pint milk; sage, pepper and salt.

DIRECTIONS FOR BONING A CHICKEN OR TURKEY.

R. E., in Household.

With a sharp pen-knife, cut the skin off your whole fowl down the back from neck to oil-bag, and cut and scrape off close to the bones, all the meat and skin; scrape, after jointing the thigh, leg and wing bones, the last joint of the wing cut off, and be careful of the skin of the second joint. When you have removed the skeleton and entrails, save all of the giblets. Make an ordinary filling of bread and butter minced fine with the giblets, and the dark meat of the fowls, and the light too, if desired; but, it is nice to leave the light for chicken salad. Fill out wherever the bones have been taken out, and shape up nicely, sewing the skin all down the back. When hot, draw out the threads, handle carefully, and serve either hot or cold. Any kind of filling may be used. The bones may be boiled up for soup.

DIRECTIONS FOR BONED CHICKEN.

Juliet Corson.

Use two-thirds as much force meat, as the chicken weighs. Lean veal, and lean fresh pork chopped fine, and for each pound, take one whole egg, one teaspoon of cloves and allspice mixed, one teaspoon salt. Instead of the veal, another fowl's flesh may be used.

After the bones have all been removed, and the fowl is laid flat down, spread on a layer of force meat, then strips of fat pork and the liver, then a layer of mushrooms. Then run a string around the edges of the chicken and draw it up like a wallet. Having sewed up the ends, then sew the cut that was first made down the back. Then roll it up in a tight bundle in a towel. Tie the ends like a sack of flour and tie two or three tapes around the middle as tight as you possibly can. Boil half an hour to the pound. Take out of the towel, wipe off, wrap in a clean towel and lay on a platter, put another over and place a weight on. The easiest fowl to bone is a year old turkey.

CURRY OF DUCK.

Juliet Corson.

A GENUINE CURRY OF THE EAST INDIES.

Cut the ducks up in small joints. Wipe with a wet towel. If lean, put a teaspoon of butter in a saucepan and brown them in it. But if fat, as is generally the case, no surplus fat will be required. Cut up a medium sized onion and brown with them. Stir in a tablespoon of flour, and as soon as that is well mixed in and brown, cover with hot water, and season with salt and pepper. A cup of grated cocoanut and a sour apple peeled and sliced must be added. Cook till the ducks are tender. It will require from half an hour to two hours, according to the age. When tender, add a tablespoon of curry powder. Serve with boiled rice. The rice may be placed around the edge of the platter, and the curry in the center, or it may be taken up on a separate dish.

CHICKEN PATE.
Mrs. E. B. B.

Two chickens boiled tender. Remove bones and skin and chop fine. Season with salt, butter and pepper. Add broth to make it moist, and press into a mold. When cold, slice thin.

PRESSED VEAL OR CHICKEN.

Stew slowly four pounds veal, or two chickens cut up small until the meat drops from the bone; then take out and chop fine. Let the liquor boil down to a cup full. Put in a lump of butter size of an egg, a tablespoon pepper, little allspice, and a beaten egg; stir through the meat; slice a hard boiled egg, lay in your mould and press in the meat. When served, garnish with celery tops, or sprigs of parsley.

CHICKEN SALAD.
Mrs. M. A. S.

Boil two chickens that weigh about five pounds. When tender, pick in small pieces. Take a coffee cup of chopped celery, and make the following dressing: Take eight hard boiled eggs and chop fine, two tablespoons olive oil, or melted butter, two teaspoons mixed mustard, two teaspoons salt, one of pepper, one tumbler of vinegar; mix, and pour over.

CHICKEN SALAD.

Joint two chickens, weighing between three and four pounds each, cover them with boiling water, set on the fire where they will merely simmer until tender, remove from the fire, and let them remain in the broth until cold; this renders the meat juicy. It is best to cook the chickens the day before the salad is required. Take both the dark and white meat for your salad, cut into pieces nearly an inch square, and one-quarter of an inch thick. To prepare the dressing for the salad, take a tablespoon of fresh butter, rub it to a cream with the yolks of two hard boiled eggs; gradually add two tablespoons of salad oil, one of French mustard, a desertspoon of powdered sugar; a teaspoon of salt, half a teaspoon of black pepper, as much cayenne as will lie on a penknife point, the yolks of two fresh eggs, uncooked, and six tablespoons of vinegar. Next fill your salad bowl with two heads of celery, cut fine—one head or bunch of celery includes three roots—two large pickled cucumbers, cut in very small slices, the whites of the boiled eggs also cut very fine. Some like two tablespoons of capers, and half a dozen olives. Now add the chicken and the dressing; mix thoroughly with a wooden fork or spoon, and as vinegar is of different strength, more may have to be added.

MEATS.

If beef is good it will be fine grained, smooth, bright red and fat.

Good veal flesh is dry, firm and white, with kidneys covered with fat.

The flesh of good mutton is dark red, with firm white fat.

Fresh killed lamb is pale red, with bluish veins in the neck.

Pork should be rejected if there are kernels in the fat. The skin should be smooth and thin.

The choicest cuts for roasting, are the sixth, seventh and eighth ribs.

If a roast is rolled by the butcher have him send home the bones for soup.

If it is necessary to freshen ham or salt pork it is recommended very strongly to put them in milk and water for several hours. Sour milk will answer as well as sweet. Rinse after taking out. This also applies to salt mackerel.

If meat is eaten when first killed it will be tender. If a little time elapses the muscles stiffen, and it will be tough. If more time elapses, the muscles relax, and it will be tender again.

Young meat of all kinds, should be cooked very thoroughly, to be healthy. It offers less resistance to mastication, hence will be less liable to be digested properly. Older and tougher meat offering more resistance, will, of necessity, be better masticated and better incorporated with the saliva; hence, will be better digested.

In cold weather, great care should be taken to heat plates, to serve at table. More especially, when mutton is used. Many a good dinner has been spoiled by a showing of cold mutton tallow on a still colder plate. If there is no warming oven to the stove, let them set in hot water for a few minutes.

[All of the following dishes credited to Miss Juliet Corson, that pioneer in culinary art in this country, are very choice, and may well be adopted by families in general. The writer feels deeply indebted to Miss

Corson for many valuable hints that are of service in everyday cooking:]

Fresh meat should be put to cook in boiling water, and if more water is needed in the pot, let it be boiling when added.

Salt meat must be put over in cold water, that the salt may be extracted in cooking. Remove the scum as soon as it rises.

To be tender, meat should cook very gently; hard boiling toughens it. The toughest meat can be made tender by boiling it a long time, or baking it in a covered dish in the oven.

Before cooking mutton, take a sharp knife and loosen the thin outside skin and remove entirely. The oil of the wool penetrates through the pores of the skin, and from this comes that strong, woolly taste, rendering mutton so objectionable. Use plenty of its own fat to cook it in.

OLD FASHIONED BOILED DINNER.

Put in a large kettle of cold water the corned beef soon after breakfast (if for noon dinner). About 10 o'clock, put in the salt pork, in a solid piece, one or two pounds, according to size of family. At the same time, wash beets very carefully and put in. If they are very large, put them in an hour earlier. At

11 o'clock, put in peeled turnips, cut in three or four pieces. Divide a head of cabbage in four parts, lengthwise, and put in at the same time, with good sized peeled potatoes, allowing a good half hour for them to boil. Beets will not injure the looks of the other vegetables if the skin is not broken. When done, put them in cold water, to remove the skin, cut lengthwise in three or four pieces, and dish up. Take up the cabbage in a vegetable dish, after draining well. A platter is scarcely large enough to hold such a variety of meat and vegetables, and it is unhandy to cut up the meat; hence, it is better to dish up in separate dishes. A piece of red pepper cooked with a boiled dinner improves it. Grated horse-radish, or any bottled sauce, should be served with boiled dinner. The best dessert with a boiled dinner is a boiled Indian pudding.

POT ROAST OF BEEF.

Get a solid piece from the round, about five pounds. Put in a medium sized kettle, that can set in the oven. Put it over the fire in hot water, to cover it. Boil slowly for three hours or more; season well; then remove the meat, and thicken the gravy with flour and water. Put the meat back in; set in the oven; put a cover over and let cook slowly till needed; two hours will not hurt. This mode of cooking will make the toughest beef tender. Serve in a large platter with part of the gravy; but dish up the greater part in a gravy dish.

PARSNIP STEW.

One pound of salt pork sliced; boil an hour or more; scrape and cut in lengthwise quarters five or six parsnips, add to the pork, and after boiling a half hour, add a few potatoes, and let all cook until the potatoes are done. The water should cook down to about a pint, when ready to dish up. (Excellent.)

BLANQUETTE OF LAMB,

OR WHITE STEW.

Have the lamb cut in pieces and put over in water to parboil. If any scum rises, skim off. When it has boiled, take out and wipe with a wet towel if any scum appears. Strain the broth. Use it for a white sauce, beginning by putting a tablespoon of butter and a tablespoon of flour in a saucepan over the fire; stir together until well mixed, and gradually add the broth in which the meat was parboiled. Season the same with salt, pepper and nutmeg. Add the meat and cook until the lamb is tender; stir in it the yolks of two eggs and a tablespoon of chopped parsley

BOILED MUTTON.

A leg of mutton boiled is a savory, juicy meat. Let the water cook down to sufficient for gravy. Boil some rice, and eat as a vegetable, with boiled mutton; or, coarse boiled hominy is equally as good. With lamb or mutton, the Southerners eat currant jelly with a sprinkling of mustard, and consider it exceedingly palatable.

MACARONI MUTTON.

Some slices of mutton, one-quarter pound of macaroni, sauce of any kind, pepper, salt, a tablespoon of vinegar, and a little water. Put all together in a stewpan, keep the lid on, and stew gently for an hour or an hour and a half.

LAMB STEWED WITH GREEN PEAS.

Cut the scrag or breast of lamb in pieces and put into a stewpan with just enough water to cover it. Cover it closely and let it stew for twenty minutes. Take off the scum; add a tablespoon of salt and a quart of shelled peas; cover and let them stew for half an hour; mix a tablespoon of flour and butter and stir in and let it simmer ten minutes; then serve. If you mix the flour with cream it makes it better. Veal is nice cooked in this way, with half a dozen small new potatoes added with the peas.

PRESSED BEEF.

Buy a shank of beef. Boil till it falls from the bone. Remove every piece of bone, boil down a little longer. Season well with pepper and salt, and a bit of sage, if liked. Pour into a form. Excellent cold.

STUFFED PRESSED MEAT.
Mrs. A. S. J.

Take a large steak, spread it with well seasoned dressing; roll up, sew it in a stout bag and boil three hours in salted water. Take it out, put a weight on it and press until cold; then slice.

TO STUFF A HAM.

Boil it very slowly. If it boils hard, it will be in strings. Let simmer all day, if necessary; then skin and remove extra fat. Make stuffing of bread crumbs moistened in water and seasoned with pepper, butter, parsley, celery, or any other, if preferred. Cut the bone out with a sharp knife. Take yolks of two or three hard boiled eggs, mix with the ham-water enough to moisten; spread over the ham, grate bread crumbs over all, and brown. Ornament with slices of hard boiled egg, fanciful cuts of pickled beets, cloves or green parsley. Slice cold. Delicious for a cold collation.

COLD BOILED HAM.

In boiling ham or corned beef to eat cold, it is far better if let remain in the water until cold. Slice on a platter, and place slices of hard boiled egg around ham, or slices of lemon. For corned beef, garnishes of pickle are nice.

ROAST BEEF.

Put in a dripping pan without water, into a very hot oven for the first half hour, that the outside may sear over and keep the juices inside. When half done, the oven heat may be lessened, and the meat salted and peppered. Pour in water and thicken for gravy when the meat is done. Fifteen minutes to the pound, if wished rare in the center, or twenty minutes will make it well done. Cranberry sauce or jelly, turnips, celery, or any kind of canned vegetables may be served with roast beef.

YORKSHIRE PUDDING.

When roasting a piece of beef set up on a cricket or muffin rings, so that the juice will drop into the pan below. Three-quarters of an hour before it is done, mix up the following and pour into the pan under the meat: One pint of milk, four eggs, beaten very light, one teaspoon salt, two cups of flour. Cut in pieces and serve with the roast.

BEEF A LA MODE.

Juliet Corson.

To make a large piece off the round tender, make holes with a steel or sharp instrument, and insert in each one a little strip of salt fat pork; run the strip with the grain. Let each end project; then put the meat in a bowl, and with it, a teaspoon of whole cloves, same of pepper corns, a bay leaf, half a teacup of carrots sliced, same of turnip and onion; not any salt; cover with vinegar and water. Let stand several hours; all the better if it stand two or three days. If the fibre is tender, take it out of the pickle, fry it brown in a pot in drippings; then put in two tablespoons of flour, turn it over and over. When brown, cover with hot water and cook slowly. Salt it when half done. A half hour to the pound usually suffices.

PORK ROAST.

Season well and roast slowly at first, allowing fully half an hour to a pound. Put some water in the pan and baste often. Cook very thoroughly. Fried cabbage is very good with pork. Any tart sauce may be used, or any canned vegetable. Turnips go nicely; celery always admissible.

Fried apples are also very nice; make gravy after pouring off the surplus from the top of the drippings.

VEAL ROAST.

Same as pork; be sure and cook well through. Squash is a palatable vegetable to serve. Stewed tomatoes are also good; currant jelly is always nice.

MUTTON ROAST.

Same as pork, but is not objectionable if a little rare. Mint sauce made by mixing half a cup of chopped spear mint, with half a cup of vinegar and a tablespoon of sugar is used by those who like it with mutton. Serve turnip with mutton.

LEG OF LAMB TO ROAST.

All lamb should be very well cooked, and not put too near the fire at first; from eighteen to twenty minutes to the pound before a clear but not fierce heat. It may be served with spinach, peas, or asparagus.

ENGLISH PORK PIE.

Make a pie-crust, not very rich, and put around the sides of a deep pie dish. In the bottom, and above, put layers of thin sliced bacon, thin sliced potatoes, onions chopped or sliced very fine; lean fresh pork cut into small pieces. Season with pepper, salt and sage. Fill the dish with any good gravy left from roasts, or with water thickened for the occasion, with some butter added. Cover with crust, and bake about an hour and a half. Cover the pie with thick paper if it gets too brown.

BEEF HEART.

Clean the heart well and stuff with bread crumbs, well seasoned, and mixed with water enough to moisten. Baste often with the liquor from it.

BEEF HEART EQUAL TO TONGUE.
A. G. S.

In the forenoon, put your beef heart into a weak brine. In the evening, change to another brine. In the morning, put to cook in boiling water and cook fully three hours. When tender, have ready a dressing of bread crumbs and stuff it. Put it in an oven twenty minutes, to cook the dressing. Let get cold, and slice very thin; season with a little salt and pepper, if necessary.

BEEF STEW.

Order two pounds of beef or veal cut up small for a stew. Cheap cuts answer every purpose. Cook two or three hours. Put in some potatoes peeled and cut in halves, and some onions, if they are liked. Season well; skim out into a platter; thicken the gravy and pour over. This will give a good dinner to six or eight persons.

MOCK DUCK.

Spread dressing, as for turkey, on a thick round of beef steak; roll up, tie and roast. Serve with gravy.

BEEFSTEAK SMOTHERED WITH ONIONS.

Cut up six onions very fine; put them into a saucepan with one cup of hot water, about two ounces of good butter, some pepper and salt; dredge in a little flour. Let it stew until the onions are quite soft. Broil the steak according to directions; put it into the saucepan with the onions and let it simmer about ten minutes.

The rules adopted by the celebrated Beefsteak Club started in England in 1734, for cooking steak:

> Pound well your meat till the fibres break,
> Be sure that next you have, to broil the steak,
> Good coal in plenty; nor a moment leave,
> But turn it over this way, and then that;
> The lean should be quite rare—not so the fat.
> The platter now and then the juice receive,
> Put on your butter, place it on your meat,
> Salt, pepper, turn it over, serve, and eat.

FRIED STEAK.

A favorite way of cooking beefsteak in the South is to take a piece off the round, fry it in a frying pan, in its own fat if sufficient, in drippings if not, and when done, pour in water and thicken with flour, and make gravy to pour over the whole in a platter.

BROILED STEAK.

Heat and grease the bars of the gridiron; have a bright fire, with live coals, at the top. Trim the steak nicely, a porter-house or sirloin, for broiling; cut off the little tough end of the porter-house. It will do better service in the soup kettle. Lay the steak on the gridiron, cover, and as soon as seared, turn over and scar the other side. Turn again during the cooking; take up on a hot platter. Season with butter, pepper and salt. A sprig of parsley, and a few slices of lemon laid at the edges garnish it nicely. A bit of onion rubbed over the platter before taking up the steak, gives a delicate flavor that is delicious, without any of the offensiveness that the onion taste imparts, if used more largely.

ROUND STEAK.
Anna G. S.

First pound it very thoroughly. Cut it into convenient pieces for serving. Season some flour with plenty of salt and pepper, and roll the steak in it, as you would fish; have your skillet hot, with some fryings in, lay in the steaks, brown slightly on both sides; pour in a little water and keep enough in the frying pan to prevent the meat from burning. Cook half an hour, and you will have a juicy steak.

SPARERIBS.

Spareribs, as they are sold in the city, are so very spare, that it is an improvement to roast them with a dressing of bread crumbs. Lay some ribs in the dripping pan; salt and pepper; spread over them a dressing of crumbs, seasoned with pepper, salt and sage; then lay on some more spareribs; put a pint of water in the pan; season; roast till well done; pour off the top for fryings; add more water and thicken for gravy. Fried apples are a nice accompaniment to spareribs.

ROAST PIG.

Scald and clean the pig carefully. Make a dressing of bread crumbs, sage, salt and pepper; stuff; sew up; fasten the legs back so that the under part will crisp nicely. Dredge with flour and put into a hot oven. Baste frequently with melted butter. When done, pour off the fat from the top of the drippings; add water to the remainder, and thicken for gravy. Serve in a gravy dish, and stand pig up on a platter and garnish with green parsley or celery tops.

BEEF TONGUE.

If it is corned it should be soaked a few hours before boiling. Cook till done, then peel. If it is to be served hot, make a sauce of a can of tomatoes, an onion, a carrot, salt and pepper, a spoon of flour well cooked and strained, and poured over. If too be eaten cold, put a weight on it, when ready to serve, cut in very thin slices.

MUTTON CHOPS.

Place in a dripping pan; season well, and set in a hot oven. This is the nicest way we have ever cooked mutton chops. The gravy may be thickened or not, just as you prefer. It is not necessary to turn them.

VEAL CUTLETS.

Fry until pretty well done; then take out and dip into beaten egg, and then in rolled cracker, with salt stirred in, and fry again, turning so as to get a nice brown on each side. Make a gravy of water and a spoonful of flour in the frying pan and pour over. Season, if not salted enough; tomatoes are nice, served with cutlets.

PORK TENDERLOINS.
Fornie.

Have the spider hot, grease it with a bit of lard, and fry both sides brown, but do not cook them through; cover with boiling water, and stew twenty minutes or a half hour; thicken the gravy, and season with pepper and salt. The meat will taste like chicken, and is every bit as good.

DEVILLED KIDNEYS.

(Devilled, means very hot.)
Juliet Corson.

Three tablespoons of oil, one of vinegar, saltspoon of salt, pinch of pepper, and a teaspoon of mustard. Dip the sliced kidneys in the above mixture and broil them. After they are broiled, sprinkle a little cayenne pepper on. Serve when plenty of water can be afforded.

STEWED KIDNEYS.

Parboil a few minutes; drain off the water and boil again for five or ten minutes; then cut up small, put in fresh water and cook until tender. Season well, and thicken the gravy.

LIVER ROLLS.

Have the liver sliced; pour on boiling water, and let stand five minutes, or so. Remove the skin; season the slices with salt and pepper. Put a little piece of fat salt pork on each slice and roll up, fastening with a string. Then brown them in a tablespoon of drippings or butter; then throw in a tablespoon of flour among them; stir them about, cover with water; season more if necessary, and cook half an hour. It may be served as a regular meat dish at dinner.

PORK AND LIVER.

Fry some nice slices of pickled pork or bacon, a nice brown, on each side; take up, pour boiling water on the slices of liver; remove the thick skin at the edges; roll in salted flour, and fry in the pork gravy. Cook slowly and thoroughly on both sides. Serve each person with a slice of each. It has been recommended to steam the liver fifteen minutes, before frying, in place of scalding. It is worth a trial.

STEWED CALF'S LIVER.

Partly cook; then cut up small and finish stewing. Season with pepper, salt and butter. Thicken with flour. Serve hot; is nice for breakfast.

ANOTHER NICE METHOD OF COOKING LIVER.

Scald and peel off the edge; put to fry, and when both sides are brown, cover with water in the frying pan; put cover over, and let stew fifteen or twenty minutes. If the liver is rolled in flour there will be a nice gravy made in the stewing.

CALVES' LIVER LARDED.
Juliet Corson.

Use fat salt pork, as it is easier to lard with than pickled. For larding small birds, the strips should be an inch and a half long and one-sixteenth of an inch thick; for chickens, a quarter of an inch thick; beef a la mode half an inch thick. These strips, called lardoons, are to be inserted in the surface of the liver with a larding needle. Wash the liver in cold water, and trim the loose pieces off, but not the skin proper. Lay it on a folded towel held in the hand, curve the point of the needle a little, take a stitch in the meat, work the needle back and forth two or three times, insert the strip of pork in the forked end of the needle and pull through, leaving half an inch or so each side of the stitch. Dot the whole surface with this culinary embroidery. Put the liver on a bed of a few scraps of pork, a little carrot, turnip, and onion in a baking-pan. In baking, put a buttered paper over it until nearly done; then remove the paper, and let the lardoons brown. The vegetables should be rubbed through a sieve, and the drippings found in the bottom of the pan used as a basis for sauce or gravy.

CREOLE SAUSAGES.

Juliet Corson.

Prick the sausages all over, and put in the bottom of a saucepan; add a very small bit of garlic. After the sausages are browned, add a quart of tomatoes peeled and sliced; season with salt and pepper, and stew for half an hour slowly. Serve all together on a platter It answers as a regular meat course at dinner. A combination of garlic and tomatoes always gives the name Creole to a dish.

A nice addition to the above, is dumplings, made as follows: A cup of flour, half teaspoon baking powder, same of salt, enough water to make a soft dough, like biscuit dough, drop into the sausage and tomatoes, being sure that there is about a pint of liquid, adding water, if necessary; cook covered, about fifteen minutes.

POTTED TRIPE.
Juliet Corson.

Boil, clean and cut up fresh tripe. Three pounds of tripe; one very large carrot, turnip, onion, all peeled, a teaspoon of whole cloves, same of whole pepper, two bay leaves, a sprig of parsley. Put in a jar. Half cover with broth or water. If broth is used, fill up with water, having a half gill of vinegar in it. Paste the cover on with flour and water, and bake six hours.

CURRIED TRIPE.
Juliet Corson.

Take the tripe, as it ordinarily comes from the market; (it is generally cooked;) parboil it for a few minutes, putting it on in cold salt and water. Pour off that water and put on another, boil for fifteen minutes; take it out, and put in that water some rice to boil — the proportion is half a pound to a pound of tripe. Boil the rice until just tender. At the time of putting in the rice, slice and fry brown in a saucepan a couple of onions in butter or drippings; then add the tripe and enough hot water to cover. Season with salt and pepper, and let it cook until the rice is done; add a tablespoon of curry powder to the tripe. Stir it up, and dish the tripe with the rice around it. If the tripe is not pickled, add a tablespoon of vinegar before taking up.

SWEET BREADS.

Soak in cold water and salt for an hour; then put on in a quart of cold water and a tablespoon of salt, and let come slowly to a boil; then put in cool water to cool sufficiently to handle; then lard them with little strips of dry salted fat pork, about one-sixteenth of an inch thick. After they are larded put in the oven for fifteen minutes; brown them a little, and in the meantime, make a garnish of whatever you wish. French green peas, mushrooms, stringbeans, or a plain white sauce.

STUFFED VEAL.

Have the butcher make an incision for dressing. Use bread crumbs, a taste of onion, a raw egg beaten up, and any herbs that are desired. Stuff and cook in a moderate oven till well done, about twenty-five minutes to the pound.

VEAL LOAF.
Mrs. M. A. S.

Three pounds uncooked veal; three-quarters of a pound of salt pork; chop both fine; one cup of rolled cracker; two eggs, well beaten; one teaspoon of sugar; four of salt; two of pepper. Bake two hours.

VEAL CAKE.
Mrs. L. S. H.

One pound of salt pork; two pounds of lean veal, both chopped fine; three Boston crackers rolled fine; salt and pepper; two small nutmegs; three eggs; mix well; put into a deep tin and bake two hours.

MARBLED VEAL.
Mrs. D. A. Bradford.

Take some cold, roasted veal; season with spice; beat in a mortar. Skin a cold boiled tongue; cut up and pound it to a paste, adding to it, nearly its weight of butter; put some of the veal into a pot; then strew in lumps of the pounded tongue; put in another layer of the veal, and again, more tongue; press it down and pour clarified butter on top. This cuts very prettily, like veined marble. The white meat of fowls may be used instead of veal.

DRIED BEEF.

Chip half a pound of dried beef fine; put it in a stewpan, well covered with cold water. When it comes to a boil, pour off, and put over it a pint and a half of milk. Thicken this with a good tablespoon of flour wet with cold milk or water. Put in a bit of butter and pepper, and serve with baked potatoes. A nice breakfast or lunch for home people.

SWEET BREADS.

Parboil them as soon as you get them. Remove the tough parts carefully. Let them lie in cold water a short time before using, then roll in cracker crumbs. Season with salt and pepper, and fry.

FRIED TRIPE.

Scrape the tripe. Cut it into squares of three inches; boil in salted water; when very tender, take out; cut up smaller; season, roll in flour and fry brown in hot lard. When done, pour a cup of water in the frying pan, and thicken with flour mixed smooth, with vinegar; pour over the tripe, hot. Good for breakfast.

RHODE ISLAND DUMPLINGS.

One quart of corn meal, half teaspoon of salt, wet up with cold water stiff. Pat with the hands, into little balls. Put them on the bottom and around the sides of a kettle, and pour boiling water over them and boil briskly an hour. To be eaten with meat gravies. You can cook potatoes with them.

TO KEEP FRESH PORK.

Roast as many pieces as you wish to keep, all ready for the table; then put them away in lard. All that is necessary is to heat through when wanted, and the lard is just as good as any for frying doughnuts or mush.

HEAD CHEESE.

Clean the head well, and soak in brine twenty-four hours; then boil it till very tender. Remove all bones, and add to it a boiled heart, tongue, and part of a liver; chop very fine; add salt, pepper, sage and onion, if wished. Mix well; put in a colander and set over hot water at night. In the morning, put it to press.

SAUSAGES.

Use the proportion of one pound of fat pork to two of lean fresh pork; three good teaspoons of sage; two teaspoons of salt; same of pepper; good half teaspoon of cloves, and a pinch of nutmeg. Chop very fine, and mix well. To keep it any length of time, pack it in a jar and pour over it hot lard.

TO PRESS CORNED BEEF.

Put over in cold water and boil till the bones fall out. Let it cool in the water; then remove, wrap it tightly in a towel, put in a cool place with a weight on it. Slice very thin.

SOUSE.

Put the pigs' feet and ears when well cleaned, over the fire in cold water. Boil till tender; pour over them in a jar a pickle made of cider vinegar, whole peppers, cloves and mace, boiling hot. They will be ready to eat in three days, or less.

HOW TO COOK PIGS' FEET.

After they are well cleaned, wrap each foot in a cotton bandage wound around it two or three times, and secured with cord; then boil them four hours; keep them in the cloths till needed to fry, broil or pickle. If cooked in this way, the skin will hold it together while cooking, and they will be found very delicate and tender.

BEEF PICKLE.
Mrs. E. B. B.

One hundred pounds of beef; four pounds of coarse salt, made fine; four pounds of sugar; four ounces of saltpetre; mix the salt, sugar and saltpetre well together, and rub the meat all over with it, and pack the pieces closely in a barrel. It will make its own pickle. Put no water in, as it will spoil the meat. In warm weather, if a scum rises, skim it off and add a little fine salt. This will preserve it, with no further trouble. The beef should be kept till juicy, before attempting to pack it at all. This is very necessary to have it tender and keep well. At first, turn it, and rub the mixture in quite often. (Excellent.)

CURING HAMS.
Mrs. E. B. B.

Nine pounds of rock salt, or coarse salt; two pounds of allspice; three and a half pounds of brown sugar; two ounces of saltpetre; one and a half ounces of soda; six gallons of water; one hundred and fifteen pounds of ham.

CURE FOR DRIED BEEF AND HAM.

Half pound of rock salt; half a pound common salt; one pint of molasses; one ounce of black pepper; one ounce of saltpetre. This is enough for eighteen pounds of meat. It should be rubbed into the meat every day, in the tub, and the meat turned over and over.

HASH.

If a medium sized family has meat twice a day there can easily be gotten drippings enough for frying all the potatoes, French toast, mush, wonders and scrapple they may serve from time to time.

In clearing a table, every scrap of meat or bone with a particle of fat on it should be saved in a tin can or basin. The meat remnants on the plates may be mixed with other food, but they should be rinsed and saved, nevertheless. It is more nice than wise to throw them into the garbage. Keep these accumulations for a couple of days, then put them in the oven, and in an hour or two all the grease will be tried out. It can then be strained, and is purer and more wholesome than the lard sold by the average butcher. A raw potato peeled and sliced and cooked in a quart of drippings will clarify it very successfully. The fat that rises on the water that corned beef has been boiled in, makes very nice cookies. It can be melted and strained with other drippings to make it clearer.

CORNED BEEF HASH.

Take the clear pieces of cold corn beef, removing all gristle and bone. Chop fine, add twice the quantity of cold chopped potatoes. Moisten with some of the water the beef was cooked in, grease the spider with the fat that rises when cold. Warm well through. It may be moistened with milk, if preferred.

WONDERS.
Mrs. J. E. M.

Take any bits of cold meat and chop fine. Take half as much potatoes as meat, and the same quantity of bread broken fine and moistened with hot water. Good tablespoon of flour made into smooth paste for thickening, two or three beaten eggs, any cold gravies that may be left over. Season well. Drop from a spoon into a hot, well greased spider. Drippings will answer.

PHILADELPHIA SCRAPPLE.
Mrs. C. S. J.

Take bits of cold fowl or any kind of cold meat, or two or three kinds together. Cut up small, put in a frying pan with water to cover. Season well. When it boils, thicken with corn meal stirred in carefully like mush, and about as thick. Cook a short time, pour into a dish to mould, slice off and fry for breakfast.

VEAL CROQUETTES.

Mrs. S. Gebhart.

Mince cooked veal very fine, add one chopped onion, mix half a cup of milk with a teaspoon of flour. Butter size of a walnut. Cook until thickened and stir into the meat. Make into balls. Dip into beaten egg, roll in bread crumbs and fry in plenty of hot lard.

UNION HASH.

Chop up cold meat and season with pepper, salt, butter, and a cup of gravy if you have it; if not, add a cup of water to a pint of minced meat. Put in a baking dish and cover with mashed potatoes. Bake half hour in a well-heated oven.

DELICIOUS MINCED VEAL.

Chop cold roast veal; season with pepper, salt, nutmeg and lemon peel; moisten with a beaten egg and gravy or water. Put into a buttered dish, press down, cover, and set in a vessel of boiling water for an hour or more. Spread a beaten yolk of egg on the top and strew sifted bread crumbs over. Brown in the oven. Pour a little melted butter over and garnish with slices of lemon.

BEEF PATTIES.

Mince cold cooked beef, fat and lean, very fine; season with chopped onion, pepper, salt and gravy.

Half fill patty pans with this and then fill them with mashed potatoes; put a bit of butter on each and brown in a hot oven.

CHICKEN CROQUETTES.

Juliet Corson.

Put a tablespoon of butter in a saucepan over the fire. Fry in it a teaspoon of chopped onion and a heaping tablespoon of flour. Add a pint of milk or water slowly, to the consistency of a sauce that will cling to the spoon. Season with salt and pepper. Put in it three-fourths of a pound of cooked chicken and one-fourth pound of mushrooms cut in small pieces but not chopped. Let cook a minute, then remove and stir in the yolks of two or three eggs and a half glass of cooking wine, if desired. Pour into a well buttered deep plate, well rubbed with oil. Pour a few drops of oil on top to keep the chicken from hardening. Let cool several hours before breading and frying the same as fish croquettes

MEAT PIES.

Chop up cold roast beef or other meat. Heat it with a cup of water in a spider. Season with pepper, salt, and a bit of sage, and thicken with a spoonful of flour mixed in a little cold water. Pour this into a deep pan and make a crust a trifle richer than biscuit dough, which spread over the top, make an opening in and bake. Cold potatoes may be added to the meat.

MEAT DUMPLINGS.

E. H.

Take cold meat prepared as for meat pie described above. Make a biscuit dough, cut into as many pieces as you want dumplings, roll each about a quarter of an inch thick, and as large as a pint bowl. Put a small tablespoon of the meat in the center, gather up and pinch the edges together, set close together on a buttered plate and steam in a closely covered steamer twenty minutes. Serve any gravy there may be in a hot gravy dish.

MINCED MUTTON.

Take cold mutton, chop fine, heat it in gravy, and add a spoon of catsup and a bit of butter. Thicken with a little flour made smooth in water, and serve on a platter surrounded with mashed potatoes.

FRICASSEE OF BEEF.

Cut thin slices of cold cooked beef and heat quickly in some butter, already hot, in a frying-pan. Season with salt, pepper, parsley, and lemon juice. Serve hot, with Saratoga potatoes.

MEAT OMELET.

Mince up any cold pieces of meat, add a few crumbs of bread or crackers, and enough beaten egg to bind them together. Season well and pour into a well buttered hot frying pan. If it is difficult to turn it whole, a hot shovel may be held over the top until it is browned.

RAGOUT.

Take pieces of any cold meats, cut small, put into a stewpan with water to cover. Put in a minced onion or two if liked, and some cold boiled potatoes sliced. Heat up, and when at a boiling point, thicken with flour. Season with pepper and salt. A dash of cayenne pepper improves it. Unless the onion is minced very fine, it must be cooked alone before putting into the stew. Meats to be hashed up should only be heated through, not boiled.

SAUCES, CATSUPS AND SALADS.

CARAMEL.

Miss Juliet Corson.

Caramel for coloring soups, gravies and sauces, is made by putting a tablespoon of any kind of sugar in a dry saucepan. Place over the fire and burn slightly. When very dark brown, pour in a very little water. Keep stirring, and gradually add a cup full. If the sugar is not entirely dissolved, add a little more water. This imparts a rich color, and is better than browned flour.

A small wooden stick or paddle is much better to use in making gravies and mush than a spoon. It can scrape the bottom of a kettle without scratching or marring.

White pepper is considered better for table use than black. In salads and any delicate cookery, it is to be preferred.

In all salads where butter is called for salad oil may be used instead, bearing in mind to use about half the quantity.

CURRY POWDER,

FOR GRAVIES WITH DIFFERENT KINDS OF MEATS, AND FOR DUCKS.

Mrs. D. W. S.

One ounce each of ginger, mustard and black pepper, three ounces each coriander seed and tumeric, one-quarter ounce cayenne pepper, one-half ounce each cardamon, cummin seed and cinnamon. Pound very fine, sift, and keep tightly corked in a bottle.

MUSTARD FOR TABLE USE.

Take one-half of a quarter pound of mustard, to this add a teaspoon of sugar and one-half teaspoon of salt. Use the best cider vinegar to wet it, and stir to a smooth paste. When this is done, make it quite thin with vinegar and cook it, stirring all the time; it will thicken like flour paste. When cool it is fit for use.

DRAWN BUTTER SAUCE.

Half cup butter, dessertspoon of flour rubbed well together. Put into a saucepan with one cup water or stock. Cover and set in a larger vessel of boiling water. Keep moving the saucepan. Season with salt and pepper. When thoroughly mixed, take off. Do not let boil.

DUTCH SAUCE FOR MEAT OR FISH.

Put six spoonfuls of water and four of vinegar into a saucepan warm, and thicken it with the yolks of two eggs. Make it quite hot, but do not boil it; squeeze in the juice of half a lemon, and strain it through a sieve.

CELERY SAUCE FOR BOILED FOWLS.

Cook in a pint of water two heads of celery cut up small. One teaspoon salt. Rub together a tablespoon of flour with the same quantity of butter, and put this into a pint of cream or rich milk. Pour over the celery and let come to a boil. Remove.

MUSHROOM SAUCE.

Cut off the stalks. Put into boiling water with butter, pepper and salt. When tender, thicken with butter and flour, a tablespoon each, and add a little lemon juice.

ASPARAGUS SAUCE.

A dozen heads of asparagus, two teacups drawn butter, two eggs, the juice of half a lemon, salt and white pepper. Boil the tender heads in a very little salted water. Drain and chop them. Have ready a pint of drawn butter, with two raw eggs beaten into it, add the cooked asparagus, and season, squeezing in the lemon juice last. The butter must be hot, but do not cook after putting in the asparagus heads. This accompanies boiled fowls, stewed fillet of veal or boiled mutton.

SAUCE ROBART, FOR RUMPS OR STEAKS.

Put a piece of butter size of an egg into a saucepan, set it over the fire, and when browning, throw in a handful of sliced onions cut small; fry brown, but do not let them burn, add one-half spoonful of flour, shake the onions in it, and give it another fry; then put four spoonfuls of gravy, and some pepper and salt, and boil gently ten minutes. Skim off the fat, add a teaspoon of made mustard, and a spoonful of vinegar, and the juice of half a lemon. Boil it all, and pour it round the steaks.

QUEEN OF OUDE SAUCE.

Mrs. A. W. S., Logan, Iowa.

One peck green tomatoes, four onions, eight green peppers, ten horse-radish roots, one cup salt. Chop fine and let stand in salt over night. Drain carefully. Add one cup sugar, one tablespoon each of cinnamon, allspice and cloves, cover with vinegar and cook four or five hours. (This is a very fine sauce.)

CHILI SAUCE.

Mrs. Hollett, Independence, Iowa.

Twenty-four good sized tomatoes, eight large onions, eight green or ripe peppers, eight tablespoons salt, four cups vinegar, ten cents worth mustard seed, one-quarter teacup spice pounded, one-quarter teacup cloves pounded. Boil one hour. If too thick, add vinegar to taste, same with salt. Double this quantity will make six quarts sauce.

WALNUT CATSUP.
Mrs. E.

The only catsup to serve with fish. Take young, tender walnuts, prick them and place in a jar with sufficient water to cover them, add a handful of salt to every twenty-five walnuts, stir them twice a day for fourteen days, drain off the liquor into a kettle. Cover the walnuts with boiling vinegar, crush them to a pulp and strain through a colander into the juice. For every quart take two ounces each of white pepper and ginger, and one each of cloves and grated nutmeg, a pinch of cayenne pepper, a small onion minced fine, and a teaspoon of celery seed tied in muslin. Boil all together for one hour. When cold, bottle.

CAPER BUTTER.

One tablespoon chopped capers, one table spoon butter, one saltspoon salt, a pinch of pepper. Serve with boiled fish.

TOMATO CATSUP.
Mrs. L. S. H.

One bushel ripe tomatoes, boil until soft, and strain through a sieve. Add two quarts vinegar, and a half pint salt, one ounce cayenne pepper, five heads garlic skinned and parted, two ounces whole cloves, four ounces whole allspice, and three teaspoons whole black pepper. Mix and boil three hours. Bottle without straining. The tomatoes will keep their own color if the spices are put in whole.

TOMATO CATSUP.
Mrs. Hollet.

Two quarts skinned tomatoes, two tablespoons salt, one tablespoon allspice, four pods red pepper, two tablespoons ground mustard. Mix and rub thoroughly, and stew in a pint of vinegar for three hours, then strain through a sieve and simmer it down to one quart. Pour in bottles and cork tight.

CUCUMBER CATSUP.

Grate full grown cucumbers, sprinkle with salt and let stand over night. Drain well, season with celery seed, add vinegar till about the consistency of the cucumber when first grated, and bottle for use.

CURRANT CATSUP.

Five pounds currants crushed, three pounds light brown sugar, one pint good vinegar, two tablespoons ground cinnamon, one tablespoon ground cloves, one tablespoon ground allspice, one-half teaspoon salt, one teaspoon black pepper. Boil fast one hour, cool, **and bottle tight.**

GOOSEBERRY CATSUP.

Pass through a colander four quarts stewed berries. To the pulp add one and a half pints vinegar, one tablespoon each of cloves, cinnamon and allspice, and three pounds sugar. Stir ten or fifteen minutes. Common red plums are nice this way.

SPICED CURRANTS.

Mrs. F. W. Van B.

Five pounds currants, three pounds B sugar, one pint vinegar, one tablespoon each of salt, cloves, allspice and cinnamon. Boil the sugar, vinegar and spices ten minutes. Then add the currants crushed, and boil hard twenty minutes.

SPICED PEACHES.

A. H. H.

One peck peaches, two quarts vinegar, four pounds sugar, three nutmegs, one tablespoon cloves and cinnamon. After paring the peaches place in a jar, strewing spices through them. Boil vinegar and sugar together, and pour over them three days in succession, the fourth day boiling altogether twenty minutes.

GREEN TOMATO SOY
Mrs. E. B. B.

Two gallons green tomatoes sliced, twelve large onions sliced, two quarts vinegar, one quart sugar, two tablespoons salt, two tablespoons ground mustard, two tablespoons black pepper ground, one tablespoon allspice, one tablespoon cloves. Stew till tender, seal in glass jars.

DRESSING FOR CABBAGE.
No. 1.

One quart vinegar, four tablespoons butter rolled in flour, one teaspoon salt, one saltspoon cayenne pepper. Put on the fire, and as soon as it boils stir in the beaten yolks of four eggs. Pour over cut cabbage while warm. Eat cold. Good for salads.

FRENCH SALAD DRESSING.
FOR ANY VEGETABLE SALAD.

One tablespoon vinegar, three tablespoons salad oil, one saltspoon salt, one-quarter saltspoon pepper. Stir together. Less oil is preferred by many.

MAYONAISE SALAD DRESSING.
Juliet Corson.

For one pint, use the yolk of one egg, a saltspoon or more of salt, half of pepper, a dust of cayenne pepper, a level teaspoon of dry mustard, a teaspoon of lemon juice or vinegar. Mix to a smooth paste, then add salad oil and vinegar (or lemon juice), a very few drops at a time, first of one then of the other, stirring constantly until three gills of oil and four tablespoons of the lemon or vinegar have been added. Make in a cool place. If it curdles, stir in half a teaspoon of the vinegar or lemon alone. Mix well, and if that does not bring it right, set it in the ice box for a while. If it still curdles, take another yolk and begin over again, and gradually stir in the curdled sauce, and it will come out all right. If a white mayonaise is desired, use the white of the egg. It will keep a long time. Set on ice a short time before using.

DRESSING FOR COLD SLAW.

No. 2.

Mrs. Nellie Roe, Sac City, Iowa.

One teaspoon black pepper, one teaspoon mustard, two tablespoons white sugar, one-half cup sour cream, one-half cup vinegar, one-half teaspoon salt. More sugar if your taste requires. Pour over cold.

CABBAGE DRESSING.

No. 3.

Mrs. L. S. H.

One teacup vinegar, one tablespoon butter, same of flour, two small tablespoons sugar, pepper and salt.

Cook, pour over chopped or sliced cabbage while **hot**. Cover closely, and eat cold.

ANOTHER.

No. 4—Mrs. M. A. S.

Half pint vinegar, butter size of egg, one egg, two teaspoons sugar, one each mustard and salt; pepper. Boil vinegar, take from stove and stir all ingredients together quickly and pour over the cabbage.

LETTUCE DRESSING.

Yolks of two hard boiled eggs, two tablespoons sweet cream, teaspoon pepper, sugar, and mustard, half teaspoon salt. Rub together, let stand five minutes, add vinegar, and pour over lettuce cold.

MAITRE D'HOTEL SAUCE.

Cup melted butter, teaspoon chopped parsley, juice one lemon, pinch cayenne and salt; simmer.

TARTAR SAUCE.

First make a Mayonaise; mix with it one tablespoon each of chopped parsley, capers and gherkins and one teaspoon chopped onion.

PLAIN WHITE SAUCE.

Tablespoon each butter and flour made smooth in a saucepan and a pint of milk or water added slowly. If it seems too thin, cook longer.

ORANGE SALAD.

For eight or ten persons, peel and slice in round slices half a dozen oranges. Grate the rind of one, squeeze the juice from one lemon, mix together the juice of lemon, the rind of orange, and three tablespoons salad oil, and a pinch of cayenne pepper. Pour over the sliced oranges. A very nice accompaniment to roast duck or game. Its place is with game.

SALMAGUNDI.

Juliet Corson.

Dress this salad on a standing salad dish or a fruit dish. Use chopped veal or chicken, hard boiled eggs, white and yolk chopped separately, sardines or anchovies, tongue, pickled beets or red cabbage, chopped pickles or capers, and parsley or water cresses. Prepare all of these separately, and arrange them in little rows, placing the colors so they will harmonize. Dress with plain French salad dressing, using three times as much oil as vinegar or lemon juice. If sardines are used, get the boneless sardines at a trifling excess of cost. Grated orange or lemon rinds are nice additions. Salmagundi is specially adapted for night suppers.

RUSSIAN SALAD.

Take at least three colors of vegetables, beet, carrot and turnip. Cut the carrot and turnip in slices over an inch thick, then take an apple corer or a smaller cylinder and cut through the slices as many pieces as can be gotten. When enough are cut, boil each kind separately in a little vessel, putting over in boiling salted water. When just tender, drain and lay in cold water. Beets are not to be soaked in cold water, but boiled whole and cut up when ready to serve in the salad. Lay the colors around on a small salad platter rather than a high salad dish, in little groups, and pour over a plain French salad dressing.

POTATO SALAD.

Cold boiled potatoes sliced in thin slices in alternate layers with onion sliced very thin. Pour over cabbage dressing No. 4, and garnish with parsley and hard boiled egg.

POTATO SALAD.

Cold boiled potatoes cut in slices. If liked, mix with bits of cold boiled fish. Put on a platter, make a salad dressing of three tablespoons melted butter or olive oil, three of cream, large teaspoon salt, half teaspoon white pepper and half a teaspoon mustard. Mix this into half a cup of vinegar. When thoroughly cooked together add a couple of well beaten eggs. Take off directly and stir two or three minutes. Pour over cold. Chop parsley very fine and strew across the top in the form of vines. Lay sliced cucumbers or green pickled tomatoes around the edge. This is for about six good sized potatoes.

VEGETABLES.

Green vegetables when boiling, should be kept at the boiling point, else by stopping, the lowered temperature will soften them, and detract from their color.

After washing vegetables, lay them in cold water till time to put over to cook. Put them into boiling water unless otherwise directed. A pinch of salt, pepper or spice, means about a quarter of a saltspoon.

BOILED POTATOES.

If they are to be served whole, wash well, (it is easier to wash with a cloth,) cut an end off, or a narrow strip entirely around. This makes them mealy. When done, pour off the water and set on the back of the stove with a towel laid over them.

POTATOES COOKED WITHOUT WATER.

When potatoes are first washed, they may be cooked without any water, by putting them into a closely covered stewpan. The cover must fit perfectly, and the vessel must set flat on the stove. I have cooked them that way many times. Set the stewpan on top of the stove, shake occasionally, but do not lift the cover under half an hour. **Try it.**

MASHED POTATOES.

Peel, cut in two, and cook tender; drain; mash fine with a large fork, or, what is still better, the Victor vegetable masher. The latter renders them extremely mealy. Season with butter and salt. Pour in a cup of sweet cream or milk for a family of half a dozen persons. Beat in thoroughly with a wooden spoon; keep beating till your potatoes are a foamy white. Take up in a tureen. Dash a little pepper on in spots, if liked. Serve hot, with any kind of meats used at dinner.

QUIRLED POTATOES.

Peel, boil, season and mash potatoes, then put them through a colander into the dish you wish to serve them. Brown in the oven.

POTATO PUDDING.

Scrape or pare six good sized potatoes, place in a chopping-bowl, scatter over them flour enough to fill a teacup, add salt, pepper, and butter to taste, chop fine and mix well. Grease a deep pie-tin, spread the mixture in it, and cover with cream; bake slowly half or three-quarters of an hour.

SARATOGA POTATOES.

Peel and slice thin into cold water. Drain well, and dry in a towel. Fry a few at a time in boiling lard. Salt as you take them out, and lay them on coarse brown paper for a short time. They are very nice cold for lunch, or to take to picnics.

BAKED POTATOES.

If the potatoes are wiped dry, they will bake much sooner than if put into the oven wet from washing them.

POTATOES A LA CREME.

Put into a saucepan three tablespoons of butter, a small handful of parsley chopped small, salt and pepper to taste. Stir up well until hot, add a small teacup of cream or rich milk, thicken with two teaspoons of flour, and stir until it boils. Chop some cold boiled potatoes, put into the mixture, and boil up once before serving.

POTATO CROQUETTES.

Season cold mash potato with pepper, salt and nutmeg. Beat to a cream, with a tablespoon of melted butter to every cup of potato. Bind with two or three beaten eggs, and add some minced parsley. Roll into oval balls, dip in beaten egg, then in breadcrumbs, and fry in hot lard or drippings. Pile in a pyramid upon a flat dish, and serve.

POTATO PUFFS.

Two cups mashed potatoes, with two spoons melted butter, beaten until creamy. Then add two well-beaten eggs and a cup of cream or milk, a little salt, beat well. Pour into a baking dish, spread butter over the top and bake quickly a delicate brown.

POTATO BALLS.

Take the remains of mashed potatoes; make into flat balls, dip in beaten egg and fry a nice brown in drippings.

LYONNAISE POTATOES.

Boil, peel and slice about one-fourth of an inch thick. For six potatoes, use one onion. Put the sliced onion into a hot buttered frying pan. When a little brown, put in the potatoes. Season, and when a golden brown, sprinkle over them a tablespoon of chopped parsley. A combination of onion and parsley always means Lyonnaise.

PARISIAN POTATOES.

Pare and cut raw potatoes in balls, like walnuts. Boil them in salted water till tender. Drain them; lay them on a towel to dry, for a moment, and then brown in hot lard, the same as doughnuts. It will take but a very short time. Take out, sprinkle with a little salt, and serve on a platter with broiled beefsteak.

SCALLOPED POTATOES.

Pare the potatoes, cover the bottom of a baking dish with bread crumbs; then add a layer of sliced potatoes, bits of butter, salt and pepper; fill the dish with alternate layers; wet the whole with milk and bake for an hour and a half.

In cooking sweet potatoes, they will be made mealy if boiled and then put into the oven to dry thoroughly.

STEWED TOMATOES.

Scald and skin the desired number, and place in a stewpan without water; let them simmer for half an hour. Add pepper, salt, and a good sized piece of butter. Grate a few bits of stale bread over all; boil up once, and serve very hot.

BAKED TOMATOES.

Select large ripe ones. Make a hole in the center and stuff with bread-crumbs, seasoned with butter, salt and pepper. Place them in a deep pan and bake. Put a cup of water in the pan.

FRIED GREEN TOMATOES.
J. E. O.

Slice rather thick, and roll in corn meal. Salt and pepper, and place in hot frying-pan, well buttered. Cover closely and fry until perfectly tender and nicely browned. If you don't really like them the first time, try again, as they seem to require a cultivated taste.

SCALLOPED TOMATOES.

Peel and slice nice smooth ripe tomatoes. Place in a baking dish a layer with salt and pepper; then a layer of bread or cracker crumbs, with small lumps of butter. Repeat till the dish is full; bake about an hour; onion may be added, if liked.

TOMATOES AND RICE.

In cooking tomatoes for half a dozen persons, put in two tablespoons raw rice, when first put over to stew. It will be found a very palatable dish, cooked until the rice is well done, and seasoned with butter, pepper and salt.

METHOD OF COOKING RICE.
Juliet Corson.

Put a teacup of rice into a quart of boiling water, with a tablespoon of salt. Boil twelve minutes; drain off the water and cover and set back for ten minutes. Very nice.

HOW TO COOK RICE.

An American in Japan writes that they do know how to cook rice there. They put just enough cold water on to keep from burning, cover closely and cook over a moderate fire. When nearly done, take off the cover and allow the surplus moisture to escape. The rice turns out in whole kernels, snow-white, and very superior to the American way of cooking it.

A NICE WAY TO COOK SWEET CORN.
Mrs. A. S. J.

Take six plump ears of sweet corn and grate from the cob. Beat one egg, stir into it one tablespoon each of flour and milk, pinch of salt and pepper; mix all together, and fry in melted butter in a hot frying-pan; a spoonful in a place; turn as it gets brown.

GREEN CORN PATTIES.
Mrs. E. B. B.

One dozen ears of corn grated, or cut off fine; one quart of flour; three eggs; salt; two teaspoons of baking powder. Make very thin with water, and bake on a griddle with butter and lard.

BAKED CORN.

Take twelve ears of sweet corn, cut the grain partly off and scrape the rest. Add one tablespoon of butter, one of sugar and one teaspoon of salt. Rub these well together and add a pint of new milk, then put in the oven and bake.

GREEN CORN PUDDING.

Twelve ears of green corn cut off cob; one and a half pints of milk, four beaten eggs, one and a half cups of sugar. Bake three hours.

TO CAN GREEN CORN.
Aunt Addie.

To every six quarts of corn take one ounce of tartaric acid dissolved in boiling water. Cut the corn from the cob and put in sufficient water to cook. When the corn is cooking put in the acid-water and seal in air-tight cans. When you wish to use it pour off the water from it, put in fresh water and a small quantity of soda; let stand a few moments before cooking. When nearly cooked, say about ten minutes, add cream or rich milk, butter, pepper and salt. [A lady tells me that in thirty-five cans put up this way, not one proved a failure. Ed.]

SUCCOTASH.

Cook the shelled beans two hours. In the meantime, cut the corn from the cobs and put the cobs in with the beans for a half hour, to extract the sweetness. Use double the quantity of corn that you do beans. At the end of the two hours, put the corn in with the beans and cook a good half hour. Season with salt, pepper and butter and a cup of cream or milk thickened with a little flour.

LIMA BEANS.

Boil, and when tender, drain. Season with butter and pepper and cream, if you have it.

TO COOK STRING BEANS.

String the beans, cut them in pieces of less than half an inch, wash them and put them over to cook in boiling water, adding a level teaspoon of soda to a good sized mess of beans, let them boil fifteen or twenty minutes, drain off the water, put them over to cook in boiling water, and as soon as they begin to be tender, salt them, then boil until they are very tender,—it takes a long time to cook them properly—after which add butter and pepper to taste, and stir in some sweet cream. Or rich milk may be substituted, dredging in wheat flour to give it the thickness of cream. Some prefer them without either, using more butter instead.

BAKED PORK AND BEANS.

Put on one quart of dry beans to boil in cold water. In about half an hour after they begin to boil, put in half a teaspoon of saleratus. Let boil up, and pour off the water. Put on fresh water, hot or cold, let boil till the beans are tender, but not mashed. Take a pound of salt pork, clean it well, score the rind, and put it in the center of the beans, in a large dripping pan. Bake in a slow oven till all are nicely browned on top.

BOSTON BAKED BEANS.

Take one quart of beans; put to soak over night. In the morning put one pound of salt pork in the bottom of the bean pot, put the beans in, with plenty of water to cover, two good tablespoons of molasses, a teaspoon of salt, and place in the oven. Bake slowly all day, being careful to keep the beans covered with hot water from the tea-kettle. If the oven is wanted, the bean pot can be set on the back of the stove for any length of time, without harm. This quantity will make over two quarts when done.

CAULIFLOWER,

Is better wrapped in a cloth for boiling. Cook in salted water. Then serve with drawn butter.

ANOTHER METHOD.

Boil in salted water, just enough to cook it; then put in a cup of milk or cream and a very little thickening, and season with butter, pepper and salt.

TO COOK GREENS.

Look them over carefully, wash them and put them in a kettle of boiling water to which has been added a handful of salt. Let them boil without cover until tender, then put them in a colander, press out all the water you can, and put them into the dish in which you serve them—a tureen or some deep dish is preferable; cut them down each way, season with pepper and plenty of butter, adding salt if necessary. Greens are very nice boiled with ham.

SAUERKRAUT.

Squeeze the sauerkraut out of the brine; wash it in one or two cold waters; drain; place it in a porcelain-lined or earthen vessel; cover with cold water; boil two hours; pour into a colander; press out the water; replace in vessel; prepare a dressing of one tablespoon of lard and one of flour; stir thoroughly in a frying-pan over the fire until it assumes a light brown color; mix this well with kraut, and serve. Some like the addition of a few caraway-seed. The above is the proportion for one quart of sauerkraut.

FRIED CABBAGE.

Slice thin or chop fine. Put into a frying-pan, with some salt pork gravy, and a very little water. Season with salt and pepper. Cover closely. Cook slowly on top of stove. When done, add half a cup of vinegar, if liked.

SPICED CABBAGE.
Juliet Corson.

Half a cup of vinegar, tablespoon of sugar, teaspoon of whole cloves, same of whole pepper, some salt, put in the cut cabbage, cover, and cook slowly until tender. It is very nice served with a flank of beef cooked as follows: Take some stale bread, soak in cold water, season highly; spread on the flank and roll up; put some drippings in the pot; brown the flank in it; then add water, cover and cook until tender.

CABBAGE A LA CAULIFLOWER.

Take a small solid head of cabbage. Boil it whole, very gently; season it with salt and pepper and a cup of milk or cream. Serve hot. It is much nicer cooked whole, than cut.

DELICIOUS WAY OF COOKING CABBAGE,

SO IT MAY BE EATEN BY A DYSPEPTIC.

Slice or chop fine, a small head, and season with salt and pepper; cook in a kettle in just enough water to keep it from burning. Take half cup sour cream, half cup of vinegar, two eggs, butter, size of an egg, beat together, and pour it over the cooked cabbage in the kettle. Let it boil up once, and serve. Very nice.

CREAM CABBAGE.

Slice nicely, cook in a saucepan with just water enough to cook it. Season with salt. When tender, drain, if any water is left. Pour over it a cup of cream or milk, a tablespoon of butter, and a tablespoon of flour made smooth with milk. Let boil up, and serve.

SPRING CARROTS.

Leave stalks on. Scrape and boil in salted water till tender. Dress them with a plain white sauce, adding a teaspoon of chopped parsley and half as much lemon juice. This is known as maitre d'hotel carrots.

RICE CROQUETTES.

Take cold boiled rice; allow a small spoon of butter and a beaten egg to each cup of boiled rice. Roll into oval balls, with floured hands. Dip in beaten egg, then in sifted bread or cracker crumbs, and fry in hot lard like doughnuts. Good with maple syrup.

JERUSALEM ARTICHOKES.

Clean well and put to cook in plenty of boiling salted water. It will take one and a half or two hours. Drain, and serve in melted butter.

TO COOK BEETS.

Boil and slice, and put in a saucepan on the stove. Take a small cup of vinegar, tablespoon of butter, tablespoon of sugar, little salt and pepper, heaping teaspoon of corn-starch dissolved in little water; stir all together, till it boils, then pour over the beets, stirring carefully. Serve very hot in a covered dish.

BOILED BEETS.

Wash without breaking the skin. Put to cook in boiling water. Boil till done. Slice and season with butter, salt and pepper in the vegetable dish. Do not put on vinegar, as many prefer them without. Eat hot. Keep out enough whole ones to cut up for pickles.

TURNIPS.

Mrs. A. S. J.

Peel, cut in slices, and steam. When done, mash; add salt, teaspoon of sugar, two or three tablespoons of milk or cream, and a little butter. This will make old turnips taste like new. Turnips are also very nice cut in slices and cocked in boiling salted water, and served in slices seasoned with butter and pepper.

MACARONI.

A delicious breakfast dish. Take a pint of Italian macaroni broken up into inch pieces. Put it into more than a gallon of boiling water, and let it boil twenty minutes; drain in a colander; put in a basin or pudding dish, with three pints of milk, season with butter, pepper and salt, and bake thirty minutes.

MACARONI AND CHEESE.

Break half a pound of macaroni into inch pieces and put into a saucepan of boiling water and boil twenty minutes; add a little salt while boiling; drain, and put in a well buttered dish a layer at a time, with plenty of grated cheese sprinkled over each layer, with pepper to suit taste, and bits of butter. When the dish is full, pour over half a cup of good milk, or better still, cream. Bake half an hour, and serve in the dish it is baked in.

ASPARAGUS.

Get the stalks of equal length if you can. Tie up. Boil in salted water not quite half an hour. Lay on buttered toast, and pour drawn butter over it.

Asparagus is very nice cut up into half inch pieces and cooked same as green peas.

PARSNIPS.

Scrape them clean, cut in slices lengthwise and boil in a stewpan or skillet till tender. Drain, and dip into a batter made of half a cup of milk, one egg, half a teaspoon of baking powder in flour enough to thicken like griddle cakes. Fry in hot drippings or butter.

GREEN PEAS.

If the pods are boiled well and the water strained, it will be found to contain a great deal of sweetness and nutriment. The peas may be cooked in this water. Season with butter, pepper and salt and cream if you have it. If the peas are old, a little sugar improves them.

VEGETABLE OYSTER.

Cut into inch pieces and throw into cold water for a short time. Boil the same as green peas. Drain the water off and pour over milk or cream, thickened a little with flour. Season with butter, pepper and salt.

FRIED EGG PLANT.

Pare and cut in slices half an inch thick. Sprinkle a little salt on each slice and press down for an hour; then rinse in clear water and dry well with a towel. Dip in egg and rolled cracker and fry a nice brown. Season more, if required.

STUFFED EGG PLANT.

Take a full grown egg plant; cut in two lengthwise; take out the inside, leaving a half inch of the peeling. Chop fine, and mix with an equal quantity of bread crumbs. Salt and pepper, to taste. A very little sugar. Cook this mixture in butter in a hot frying pan, stirring it to keep from burning. Let cook about ten minutes; fill the shells with this, and bake in the oven half an hour. Serve in the shells.

[To peel an onion so it will not break, trim off the root carefully, but not closely. Take off the outer dry layer and leave the others intact. Do not cut the stalk. In this way, it will not boil to pieces. Juliet Corson.]

BOILED ONIONS.

When peeling onions keep them under water, and all weeping of the eyes will be avoided. Put to cook in boiling water. Boil a few minutes, then drain off the water; put on more water and boil again; and, still a third, where they may remain till tender. This renders them mild in flavor. When the last water is poured off, add a cup of milk and seasoning of butter, pepper and salt. Boil up and serve. The milk helps to relieve them of their offensiveness. Onions are very healthful, and it would be better for the generality of people, if they ate them oftener.

SUMMER SQUASH.

Grandma Owens.

Take them when the skin is tender and can be easily punctured with the finger nail. Cut up small and cook in as little water as possible. Cook without covering, so there will be more rapid evaporation. Stir often. When they are sufficiently cooked, they will generally be mashed enough for the table. Season well with salt, pepper and butter. Some like a little cream or milk added last.

HUBBARD SQUASH.

Cut in large pieces, scrape clean, and bake. When done, they may be served in the shell, or mashed, just as preferred. They cleave from the peel very easily. Season with butter and salt. If mashed, smooth them nicely on top with a knife, and put little lumps of butter and dashes of pepper here and there. Squash may be steamed if preferred.

BREAD.

Good bread is the staff of life. It can not be made from poor flour. The new process or patent flour is the most uniformly satisfactory for bread. Ordinary spring wheat makes good sweet bread, but is sticky and disagreeable to work up. It takes more of this flour than of winter wheat. Small loaves are better than large, and make less waste. Never set a bread bowl of sponge when it is so hot you can not rest your hand for a moment. Let loaves rise to twice the original size before baking. When bread is taken from the oven, turn it out on a bread cloth. Take the pan off, lay an end of the cloth over the bottom of the loaf. Replace the pan for ten minutes. It helps to make the crust tender. If baked quite hard, it is best to brush them over with butter. Cut warm bread or cake with a hot knife, to prevent clamminess.

If at any time it is desired to have bread rise more quickly than usual, use double the quantity of yeast and it will come up accordingly.

A half cup of sugar in a batch of bread will keep it moist, and make it much nicer.

The following recipes for yeast are excellent, and may be implicitly relied upon:

THE VERY BEST HOME-MADE YEAST I EVER SAW.

Mrs. W. P. Carr, New Lisbon, Wis.

Take three large potatoes, peel and grate them as rapidly as possible, so they will not turn dark. Pour on one quart boiling water and cook half an hour. Add one-half cup sugar, one-half cup salt, shortly before it is done. When sufficiently cool, put in any good yeast to raise it; the next day it will be as light as a foam. A teacup of this yeast will be enough to raise four or five loaves of bread. It should be kept in a cool place, and in summer renewed every fortnight.

HOP YEAST.

Mrs. P.

Nine large or twelve small potatoes, one teacup hops, one teacup sugar, one teacup salt, one teacup old yeast. Pare and slice the potatoes, tie up hops in a cloth, and boil together in bright tin or porcelain. Put through a colander, add enough cold water, washing the hop bag in it, to make a gallon. When cool, add sugar, salt and old yeast.

INDIAN MEAL YEAST CAKES.

Six potatoes and a handful of hops, boil together and strain on some corn meal, thoroughly scalding it. When cool, put in tablespoon ginger, and yeast. Let rise, then make into cakes and dry.

VERMONT YEAST CAKES.

Mrs. A. S. J.

Stir into a pint of good lively yeast a tablespoon salt, and wheat flour to make a thick batter. When risen light stir in some corn meal till thick enough to roll out. When again risen, roll very thin, cut into cakes and dry in the shade in clear, windy weather. When perfectly dry, tie in a bag and hang in a cool, dry place.

POTATO YEAST.

Mrs. Nellie Roe.

Six or eight large potatoes boiled and put through a colander, one cup sugar, one-half cup salt. Pour on boiling water till about as thick as griddle cakes. Let cool, and when lukewarm, put in one pint good yeast. When risen, stir down several times, keeping in a warm place all the time. Then put into jugs, cork, and keep in a cool place.

EASY BREAD MAKING.

One quart boiling water, one quart cold water, flour enough to make a batter. When sufficiently cool, put in half a cup yeast, teaspoon salt, and flour enough to knead. Knead smooth and place in a well greased pan. In winter cover with a dish, in summer with a cloth; do this at night. In the morning make into loaves without using any more flour than barely necessary to handle, place in the baking tins, greasing the top and sides of each loaf with butter or sweet lard. Let it rise until little holes may be seen when it is pressed gently back from the tin, and put in the oven. The oven should be so hot as hardly to bear your hand half a minute, and the heat uniform, for from thirty to forty-five minutes. This bread is just as good as if kneaded for half an hour or more.

EASY BREAD MAKING.
No. 2.

In the first place, take three tablespoons flour, two tablespoons salt, two tablespoons sugar, and scald by pouring on one pint boiling water. Let it stand till cool, then add two yeast cakes or soft yeast of equal quantity and let rise. Take one dozen good sized potatoes, boil and mash, add three quarts hot water, when cool enough put in the above yeast, and let stand over night. Now all that is necessary is to take a quart or more, according to the number of loaves you want, stir it into the flour, knead it into loaves and put it into your tins, let it rise, and bake. No sponging nor fussing. The mixture will keep two weeks. If your family is large and you require more loaves of bread, make up more of the yeast at a time. If you want raised biscuit for tea, just stir a pint or more of the yeast with a little shortening into your flour, make into biscuit, let rise, and bake. The contributor of this says it is the nearest to perfect bread that she ever tried.

MILK YEAST BREAD.

Take a pint of wheat middlings, stir into it one tablespoon white sugar, one tablespoon ginger, one teaspoon salt, one teaspoon soda. Put this in something that will exclude the air. The day before you want to make bread take two tablespoons of this dry mixture, put it in a cup, pour boiling water on it to scald, make it about the consistency of yeast, and set it where it will keep warm. Do this at noon, and by night it will be light, though it will not rise high. The next morning take a cup of new milk and one of boiling water, a little salt; stir in flour till as thick as fritters, add the yeast set the day before. If it looks dark it will not discolor your bread. Set it in a kettle of water as hot as you can bear your hand in, and in two or three hours it will be up and foaming, then mix your bread, put in the pans to rise, which will take about an hour, and then bake.

GRAHAM BREAD.

Make a rather thick sponge of white flour, yeast, water and salt. When light, stir in Graham flour till it is as thick as can be stirred with a spoon. To about three loaves put in one cup sugar or molasses. Put immediately into the pans to rise for baking. It requires a slow oven and takes over an hour to bake. Sometimes if the sponge is not quite as thick as intended, it is necessary to use more white flour when stirring to put into the pans. Graham bread should **never** be kneaded.

NOTE.—Water may be substituted for milk in the following recipes, and baking powder for soda and cream of tartar.

INDIAN BREAD.

Two cups Indian meal, two cups rye and two cups Graham, one cup molasses, one-half cup yeast, one teaspoon soda, salt, mix not very stiff with tepid water, let rise, and bake slowly three hours. (Excellent.)

NEW ENGLAND RYE AND INDIAN BREAD.
Mrs. O. Jones.

Scald one quart Indian meal. When cool, add same quantity of rye, one-half teacup molasses, teaspoon salt, a teacup good lively yeast, and small teaspoon soda. Mix well, add more water if needed. When risen, bake two hours or steam three hours. Graham will answer in place of rye.

PRISON MISSION BROWN BREAD.*
Mrs. J. B. Wheeler, Peoria, Ill.

1 pint sour milk, 1 cup each corn meal, Graham flour and white flour, $\frac{1}{2}$ cup molasses, 1 teaspoon salt, same of soda. Steam 2 hours and bake 1 hour, in a two-quart basin.

* This recipe was given me by the wife of our United States Prison Missionary, Rev. W. D. A. Matthews, Onarga, Ill., who is doing so much for the welfare of prisoners.

PAULINE'S BROWN BREAD.
Mrs. Dr. Cory.

Four cups meal, two and one-half cups flour, two cups sour milk, one and one-half cups sweet milk, two and one-half teaspoons soda, one teaspoon shortening, salt. Steam two or three hours.

ELECTION BREAD.

Two quarts flour, one pint corn meal, two tablespoons lard, one-third cake of yeast, a teaspoon of salt; mix with water to a stiff batter; pour into a deep bread pan. Let rise over night and bake in the morning.

VERMONT BROWN BREAD.
Mrs. A. C. Hastings, Middletown, Vt.

Two teacups sour milk, two teacups sweet milk, one scant teacup molasses, three teacups Indian meal, two teacups rye or wheat flour, two teaspoons soda, one teaspoon salt. Put in a two quart basin, place in a steamer and steam three hours, then bake one-half hour, or till a light crust is formed. (Excellent.)

RUSK.
Mrs. L. D. R.

One cup butter, two cups sugar, two cups new milk, one cup good yeast, three eggs. Stir as stiff as possible with a spoon. Set in warm place to rise over night. Ought to rise twice the size of the first. Cut off little bits, make into balls with the hands, using no more flour than necessary. When very light bake twenty minutes.

RAISED BISCUIT.

On baking day save out enough of the bread dough for a large pan of biscuits. Mix in two eggs, two tablespoons shortening, same of sugar. Use flour enough to knead all well together. Let it rise in a bowl and chop down with a chopping knife or carver. It will soon come up again. Keep chopping it down. It rises sooner after each chopping. Make into small round balls for supper. Put a little butter between them, let rise and bake. Then take them from the oven, brush them over with milk and sugar.

ROLLS.

Mrs. A. S. Johnston.

One pint of sweet milk warmed; add half a teacup melted butter, two tablespoons of sugar, small pinch of salt, penny's worth of good yeast. Stir in flour and knead it on the board five minutes. Set in a warm place. When risen, knead it for ten minutes and put on the board and chop it fine with carving or chopping knife. Let rise again; then roll it out, cut, as for biscuit, spread lightly with melted butter; lap one side over the other; let rise, and bake. The best I ever ate.

SARATOGA ROLLS.
Mrs. E. B. Baldwin.

Two quarts of flour; one quart of milk; half a cup of butter, two large tablespoons of yeast, salt. Sponge over night, and make into rolls in the morning; let rise, and bake.

CORN MEAL ROLLS.
Mrs. A. S. J.

If you wish the rolls for breakfast, make a quart of mush at noon, the day before. Salt it well; add while warm, one teacup of lard or butter, one-half cup of sugar. Mix thoroughly; when cool enough, add a small cup of lively yeast, and set to rise in a warm place. When risen well, stir in flour and knead it a few minutes; then set to rise again. Before bed-time, knead again. In the morning, roll and cut out like biscuit. Butter and lap one side over the other; let rise, and bake. In hot weather, add a small teaspoon of soda, well dissolved. If wanted for very early breakfast, roll out the night before, and they will be ready to bake when the oven is ready. (Very fine.)

FLANNEL ROLLS.

Mrs. M. A. Smith.

One quart of sweet milk, five eggs, salt, small spoon of butter; beat eggs well, add butter, salt, milk and flour enough to thicken sufficiently to pour. Bake in gem irons. (Excellent.)

CORN MEAL GRIDDLE CAKES.

Mrs. E. B. B.

One cup of white corn meal; two cups of flour, two cups of milk, one quart of boiling water, two tablespoons of yeast, one tablespoon of brown sugar, one-quarter teaspoon of soda; one teaspoon salt. Scald the meal at night, with the boiling water. Beat well; while yet warm, stir in flour, sugar, milk and yeast. Let rise all night; then add soda and salt. Leave a cup full for the next rising.

BREAD PANCAKES.

Take all the little crusts, crumbs and pieces of bread that are left in the bread box, or gathered from the table. Soak in water till soft, press through a colander; add milk, as many eggs as you can afford, salt, flour and baking powder, and your griddle cakes will be praised.

ECONOMICAL CORN CAKES.

Take one pint of corn-meal and scald with not quite a quart of boiling water; when cool add another pint of meal and a large handful of flour, salt, and a tablespoon of liquid yeast. Before baking add one-fourth of a teaspoon of soda dissolved in hot water; bake as other corn cakes. Let them raise over night if for breakfast.

MILK TOAST.

Put one quart of milk over boiling water to heat. When nearly boiling hot, stir in a spoon of flour mixed smooth in a little cold milk. Let cook a minute; season with salt and butter, and pour over slices of toast in a deep dish. If the toast is made from very dry bread, moisten it in hot water before pouring gravy over.

FRENCH TOAST.

Mrs. A. S. J.

Make a batter of two eggs, one-half cup of milk, pinch of salt, and teaspoon of corn-starch. Dip thin slices of bread in and fry brown in a well buttered frying-pan. If the bread is very dry, dip in water first.

MOBILE BISCUIT.

One and a half tablespoon each of butter and lard, three eggs, one yeast cake, one and a half quarts of flour, one teaspoon of sugar, two teaspoons of salt, and work up with warm milk. Stir lard, butter and sugar together, and then beat into the flour. Beat the eggs into this batter. Dissolve the yeast in a little warm water and add. Sift the salt through with the flour. Lastly, mix with warm milk into a soft dough. Set over night; make into rolls in the morning, and raise a half hour before baking.

BAKING POWDER BISCUIT.

Two quarts flour, with 5 or 6 teaspoons baking powder sifted through it; rub in 2 tablespoons lard and 1 teaspoon salt; stir in with a spoon $1\frac{1}{2}$ pints cold water; if too soft to roll out, flour the board well; roll soft, cut out, and bake in a quick oven.

SODA BISCUIT.

Mrs. A. S. J.

To one quart of flour add two good teaspoons of cream of tartar, and one of soda, and a pinch of salt. Sift all together. Mix soft, with sweet skim milk. Bake quick in a hot oven.

GRAHAM BISCUIT.

One cup of sour milk, one egg, half a cup of sugar, one tablespoon of lard, one teaspoon of soda, salt, Graham flour; stir to a thick batter. Do not roll out, but drop with the spoon into a greased dripping-pan.

KENTUCKY BISCUIT.

One quart of flour, half a cup of butter, a pinch of salt; make a stiff dough with milk; knead it a little, then beat hard with a rolling-pin, fifteen or twenty minutes. Roll out and cut into small round biscuits. Prick with a fork and bake in a hot oven.

SOUR MILK BISCUIT.

A half teaspoon soda powdered fine and rubbed into a quart of flour; mix in a large spoon of shortening and a saltspoon of salt; then stir in a cup of sour milk, roll soft, and bake in well-heated oven.

RICE WAFFLES.

One cup of boiled rice, one pint of milk, two eggs, butter the size of a walnut, one-half teaspoon of soda, one teaspoon cream of tartar, flour for a thin batter.

RAISED WAFFLES.

Mrs. E. B. B.

One quart of milk, one heaping quart of flour, two eggs, five large spoons of yeast, one large spoon of melted butter, one teaspoon of salt; mix the milk, flour, yeast and salt over night. In the morning, add the eggs and butter, and bake in waffle irons.

WAFFLES.

Four eggs, tablespoon melted butter, one pint of milk, pinch of salt, two teaspoons of baking powder, in flour enough to make thick batter. Heat irons well, before filling.

JOHNNY CAKE.

When baking johnny cake, after it begins to brown, baste it often, with a rag tied to a stick, in melted butter. A great improvement.

CORN-CAKE FOR BREAKFAST.

One pint of sifted corn-meal, one pint of sweet milk, two tablespoons of flour, one tablespoon of sugar, two tablespoons of melted butter, one-half teaspoon of salt, two teaspoons of baking powder, one egg. Mix into a nice smooth batter, and bake in a hot oven twenty minutes, and serve immediately. It is excellent when steamed three-quarters of an hour, and served at dinner with the meat course.

JOHNNY CAKE.

Mrs. M. A. S.

One pint of sour milk, three eggs, one tablespoon of sugar, one teaspoon of soda; corn-meal, to make it as thick as griddle cakes.

HOE CAKE.

Make a very stiff batter of water and corn-meal. Salt it; grease a griddle, and put on a large cake, pat it down, and cook slowly; turn it. When done, send it to table on a large plate, and let each one break off as much as he wishes.

GRAHAM GEMS.

One cup of Graham flour, two tablespoons of white flour, one teaspoon of sugar, one teaspoon of baking powder; water to make a batter a trifle thicker than griddle cakes. Heat gem irons quite hot, grease them well; fill two-thirds full, and bake in hot oven. (Good.)

GRAHAM GEMS.

One egg, half cup of sugar, beat together; one cup of sour milk, one teaspoon of soda, one heaping cup of Graham flour, one tablespoon melted butter, little salt. Bake in gem pans.

CORN GEMS.

Two cups of corn meal, two cups of flour, two cups of sweet milk, half a cup of shortening, half a cup of sugar, two eggs, three teaspoons of baking powder. Bake in gem pans.

LAPLANDERS.

One egg, one cup of milk, one cup of flour, pinch of salt; beat well. Pour into hot gem irons well buttered, and bake quickly. No baking powder required. Fill irons a little more than half full

HOMINY MUFFINS.

Wash a pint of fine hominy through several waters. Pour boiling water on it, cover and let it soak half a day. Then boil it in a saucepan in half a pint of water, till soft enough to mash. Drain it, and mix it with a pint of corn-meal or wheat flour, a little salt, and one and a half pints of milk, and two tablespoons of melted butter. When the batter is cool enough, add four tablespoons yeast; cover, and keep warm until very light, with the surface covered with bubbles. Grease some muffin rings, set them on a hot griddle, fill them two-thirds full, and bake them brown on both sides. Send to the table hot, to be buttered quickly.

OATMEAL MUSH.

One pint oatmeal, 4 pints water, 1 teaspoon salt; cook in oatmeal cooker, or, if you have none, use a tin pail set in boiling water; stir from the bottom; will cook in 1½ hours, but is better if cooked longer.

RAISED MUFFINS.

Mrs. Dr. Baker.

Three cups of milk, three large spoons of melted butter, three large spoons of good yeast; sugar and salt to taste. Mix very stiff at night. In the morning, dip the batter into iron muffin moulds, let rise, and bake.

MUFFINS.

Mrs. J. B. DeLon.

One egg, one large tablespoon of sugar, three cups of flour, half a cup of milk, two teaspoons of cream of tartar, one of soda.

RAISED MUFFINS.

Mrs. M. A. S.

One and a half pints of sweet milk, one quart of flour, two eggs, two tablespoons of butter, half a cup of yeast. Set over night.

CORN MUFFINS.

Mrs. E. B. B.

Two cups of flour, one cup of corn-meal, two cups of sweet milk; half a cup of sugar, one-third cup of butter, salt, two teaspoons of baking powder. Bake in muffin rings or gem pans.

MUSH MUFFINS.

Make mush as you ordinarily do, and when cold, take 2 cups mush, 2 cups flour, 2 cups milk, 2 teaspoons baking powder, 1 of salt, 1 tablspoon melted butter, 3 eggs; bake in gem pans.

RICE FRITTERS.

One or more cups of cold boiled rice, half a pint of milk, two or three eggs, flour to make stiff batter, with good spoonful of baking powder. Fry in hot drippings. Hominy may be similarly prepared. Eat with butter, syrup, or jam.

MUSH.

When the water is boiling, stir the meal in by the handful, having salted the water well. Make it a thick smooth batter, and at the last stir in a good handful of flour; it helps bind it, and is better for frying.

FRIED MUSH.

When hasty pudding is made, it should be put into a baking tin to mould for frying. Cook slowly in drippings, or lard and butter. Fry to a crisp brown on both sides. Eat with syrup. Many prefer frying the mush when it is first made fresh, **by dropping it in pats in hot drippings.**

BUCKWHEAT CAKES.

Put in a jar tepid water, with salt and yeast; half a cup of home yeast, or half of a two cent cake of compressed, will be sufficient for two or three quarts of water. Make a smooth batter with buckwheat flour of medium thickness. In the morning, beat well, but do not add any soda for the first or second bakings. Save a pint of batter for the next rising. It is better to take out the batter that you wish to keep before the soda is added, that it may not become too strongly impregnated with the soda.

GRIDDLE CAKES

Of buckwheat, wheat or Graham, may be made with sour milk and eggs, and are very palatable. To the above, two or three quarts, use three eggs and a teaspoon of soda.

POP-OVERS.

Euchre.

One pint of sweet milk, three eggs, nine table spoons of sifted flour, teaspoon of salt. Pour the milk upon the flour scalding hot, and stir until free from lumps. When cool, add the eggs, beaten to a foam. Bake half an hour in cups, and take from the oven immediately. Serve with cream and sugar, or sauce.

CRUMPETS.

One quart warm milk, half cake yeast, little salt, flour to make a stiff batter. Let rise, add half cup melted butter and bake in muffin rings.

FRENCH PUFFS.

One pint of sweet milk, six ounces of flour, four eggs, half a saltspoon of salt; scald the milk and pour over the flour, beat until smooth, whisk the eggs to a froth, and add to the flour and milk when sufficiently cool. Have ready a kettle of boiling lard, and drop one teaspoon of the batter at a time into the lard, and fry a light brown; sift white sugar over them, or eat with syrup.

PIES.

Good flour and sifted, good butter and sweet lard are essentials to good pie crust. Use very cold water for wetting and roll the crust from you. A quick oven is necessary for almost all kinds of pies.

If a little beaten egg is rubbed over the bottom crust of a pie it will prevent juice from soaking through it.

The yolk of eggs binds the crust much better than the whites. Apply it to the edges with a brush.

In all juicy pies, or when there is a tendency for the juice to run out, take some stiff white writing paper, make a roll about as large round as a penny and stand upright in a hole cut in the upper crust. Let it rest on the lower crust. Push the fruit aside to make room for it. Bake with this funnel in and the refractory juice will collect in it instead of on the oven bottom. It is not necessary to paste the paper together. It will keep its place without any trouble, and may be removed when the pie is done.

GOOD PIE CRUST.

One cup flour, one pinch of salt, scant teaspoon baking powder, sift together, and rub well into a piece of butter size of an egg, with cold milk.

ANOTHER.

One cup lard, half cup cold water, half teaspoon salt; mix the lard well in the flour, and add the water a little at a time, stirring with a knife.

PIE CRUST—PLAIN.

Three cups of sifted flour, one cup of lard, a little salt, a half cup of very cold water; handle as little as possible. Do not grease your pie-plates, they are more likely to stick if you do; you will find this just right.

PIE CRUST—VERY LIGHT.

Mix the flour and water together (same proportion as above), roll the paste out and lay bits of butter upon it, beat up the white of an egg and brush it all over the paste, fold it, roll it out again, and repeat the process till the whole of the white of egg is used; it will make the paste rise and become very flaky.

VERY RICH PIE CRUST FOR FRUIT PIES.

Take one pound of dried flour and one pound of butter. Break the butter with your fingers among the flour as fine as possible, and then with a little cold water mix into a tolerably stiff paste. Gently roll it passing the roller in one direction only—from you: After this lightly fold it over, and set it aside for a quarter of an hour in a cool place; then repeat the rolling in the same manner, and let it stand another quarter of an hour. This is to be repeated once more. Be sure to handle it as little as possible, and to keep it cool. Bake in a quick oven.

Many of the best cooks of the present day make their pies without sugar. When done they remove the upper crust and sweeten. It is a well known fact that it takes less sugar than if it is cooked in the pie.

MINCE PIES.
Mrs. L. Currey.

4 pounds lean meat, chopped fine after being cooked tender.

3 pounds chopped suet.
8 pounds chopped apples.
2 pounds currants.
2 pounds raisins.
1 pound citron.
6 pounds brown sugar.
1 lemon chopped up entirely, except the seeds.
$\frac{1}{2}$ ounce mace.
1 tablespoon cinnamon.
1 tablespoon allspice
1 tablespoon cloves.
2 tablespoons salt.

Wet with boiled cider and cook together.

MINCE PIES.

2 pounds lean fresh beef, after it is chopped.
1 pound beef suet.
5 pounds apples chopped fine.
2 pounds raisins—part of them chopped.
1 pound sultana raisins.
2 pounds currants.
$\frac{1}{2}$ pound citron or candied lemon peel sliced thin.
$2\frac{1}{2}$ pounds brown sugar.
2 tablespoons cinnamon.
1 tablespoon cloves.
1 tablespoon allspice.
1 tablespoon fine salt.

1 nutmeg.
1 quart cider.
1 pint molasses.

Mix and cook till the apple is done.

Apples may be used for mince pies without peeling. Chopped fine, the omission will be unnoticed. A lady of well-known culinary ability says chopped potatoes may be used instead of apples. Soak over night in vinegar; no one will know the difference

SUMMER MINCE PIES.
Mrs. E. B. B.

4 Boston crackers soaked soft in cold water.
1 cup molasses.
½ cup vinegar.
2 teaspoons cinnamon.
1 teaspoon cloves.
1 teaspoon allspice.
Raisins, currants, butter or suet.

Sweeten to taste. This makes three pies.

TOMATO PIE.
Mrs. A. S. J.

Take half-ripe tomatoes, pare and slice them, season with ginger, nutmeg, and cinnamon and plenty of sugar.

RIPE TOMATO PIE.

Aunt Lou.

Prepare your pastry as for an apple pie; slice in as many ripe tomatoes as will fill the plate; sprinkle a single handful of flour over it, also two teaspoons lemon extract and one teacup white sugar; wet the edge of the bottom crust before covering with the top crust. The fruit will be cooked when the crust is baked sufficiently.

RHUBARB PIE.

Grandma Graves.

Peel the stalks. Cut into half inch pieces. Pour boiling water over and let remain until cold. This takes the bitter sour from the rhubarb, thus saving much sugar. When cool, strew lavishly with sugar, a little butter and a sprinkling of flour. Half an orange improves the flavor.

[Canned pie plant is one of the most useful adjuncts to a winter supply of fruits. Nothing tastes better than a pie made of it in mid winter.]

DRIED APPLE PIES.

Soak the apples until quite soft. Then stew till soft enough to go through a colander. Season with lemon, add sugar to taste and one beaten egg for every two pies, and a teaspoon of butter to each pie. A tablespoon of cream may be added. Mix and bake with two crusts. This makes just the nicest pie of dried apples I ever saw or tasted.

GRANDMA GRAVES' APPLE PIE FOR WINTER.

Four or five tart apples peeled and quartered. Slice small and lay evenly around on the pie paste. Take one cup sugar, small pieces of butter, some cinnamon and a sprinkling of flour over the whole, and two spoons water. Cover with rich paste and bake slowly. Green apples should be stewed before making into pies.

ENGLISH CURRANT PIE.

Take the large English currants, cleanse carefully, and stew in plenty of water. Sweeten, and thicken with flour till of the consistency of rich cream. Bake with two crusts. A very good pie in the spring when pie material is scarce.

PUMPKIN PIE.

Remove the seeds of the pumpkin, cut into small pieces, steam till tender, then remove peel and mash fine with Victor vegetable masher. Or, cut up, peel, and boil in a very little water till well done **and dry.** After mashing, to each quart add one quart of milk, two teacups of sugar, one teaspoon of cinnamon and ginger, one teaspoon salt, four tablespoons of corn starch or three eggs; bake in a custard pan with an under crust.

SQUASH PIES.

Boil and sift a good dry squash, thin it with boiling milk until it is about the consistency of thick milk porridge. To every quart of this add three eggs, two great spoons of melted butter, nutmeg, or ginger if you prefer, and sweeten quite sweet with sugar. Bake in a deep plate with an undercrust.

SWEET POTATO PIE.

Boil till tender; rub through a colander or mash fine, and proceed as for squash pies.

CREAM PIE.

Mrs. L. S. Hodge.

One-half pint milk, one egg, one tablespoon corn starch. Sweeten to taste and flavor. Cook over water. Bake the crust alone in the pie plate. Put the mixture in and no more cooking is required.

COCOANUT PIE.

One cup sugar, one and one-half cups sweet milk,

one-half cup sweet cream or a tablespoon melted butter, one egg, one cocoanut grated. Bake without upper crust. Desiccated cocoanut is nearly as nice as the fresh.

RAISIN PIE.

Mrs. E. B. B.

1 cup raisins—seeded.
Stew until soft. Thicken with flour, like gravy. Sweeten to the taste and bake with two crusts.

BERRY PIE.

Mrs. E. B. B.

1 tablespoon flour.
$\frac{2}{3}$ cup cream.
$1\frac{1}{2}$ cups sugar. Make a crust as for custard pie and fill with fresh fruit and pour mixture over. Bake immediately.

ORANGE PIE.

Mrs. M. A. S.

One large or two small oranges, grated rind and juice, yolks of three eggs beaten with one cup sugar. Mix this with orange and add one cup milk or cream. Bake till the pie paste is done. Beat the whites with little sugar and put on top and brown.

LEMON PIE.

Juice and grated rind of one lemon, one cup sugar, one cup water, one tablespoon corn starch or two of flour, yolks of two eggs well beaten. Mix all together and cook in a basin over water. Line a pie plate with paste, put in the mixture and bake till the crust is done. Then whip the whites of eggs to a stiff froth add a tablespoon of sugar, spread over and brown in the oven.

LEMON PIE.

Miletus Swinney, Monmouth, Ill.

Two lemons, four eggs, two spoons melted butter, eight spoons sugar, squeeze the juice of both lemons and grate the rind of one. Stir together the yolks, sugar, butter, juice, and rind. Cover the pan with crust, pour the mixture in and bake till the crust is done. Beat the whites to a stiff froth, stir in four spoons sugar, put it on the pie and set it in the oven for a delicate browning. This is for two pies.

LEMON-POTATO PIE.

One raw potato grated; one lemon grated, with juice; one cup sugar; one cup water; bake with two crusts.

ANOTHER LEMON PIE.

WITH TWO CRUSTS.

For three pies take three lemons, grated rind and juice, three tablespoons sugar, same of flour, three eggs, one pint of syrup, mix well. (Excellent.)

EMANCIPATION PIE.

Mrs. A. S. J.

For two pies take two lemons, squeeze out juice; remove seeds. Chop rind and pulp very fine with one cup of seeded raisins. Add juice and one-half cup sugar and one cup water. Spread a layer of this mixture on the bottom crust, then roll out a very thin crust and lay on. Then another layer of the mixture, then the top crust. The best pie I ever ate.

[We think a little thickening improves it.—Ed.]

Wild grapes may be put up for winter use in sorghum or molasses. Fill a jar with grapes and pour the molasses over until covered with it. Tie a cloth over and in winter it will be found to be of a very rich color and flavor, and is delicious for pies.

APPLE CUSTARD PIE.

One cup milk, yolks of two eggs, three or four grated apples, small spoon of melted butter, half cup sugar, nutmeg to flavor, small pinch of salt. Bake in one crust. Make a frosting with the whites of eggs and two spoons sugar. Brown delicately.

CUSTARD PIE.

Three eggs, not quite a pint of milk, pinch of salt, three tablespoons sugar, flavor with nutmeg. Bake in a large pie plate with one crust. The whites may be left out for frosting if preferred.

CUSTARD PIE,

THAT MAKES ITS OWN CRUST.

Three eggs, three tablespoons sugar, one-half cup Graham flour, salt and flavor. The flour settles to the bottom and forms a good crust. Fill the pie pan with milk, mixing a part of it with the other ingredients first.

PEACH PIE

Cut the pared peaches and spread the same as apples. Sprinkle with sugar and a little flour. If the peaches are very juicy no water will be required. Bake with two crusts.

CRANBERRY TART PIE.

Stew cranberries—allowing a pint of sugar and a pint of water to a quart of berries. Line a pie plate with paste. Fill with the stewed berries. Put narrow strips of pie crust across the top. A quart should make two good pies.

CURRANT PIE.

This fruit makes the best pie when green. The main thing is to put in sugar enough. Dredge with a small handful of flour and put in about two tablespoons water. Bake with two crusts, fifteen or twenty minutes.

HUCKLEBERRY PIE.

This pie is improved by mixing currants with the berries. It is made in the same manner as the above. If no currants are at hand put in a little vinegar.

CHERRY PIE.

Of course it is nicer when eating to have the cherries pitted, but either way is admissible. Put in the pie-plate plenty of fruit, sweeten well and sprinkle with flour. No water is needed. The cherries will cook by the time the crust is done.

CHERRY PIE.

WITH ONE CRUST.

Take half cherries (pitted), and half chopped apples; cook together; sweeten, stir in a little flour, cinnamon, and a bit of ginger. Bake without upper crust.

It is unnecessary to detail each kind of fruit in pie making. Having made one or two that are similar there is judgment enough acquired to make others.

Pie plant may be used very largely for pies as the principal filling, by using enough of other fruit to flavor. The pie plant readily takes to itself any flavor. Thus with a scarcity of currants, gooseberries, apples, etc., the bulk of the pie may be made of the rhubarb with but little of the other fruit.

FRIED PIES.

Make a good biscuit dough, roll thin about the size of a pie plate, put a spoon of nice dried apple sauce or any other kind in, turn the crust over, cut out with the edge of a saucer to shape it nicely, and fry in hot lard like doughnuts.

STRAWBERRY SHORT CAKE.

Make a very rich biscuit dough; roll out half an inch thick, and put on a round pie tin. Spread over it butter or lard and a light sprinkling of flour. Lay another crust over this, bake. When done remove the upper crust and spread on a thick layer of strawberries and sugar after buttering the crust well. Lay on the upper. Butter that and spread over more berries. If any juice is left pour it on. This will be found easier than splitting a thick short cake. And it is better to make two or more small cakes than one large one, for the reason that they can be prepared fresh for late comers, and for a large table full may be dished out by more than one person.

If strawberries are sandy they must be put in a colander and rinsed thoroughly. Then put in a bowl and sprinkled with sugar, for an hour or two before using. Mash them if large.

ORANGE SHORT CAKE.

Sprinkle sugar over the sliced oranges for two or three hours before using. One quart flour, two tablespoons butter, two teaspoons baking powder. Cold water. Bake, split open and put the orange between. Eat with sweetened cream.

Any fruit either fresh, stewed, or canned, may be used for short cake.

PEACH SHORT CAKE.
Mrs. F. B. Smith.

One tablespoon butter, two loaf sugar, one egg, three cups flour, two teaspoons cream tartar, one teaspoon soda. Bake in round tins. When done divide it, butter and cover with peaches sliced and sugared.

HARD WINTER SHORT CAKE.

In the absence of fruit of all kinds, make a rich short cake and pour over it sweetened cream. In many new farming districts there is no fruit whatever and it requires a great deal of ingenuity to get up desserts.

BROTHER JONATHAN.
Mrs. A. S. J.

To one pint buttermilk add one teaspoon soda, little salt and flour to make a thin batter. Have ready some tart apples sliced thin. Mix in the batter. Grease pudding dish and pour the mixture in. Bake slowly or steam. Sweet milk may be used with cream of tartar and soda. Eat warm with sweetened cream or any rich sauce.

APPLE POT PIE.

Fill a basin one-third full of tart apples pared, quartered, and cored. Pour on boiling water and place on stove to cook. When they begin to boil put over them a crust made as for biscuit, cover closely and cook about twenty minutes. Eat with sugar and cream or hard pudding sauce.

BOILED APPLE DUMPLINGS.

Take one quart flour, one tablespoon lard, the same of butter, one teaspoon soda dissolved in a little hot water, two teaspoons cream tartar sifted through the flour; a little salt, enough milk to make the flour into a soft dough; roll out the paste less than half an inch thick, cut it in squares and place in the center of each an apple, pared and cored; bring the corners together; place each dumpling in a small, square, floured cloth; tie the top, leaving room enough to swell; boil fifty minutes.

BAKED APPLE DUMPLING.

Pare, quarter and core the apples. Make a rich, stiff biscuit dough. Roll and cut in strips, and take four pieces of apple for each dumpling and wrap two or three strips of dough around them, pinching the ends together. Put a quart of water in a pudding or baking dish, and one cup of sugar, and a small piece of butter. Let it get to boiling on top of the stove. Then place the dumplings in and bake till crust and apples are done.

APPLE PUFFS.

1 pint of milk, or part milk and part water.
2 beaten eggs.

Make a batter rather thicker than griddle cakes. Two teaspoons baking powder, salt. If water is used put in a spoon of melted butter. Pare, core and chop apples fine. Half fill buttered cups with the chopped apple, pour in the batter till two-thirds full. Set in steamer and steam about an hour. Serve hot with cream and sugar flavored, or liquid sauce.

DEW DROP APPLES.

Pare and core, without splitting, some small sized tart apples, and boil them very gently, with one lemon for every six apples, till a straw will pass through them. Make a syrup of half a pound of white sugar for each pound of apples; put the apples unbroken and the lemons sliced into the syrup, and boil gently till the apples look clear; then take them up carefully, so as not to break them, and add an ounce, or more, of clarified isinglass to the syrup, and let it boil up; then lay a slice of lemon on each apple, and strain the syrup over them.

PEACH PANDOWDY.

Mrs. E. J. Wilber.

One quart of canned peaches. Pour into a two quart basin. Make a batter of one cup milk, one egg, butter size of an egg, melted, two teaspoons baking powder, flour to make thick enough to roll out. Cover over the peaches. Put paper over. Bake till the crust is done. Eat with sauce made of one cup sugar, one-half cup butter, three cups water, small spoon corn starch, boiled a long time. (Very nice.)

CAKE.

The "cup" used in the recipes in this book holds half a pint. (See "Weights and Measures," p. 356.)

"Cooking butter" is generally a rancid, unfit commodity for cooking in any shape. Those who use creamery for the table, can procure dairy butter several cents a pound cheaper that is good and sweet, and will do nicely for cooking.

Eggs, if whites and yolks are beaten separately, give best results. Water may be substituted for milk, and baking powder for soda and cream of tartar in the following recipes. Flour should be sifted, and baking powder or cream tartar sifted with it.

If the oven is thought to be too hot do not leave the door open, but lift one of the stove lids off a little way, for a short time.

If coffee sugar is used, roll it fine. Any sugar makes better cake by sifting it. If a broom splinter does not adhere to the cake, it is done.

If a cake has to be turned or moved, do it very gently.

Since the alarming adulterations of almost everything used in cooking, a chemist advises the use of tartaric acid in place of cream of tartar. It costs about twice as much, but half the quantity suffices, and there is no difficulty in procuring this pure.

BAKING POWDER.

6 ounces of starch.
6 ounces of bi-carbonate of soda.
4 ounces of tartaric acid.

Powder and sift several times, and you will have a cheaper article than you can buy, and will have it pure. Keep it from the air. The main thing in preparing one's own baking powder is to sift it times enough. The above is a reliable formula, and may be safely used.

Almonds are blanched by pouring on boiling water. The skins will then rub off easily. If one application is not sufficient, another will be. The skin is tough and hard to digest.

In using fruit, dredge it with flour.

The whites of eggs will beat up much better if the eggs are kept in cold water for an hour.

Do not begin to grate a nutmeg at the stalk end. It will prove hollow throughout.

Cochineal for cake or candy coloring should be dissolved in a little water, and strained through muslin. Coloring may be bought already prepared at fancy groceries.

When frosting cake, dip the knife frequently in cold water.

It will sometimes be found that a trifle more or less flour is needed than the recipe calls for. This can only be accounted for by the known peculiarities of different brands of flour.

Unless otherwise directed, work butter and sugar to a cream; add the beaten yolks of eggs, then the wetting and flour, a little at a time alternately, then the whites, and lastly the fruit, if used.

When jelly tins are to be used, butter them, and then dust some flour over them; then turn upside down and shake it off. This prevents sticking.

To beat the whites of eggs quickly, put in a pinch of salt. Salt cools and also freshens them.

Cookies and small cakes require a quick oven.

Place a rim of stiff paper about a cake to retain the frosting in place until it sets.

FROSTING WITHOUT EGGS.

Hattie.

Take one teaspoon of gelatine and dissolve it in three tablespoons of warm water; then add one cup of powdered sugar and beat until smooth. Flavor with whatever you like.

GLAZING FOR CAKE

Take the beaten white of one egg, stir it well in a basin with a little water, let boil, and while boiling, put in a few drops of cold water; then stir in a cup of powdered sugar. Boil to a foam, and then use.

FROSTING FOR CAKE.

M. A. W.

White of one egg beaten stiff, five tablespoons of white sugar, boiled twenty minutes in enough water to dissolve it. Stir in the egg froth warm; add one teaspoon of corn starch dissolved in a little water and lemon extract.

BOILED FROSTING.

Two cups of sugar boiled with little water till it will click in cold water; whites of two eggs beaten to a stiff froth; then add to the syrup.

QUICK FROSTING.

Take the white of one egg and stir into it all the pulverized sugar it will take; spread on the cake, and smooth with a knife dipped in water now and then.

BOILED ICING.

Whites of 4 eggs beaten stiff.
1 pint of sugar melted in water and boiled.
Add to it the eggs, and beat until cold.

CHOCOLATE ICING.

$\frac{1}{2}$ cake of chocolate, grated fine.
$\frac{2}{3}$ cup of sugar, $\frac{1}{2}$ cup of milk or cream.
Boiled, and stirred to a paste.

COFFEE CAKE.
Mrs. A. S. J.

1 cup of coffee.
1 cup of molasses.
1 cup of sugar.
1 cup of butter or drippings.
1 cup of chopped raisins.
1 teaspoon of soda.
1 teaspoon of cloves.
1 teaspoon of cinnamon.
1 teaspoon of nutmeg.
1 cup five times full of flour.

ANGELS' FOOD.

IN OTHER WORDS, WHITE SPONGE CAKE.

1½ cups of pulverized sugar.
1 cup of flour.
1 teaspoon of cream of tartar.
Whites of 10 eggs.

Beat the whites to a stiff froth. Sift the sugar two or three times, and add it very lightly, to the eggs. Sift the cream of tartar through the flour, after sifting the flour alone, four times. Add it very carefully, mixing it as gently as possible. Then add rose-water to flavor with. Some prefer lemon. Put it into a bright cakepan, not buttered, and bake in a moderate oven about three-quarters of an hour. Try it with a straw. Let it cool off gradually by leaving the oven door open. Turn the pan upside down on the tube, if it has one; if not, set it up on something. When entirely cold, take out. (Very delicious.)

EVERYDAY CAKE.

Mrs F. W. Van Bergen.

⅔ cup of butter.
⅔ cup of milk.
1½ cups of sugar.
2½ cups of flour.
2 eggs.
1 teaspoon of vanilla.
2 teaspoons of baking powder.

CHOCOLATE CAKE.

No. 1.

NOT IN LAYERS.

Mrs. Dr. Evans.

1 cup of sugar.
½ cup of butter, scant.
½ cup of hot water.
1½ cup of flour.
2 eggs.
2 teaspoons of baking powder.
Bake in a square tin.
Spread frosting all over the top. Cut in **squares**.

FROSTING FOR THE ABOVE.

¾ cup of sweet German chocolate.
¾ cup of sugar.
1 tablespoon of sweet cream.
1 egg, well beaten; all simmered together in **a dish**.
Set in boiling water, till it is a thick paste.

CHOCOLATE CAKE.

No. 2.

Mrs. Howlett, Niles, Mich.

1 pint of pulverized sugar.
1 half cake of chocolate.
Cooked to a smooth paste in a very little milk; 4 eggs beaten separately.

1 teaspoon of vanilla.
1 cup of flour.

Beat yolks and sugar. The whole should then be stirred slowly together, adding the flour by degrees. Bake in square shallow pan and frost. This cut in two inch squares, with white sponge cake, makes a very pretty appearance.

CHOCOLATE CAKE.
No. 3.
Mrs. Howlett, Niles, Mich.

1 full cup of butter.
2 cups of sugar.
3½ cups of sifted flour.
1 scant cup of milk.
5 eggs, leaving out the whites of two.
3 teaspoons of baking powder.

Rub the butter and sugar to a cream; add the milk; then the eggs, well beaten, and the flour lastly, with the baking powder sifted in.

Bake in a dripping pan.

The cake should be about an inch thick when done.

While hot, turn on to a perfectly flat surface, and spread with a frosting made with the whites of the two eggs, and one and a half cups of pulverized sugar, six tablespoons of chocolate, and one of essence of vanilla.

CORA BELLS' WHITE CAKE.

Cora Bell H., Niles, Mich.

½ cup of butter, scant.
2 cups of sugar.
1 cup of milk.
2¾ cups of flour.
Whites of 3 eggs.
3 teaspoons of baking powder.

WHITE FRUIT CAKE.

Mrs. O. Blackman, Chicago.

⅔ cup butter.
2 cups sugar.
1 cup sweet milk.
3 cups sifted flour.
1 cup stoned raisins, chopped.
3 teaspoons baking powder.
Whites of 4 eggs.
Flavor with lemon.

NOTE.—In the recipes given in this book, when the word "cup" is used it has reference to the teacup in common use, which holds half a pint. I have, as far as possible, given the recipes by measure, instead of by weight; but when the recipes are used which specify the amounts by weight, the table of "Relation of Weights to Measures," page 356, will be of service where scales are not convenient.

LOVE CAKE.

Mrs. L. S. H.

1½ pounds of flour.
1 pound of sugar.
½ pound of butter.
3 eggs.
½ pint of milk.
1 pound of raisins.
2 teaspoons of cream of tartar.
1 teaspoon of soda.
Spice to taste.

BLACK CAKE.

Mrs. L. Currey.

1 pound of flour.
1½ pounds of brown sugar.
1¼ pounds of butter.
3 pounds of raisins.
3 pounds of currants.
½ pound of citron.
1 cup of molasses.
1 wine-glass of rose-water.

10 eggs. Season with cloves, cinnamon, and mace, to taste. Better have too little, than too much.

ENGLISH FRUIT CAKE.

½ a cake of compressed yeast.
1 pint of flour; make a sponge.
½ teaspoon of salt.
¾ pounds of currants.
1 cup of chopped raisins.
1 cup of sugar.
½ cup of shortening.
1 ounce of citron.
1 teaspoon of lemon extract.

Let the sponge rise; then knead like bread. When light again, work in all the other ingredients; place in the pan for baking. When light, bake.

FRUIT CAKE.

Mrs. E. B. Baldwin.

2 pounds of flour.
2 pounds of sugar.
2 pounds of butter.
6 pounds of currants.
4 pounds of citron.
10 pounds of raisins.
1 pound of almonds.
20 eggs.
2 wine-glasses of rose-water.
1 ounce of mace.
1 ounce of cinnamon.

½ ounce of cloves.
2 nutmegs.

The yellow of three fresh lemons grated. Beat the butter to a cream; add the sugar; beat with the hand until very light; add the rose-water, then add the eggs (they must be well beaten), and the flour next, the spices, lemon and blanched almonds, chopped fine. Lastly add the fruit, dredged with a little flour. The raisins should be chopped not very fine, and the citron shredded fine. Bake from four to six hours.

[If fruit cake is allowed to stay in the oven till the fire dies out, it is a great improvement. Plan so as to make it after dinner, and get it about done before the fire decreases much; then leave it till bed-time. If fruit cake cracks on the top, it is because the oven is too hot when first put in. In place of wine or other liquors, you can use an extra egg and a trifle more spices.]

FRUIT CAKE.

Mrs. M. A. Smith.

1 pound of butter.
1 pound of sugar.
1 pound of flour.
3½ pounds of currants.

2½ pounds of raisins.
½ pound of citron.
10 eggs.
½ teaspoon of soda.
½ cup of molasses.
Cinnamon, cloves, mace, nutmeg, and wine-glass rose-water.

RAISIN CAKE.

Mrs. F. W. Van B.

1 cup of butter.
2 cups of sugar.
1 cup of molasses.
1 cup of sweet milk.
1½ cups of raisins.
6 cups of flour.
3 eggs.
½ teaspoon of soda.
1 teaspoon of cream of tartar.
Spice to suit taste.

POVERTY FRUIT CAKE.

Mrs. E. B. B.

1 teacup of dried apples.
½ teacup of sugar.
½ teacup of butter.
1½ teacups of flour.

½ teacup of sour milk.
1 egg.
2 teaspoons of cinnamon.
1 teaspoon of cloves.
1 teaspoon of saleratus.

Soak the apples over night and chop fine, and stew two or three hours in sugar, until they are candied a little.

VILLAGE FRUIT CAKE.

Tribune Home.

1 pound of butter.
1 pound of dark brown sugar.
2 nutmegs.
2 teaspoons of cloves.
3 teaspoons of cinnamon.
10 eggs.
2 pounds of figs (chopped fine).
2 pounds of chopped raisins.
2 pounds of currants.
2 pounds of almonds shelled, blanched, and chopped.
1 pint of black molasses.
1 teaspoon of soda.
½ pound of citron.
½ cup rose-water.
1 pound flour.

MY WEDDING CAKE.

Mrs. F. W. Van B.

1 pound of sugar.
1 pound of butter.
1 pound of flour.
1 pound of citron.
3 pounds of raisins.
3 pounds of currants.
3½ pounds of eggs, minus shells.
2 wine-glasses of rose-water.
1 cup of molasses.
4 nutmegs.
3 teaspoons each of cloves, cinnamon and allspice.

PORK CAKE.

1 pound of fat salt pork, chopped fine, dissolved in one pint of boiling water.
3 cups of brown sugar.
1 cup of molasses.
1 pound or more of raisins and currants.
2 tablespoons of cinnamon.
1 teaspoon of cloves.
1 teaspoon of soda.
2 teaspoons of cream of tartar.
2 nutmegs.
7 cups of flour.

SPICE CAKE.

Mrs. C. Butterfield.

1 cup of sugar. 2½ cups flour.
1 cup of molasses.
¾ cup of butter.
1 cup of milk.
1 cup of stoned raisins.
1 tablespoon each of allspice and cinnamon.
1 teaspoon of soda.

SPICE CAKE.

Mrs. M. A. S.

1 cup of butter.
2 cups of sugar.
1 cup of sweet milk.
4½ cups of flour.
4 eggs.
1 teaspoon each of soda, cinnamon, cloves, allspice, nutmeg and mace.
2 teaspoons of cream of tartar.

CLOVE CUP CAKE.

Mrs. A. S. J.

1 cup of sugar.
1 cup of butter. 3 scant cups flour.
1 cup of raisins chopped.
1 cup of milk or water.
2 well beaten eggs.

Dissolve 1 teaspoon of soda in the milk and sift 2 teaspoons cream of tartar in the flour.

2 teaspoons each of cinnamon and cloves.

LADY CAKE.

Mrs. O. Jones.

1 cup of butter.
2 cups of white sugar.
1 cup of milk.
6 eggs, well beaten.
1 quart of flour.
½ pound of raisins chopped.
1 teaspoon of cream of tartar.
½ teaspoon of soda.
Nutmeg, or any other flavoring.

CREAM CAKE.

Mrs. S. E. Duncan.

Break one egg into a teacup. Fill the cup with cream; a scant cup of sugar; one and a half cups of flour, a pinch of salt; scant half teaspoon of soda. This recipe is very nice for patty pans, and excellent for layer cakes. If used for the latter, break two eggs into the cup instead of one. Flavor with lemon.

SPONGE CAKE.
Mrs. S. E. Duncan.

2 cups of sugar.
2 cups of flour.
4 eggs.
2 teaspoons of baking powder. Flavoring.
¾ cup of boiling water. Flavor to taste. Add the water last. The cake may seem too thin, but will come all right from the oven.

GOLD CAKE.
Mrs. E. B. B.

½ cup of butter.
1½ cups of sugar.
2½ cups of flour.
½ cup of milk.
½ teaspoon of soda.
1 teaspoon of cream of tartar.
Yolks of 6 eggs. Vanilla.

SILVER CAKE.

1 cup of butter.
2 cups of sugar.
3 cups of flour.
½ cup of sweet milk.
½ teaspoon of soda.
1 teaspoon of cream of tartar.
Whites of 6 eggs. Lemon.

This is an excellent recipe for many kinds of **layer cakes**; also, for a light fruit cake.

CORN STARCH CAKE.

Whites of 3 eggs.
½ cup of butter.
½ cup of corn starch.
1 teaspoon of baking powder.
1 cup of sugar.
½ cup of sweet milk.
1 cup of flour.

CORN STARCH CAKE.
G. W. Ashard, Vermilion, **Dak.**

1 cup of butter.
2 cups of sugar.
1 cup of sweet milk.
1 cup of corn starch.
2 cups of flour.
Whites of 7 eggs, and yolk of **1 egg.**

1 teaspoon of soda, 2 of cream of tartar, **or 3 of** baking powder. Mix flour, starch and cream of tartar together. Flavor with almond.

MARBLE CAKE.

Light part—
  2 cups of white sugar.
  1 cup of butter

1 cup of sweet milk.
3 cups of flour.
Whites of 7 eggs.
2 teaspoons of cream of tartar.
1 teaspoon of soda.
1 teaspoon of lemon.

Dark part—
2 cups of brown sugar.
1 cup of molasses.
1 cup of butter.
½ cup of sour cream.
5 cups of flour.
Yolks of 7 eggs. Pinch of pepper.
2 tablespoons of cinnamon.
1 tablespoon each of nutmeg, cloves and allspice.

1 teaspoon each of vanilla and soda. Butter the cake tin and put in alternate spoonsful of the light and dark batter.

FEATHER CAKE.

Mrs. J. H. Wilson.

1 cup of sugar.
1 cup of milk.
2½ cups of flour. Butter, size of an egg. Lemon flavor.

½ teaspoon of soda. Teaspoon of cream of tartar. Bake slowly.

PORCUPINE CAKE.

1 egg.
½ cup of butter.
1 cup of milk.
1 large cup of sugar.
2½ cups of flour.
1½ teaspoons of baking powder.

When the cake is cold, stick a teacup of soft almonds over the top, and pour over the cream, made as follows: 2 eggs, 1 quart of milk, 1 cup of sugar, 2 tablespoons of corn starch, ½ teaspoon vanilla; cooked over hot water.

SURPRISE CAKE.
Mrs. H. F. Marvin

1 egg.
1 cup of sugar.
1 large tablespoon of butter.
1 cup of water. 2 cups flour.
2 teaspoons of baking powder.   Flavoring.

WATERMELON CAKE.

White part—
2 cups of pulverized sugar.
⅔ cup of butter.
⅔ cup of sweet milk.
3 cups of flour.
Whites of 5 eggs.
1 tablespoon of baking powder.

Red part—
  1 cup of red sugar sand.
  ⅓ cup of butter.
  ⅓ cup of milk.
  2 cups of flour.
  5 yolks of eggs.
  ½ pound of raisins.
  1 tablespoon of baking powder.
Put the red all in the center of the pan, and the white around the outside.

SNOW-BALL CAKE.

Mrs. C. B.

1 cup of sugar. 1½ cups flour.
½ cup of butter, worked to a cream.
Whites of 3 eggs well beaten.
½ cup of milk.
2 large teaspoons of baking powder.

QUAKER POUND CAKE.

Mrs. L. S. Hodge.

2 eggs. 2 cups flour.
1 cup of sugar.
½ cup of butter.
½ cup of sweet milk.
½ cup of chopped raisins.
1 whole nutmeg. Scant half teaspoon of soda.

SODA POUND CAKE.

Mrs. C. S. Johnston, Harford, Pa.

1 cup of butter.
1 cup of sugar.
2 cups of flour.
4 eggs.

Small teaspoon of soda. Flavoring. Rich and moist; will keep a long time.

AMERICAN HOME CAKE.

Stir one pound sugar and three-quarters pound butter to a cream; have some one beat the whites of sixteen eggs to a froth; add to the cream, and, before mixing, add one pound flour in which you have added one and one-half teaspoons of cream of tartar; do not beat, but stir one way gently; then add peach flavor, and half a teaspoon of soda dissolved in a tablespoon of vinegar. I set it in the oven, and at the same time a pan containing three pints of water; when it has evaporated the cake is done.

WHITE POUND CAKE.

1 cup fine white sugar.
½ cup butter.
Beat to a cream and add whites of two eggs.
Then beat ten minutes.
1 teaspoon cream tartar.

½ teaspoon soda.
½ cup sweet milk.
1½ cups flour.
1 teaspoon lemon.
Beat all together fifteen minutes.
Bake one hour in moderate oven, in a round dish.

PRESIDENTIAL POUND CAKE.

Mrs. M. A. Allen

1 pound sugar.
1 pound butter.
1 pound flour.
10 eggs.
½ teaspoon baking powder put in the flour.
2 tablespoons sweet milk.

Beat the whites of the eggs separately, and add them the last.

PRIZE POUND CAKE.

Mrs L. A H.

1 cup sugar.
½ cup butter.
½ cup milk.
1 cup chopped raisins
2 cups flour.
1 nutmeg.
1 teaspoon soda.

LEMON CAKE.

Mrs. M. A. Smith.

1½ cups butter.
3 cups sugar.
4 cups flour.
⅔ cup milk.
5 eggs.
1 teaspoon of soda.
1 teaspoon of cream of tartar. Rub butter and sugar to a cream, then add the yolks, milk, juice and grated rind of one lemon. The flour and whipped whites to be added alternately. Will make two loaves.

BIRTH-DAY CAKE.

Annie and Marrion.

1 cup of butter.
2 cups of sugar.
3 cups of flour.
4 eggs.
1 cup of milk.
1 teaspoon of soda.
2 teaspoons of cream of tartar.

Beat the butter and sugar to a cream; add the beaten yolks of eggs; the milk with soda dissolved in it; the flour with the cream of tartar sifted in it; and, lastly, the whites beaten to a froth. Bake in a large dripping-pan, and frost heavily. When the frosting is partly dry, mark it off in small squares and put half an English walnut meat on each one. (This is a very delicious cake.)

DELICATE CAKE.

Whites of 15 eggs.
1 pound of sugar.
1 pound of flour.
½ pound of citron.
½ pound of butter. Flavor to suit the taste.

SPLENDID DELICATE CAKE.

Mrs. F. W. Van B.

1 cup of butter.
2 cups of sugar.
3 cups of flour.
½ cup of milk.
Whites of 6 eggs.
2 teaspoons of baking powder.

HOLLIS CAKE.

Mrs. Nellie Roe.

½ cup of butter.
2 cups of sugar.
1 cup of milk.
3½ cups of flour.
3 eggs.
1 teaspoon of cream of tartar.

½ teaspoon of soda.
1 teaspoon of lemon.

Put soda in half the milk, the yolks of eggs in the other half. Beat whites stiff, and put in last. This cake requires a great deal of beating. Make one very large loaf, or two small ones.

1, 2, 3, 4, CAKE.

Mrs. Nellie Roe.

1 cup of butter.
2 cups of sugar.
3 cups of flour.
4 eggs.
1 teaspoon of soda.
2 teaspoons of cream of tartar.

Be sure to put in all the flour. No better is made, in my opinion, if properly beaten and baked. Is **nice** frosted.

WALNUT CAKE.

Mrs. Duncan, Sing Sing, N. Y.

½ cup milk.
1 cup butter.
2 cups sugar.
3 cups flour.
4 eggs.
1 tablespoon baking powder.
2 cups walnut or hickory nut meats.

PLYMOUTH CAKE.

Mrs. L. S. H.

1 cup of butter.
3 cups of sugar.
1 cup of milk.
3 eggs.
3½ cups of flour. Small teaspoon of saleratus.

JENNY LIND CAKE.

Mrs. L. S. H.

1½ cups of butter.
3 cups of sugar.
1 cup of milk.
4 cups of flour.
5 eggs.
½ teaspoon of soda.
1 teaspoon of cream of tartar.

BUCKEYE CAKE.

Mrs. C. S. Johnston.

3 eggs.
1½ cups of sugar.
½ cup of butter.
½ cup of milk.
2 cups of flour
½ teaspoon of soda.
1 teaspoon of cream of tartar.
milk.

SISTER JULIA'S CUP CAKE.

1 egg.
1 cup of sweet milk.
3 cups of flour.
1 cup of sugar.
½ cup of butter.
½ teaspoon of soda.
1 teaspoon of cream of tartar.

ROLL JELLY CAKE.

1 cup each of sifted flour and coffee sugar.
3 eggs; 1 large teaspoon baking powder.
Stir quickly, pour into square tin and bake in hot oven; turn on flat surface, spread with jelly, and roll.

SPONGE CAKE.

Mrs. G. G. Bennett, Washington, Iowa.

A good patty-pan, loaf or layer cake.
4 eggs.
4 tablespoons of water.
1½ cups of sugar.
1½ cups of flour.
2 teaspoons of baking powder.

SPONGE CAKE

1 quart of sugar.
1 quart of flour.

12 eggs; pinch of salt and flavoring.

Bake in a dripping-pan. Requires no baking powder, as the eggs lighten it sufficiently.

MOLASSES SPONGE.

3 eggs.
1 cup of molasses.
1½ cups of flour.
1 teaspoon of soda. Ginger and cloves, teaspoon each.

WHITE SPONGE CAKE.

Mrs. J. G. B., Sioux Falls, Dak.

Whites of 5 eggs, beaten to a froth on a large platter. Add carefully 1 cup of sugar, and ½ cup of flour, with ½ teaspoon of cream of tartar sifted through it. Stir in lightly. Flavor with rose.

DAKOTA CAKE.

Author's Recipe.

Yolks of 5 eggs.
1½ cups of sugar.
½ cup of butter.
½ cup of sour milk.
1 pint of flour.
1 teaspoon of soda. Nutmeg.

ALMOND CAKE.

1 cup of butter.
2 cups of sugar.
3 cups of flour.
1 cup of sweet milk.
Whites of 8 eggs.
1 teaspoon of soda.
2 teaspoons of cream of tartar.
1 pound of almonds.   Instead of almonds, **you can use a cup** and a half of hickory-nut meats.

WHITE CITRON CAKE.
Mrs. M. A. S.

1 pound sifted loaf sugar.
1 pound of flour.
1 pound of butter.
½ pound of almonds.
½ pound of candied lemon.
¼ pound of citron.
8 eggs.

After the butter is beaten to a cream, add the beaten eggs, and then the flour. Beat it for an hour, then add the other ingredients.

CAKE WITHOUT EGGS.
Mrs. S. L. C.

1 cup of sugar.
½ cup of butter.

½ cup of sweet milk.
2 cups of flour.
½ teaspoon of soda.
1 teaspoon of cream of tartar.

GRAHAM CAKE.

Mrs. J. B. Bryan, in Tribune Home.

If any reader of the Home
    Should like a Graham cake,
I give you here a recipe
    Which I quite often make.

First take one cup of sugar white.
    And butter one-half cup,
Together mix, then add an egg,
    And lightly beat it up.

Then take one cup of pure sweet milk,
    And well dissolve therein
A teaspoon full of soda so
    Its trace cannot be seen.

Then scatter in a little salt,
    And flavor it with spice,
A little nutmeg, if you please,
    Or lemon-peel is nice.

And then of flour you may put in
    Three even teacups full,
And when you've stirred it well around,
    Then quickly pour the whole

Into your buttered pan, my dear,
    Which ready stands the while,
Then, if you give it a good bake,
    'Twill be so nice you'll smile.

GRAHAM COMPOSITION CAKE.

1 cup of butter.
1 cup of molasses.
1 cup of light brown sugar.
1 cup of sour milk.
1 cup of chopped raisins.
2 eggs.
1 teaspoon of soda.
1 teaspoon of lemon. Graham flour sufficient to make like ginger bread. Bake one hour.

LAYER CAKE.

ALMOND NAGOUT.
Mrs. M. L. Currey, Detroit.

½ cup butter.   ½ cup milk.
1½ cups sugar.   2 cups flour.
2 eggs.   1 teaspoon soda.
2 teaspoons cream tartar.
1 teaspoon lemon extract.
Bake in four layers. For the jelly, take
1 lb. sweet almonds (blanch and chop them.)
1 cup sour cream.   1 cup sugar.
1 teaspoon vanilla.
Beat all together and put between the layers. Frost all over with the whites of 2 eggs and ¾ cup pulverized sugar. Flavor with lemon.

DOLLY VARDEN CAKE.

DARK PART.	LIGHT PART.
1 cup sugar.	Whites 3 eggs.
½ cup syrup.	1 cup milk.
½ cup butter.	1½ cups sugar.
⅔ cup milk.	½ cup butter.
2 cups flour.	2 cups flour.
Yolks 4 eggs.	2 teaspoons bak'g powder.
2 teaspoons bak'g powder.	2 teaspoons vanilla.
1 cup raisins, chopped.	
½ cup currants.	
1 teaspoon each cloves and cinnamon.	
½ nutmeg.	

Bake in square tins and put together in alternate layers with jelly between. Make a frosting of the remaining white of an egg, and 1 cup of pulverized sugar for the top.

PINE-APPLE CAKE.

1 cup butter.
2 cups sugar.
3½ cups flour.
½ cup milk.
5 eggs.
1 teaspoon soda.
2 teaspoons cream of tartar.

Bake in jelly tins; grate a pine-apple and half a cocoanut and put between the layers.

WHITE LINCOLN JELLY CAKE.

Mrs. M. A. S.

1½ cups of sugar.
½ cup of butter.
2½ cups of flour.
⅔ cup of sweet milk
Whites of 4 eggs.
½ teaspoon of cream of tartar.
¼ teaspoon of soda.

Use ½ cup of corn starch and 2 cups of flour if desired. Instead of jelly between the layers, use lemon butter as given elsewhere.

COCOANUT CREAM CAKE.

Mrs. M. A. Woodworth.

1 cup of sugar.
½ cup of butter.
2 eggs.
½ cup of sweet milk.
2 cups of flour.
1½ teaspoons of baking powder. Bake in layers.

Cream for the above—

1 cup of sweet milk.
1 teaspoon of butter.
1 dessert spoon of corn starch. Sugar to taste.

Put on warm and sprinkle with cocoanut.

ROCKY MOUNTAIN CAKE.
Mrs. J. A. Reichelt, Chicago.

½ cup butter. 2 cups sugar.
1 cup sweet milk. 3 cups flour.
Whites 6 eggs. 2 teaspoons bak'g powder.

Bake in 3 layers in deep jelly tins. Make a thin icing of whites of 3 eggs and 2 cups sugar. Ice both sides of each cake. For the fruit, take

1 fresh cocoanut. 6 large figs.
1 cup stoned raisins. ½ lb. almonds.
¼ lb. citron. 1 lb. dates.
½ cup currants.

Blanch the almonds. Grate the cocoanut. Take about ⅓ of the almonds and chop fine with all of the fruit. Mix with a small part of the cocoanut and spread the mixture on each layer of cake and sprinkle On the top layer spread fruit, and use the whole almonds for decoration, sprinkling plentifully with cocoanut. Desiccated cocoanut will not answer very well for this beautiful cake. It is not so fluffy.

CHOCOLATE CAKE.

Layers from recipe on p. 184; frosting, p. 162.

STRAWBERRY CAKE.

Layers like the above. Let a quart of the berries stand a few hours in sugar; drain off the juice and spread the berries on the cake layers. For frosting, take 5 tablespoons sugar, and boil in the strawberry juice; stir in the beaten white of 1 egg and a teaspoon of corn starch dissolved; use more corn starch if it is not thick enough.

FIG CAKE.
Mrs. L. A. Clinton.

1 cup butter. 2 cups sugar.

3 cups sifted flour.
4 eggs, whites and yolks beaten separately.
1 cup milk.
3 heaping teaspoons baking powder.
Vanilla flavoring.

Take half the batter, pour it into 3 or 4 jelly tins. On each put a layer of split figs, seeds up; bake.

To the rest add 2 tablespoons molasses, 1 cup seedless raisins, ⅓ cup currants, teaspoon of cinnamon and cloves, a little more flour; bake in 2 or 3 jelly tins.

Put the layers together with frosting, having a fig cake on top.

ICE CREAM CAKE.

A corn-starch cake, with icing between the layers.

WHITE MOUNTAIN JELLY CAKE.

Mrs. A. C. Hastings, Middletown, Vt.

½ cup of butter.
2 cups of sugar.
3 cups of flour.
1 cup of milk.
2 eggs.
2 teaspoons cream of tartar.
1 teaspoon of soda.

Stir together without separating the eggs. Put soda in milk; cream of tartar in flour. Bake in layers, with frosting put between, as for jelly cake.

CARAMEL CAKE.

3 cups of sugar.
1½ cups of butter.
1 cup of milk.
4½ cups of flour.
5 eggs.
1 small teaspoon of soda.
2 teaspoons of cream of tartar.

Caramel for filling—

1½ cups of brown sugar.
½ cup of milk.
1 cup of molasses.
1 teaspoon of butter.
1 tablespoon of flour.
2 tablespoons of cold water.

Boil five minutes; add half a cake of chocolate (grated), boil until like custard. Add a pinch of soda, stir well, and remove from fire. When cold, flavor with vanilla, and spread between the layers of cake. Cover the top with the same, and set in sunny window to dry. The above will make two large cakes.

RIBBON CAKE.

Mrs. Rice, Sioux Falls, Dak.

2 cups of sugar.
1 cup of butter.
1 cup of milk.

4 cups of flour.
4 eggs.
1 teaspoon of cream of tartar.
½ teaspoon of soda.

Have two tins alike, ready; put one-third of the mixture in each, and bake. To the other third add 3 teaspoons of molasses; 1 cup of currants, and citron and spices to suit the taste, and bake in a tin same size as the others. When done, put a layer of the light cake, then spread with jelly, then the dark cake, jelly, and the light cake on top. Lay a paper on, turn over on a plate or tin, and press with two flat irons till cold.

CONFECTIONER'S CAKE.

Mary Van B. Owens, Oak Park, Ill.

One large cup of sugar, ½ cup of butter, 3 eggs, ½ cup of milk, 2 cups of flour, 2 teaspoons of baking powder. Take out half of the batter and add to it ½ cup of stoned raisins, cinnamon, cloves and nutmeg. Bake on jelly tins, and place in alternate layers, light and dark, with frosting between.

GILT EDGE CAKE.

1 cup sugar; 2 cups flour; ¾ cup milk or water; 1 tablespoon butter; 1 teaspoon soda; 2 cream tartar; yolks 2 eggs. Bake in 3 layers. For filling, take ¾ cup sugar in enough water to melt; let boil up; add whites 2 eggs beaten stiff; mix; add ⅓ teaspoon each vanilla and lemon; put between and on top.

VARIETY CAKE.

¾ cup butter and
1 cup sugar worked to a cream; add
½ cup milk,
5 yolks of eggs well beaten, and
1 teaspoon baking powder in
2 cups flour.

Divide, and flavor one-half with orange water and the other with vanilla and enough grated chocolate to color brown. Bake in two jelly tins.

Prepare another cake batter as follows:

½ cup butter.
1½ cups sugar.
½ cup sweet milk.
Whites 5 eggs.
1 teaspoon baking powder in
2 full cups flour.

Divide, and flavor one-half with rose water and the other with lemon and color with pulverized cochineal a bright red. Bake in two jelly tins. When done, place the brown cake first, then white, red, and last yellow, with jelly between, and frost the top with boiled icing. When cold and hard, ornament the top with a funnel of the frosting.

LEMON CAKE.

½ cup butter.   3 eggs.   For the jelly—
2 cups sugar.   1 cup sugar.   1 egg.
1 cup milk.   1 tablespoon butter.
3 cups flour.   Grated rind and juice 1
2 teaspoons bak'g powd'r. lemon.
   Bake in jelly tins.   Boil till thick.

ORANGE CAKE.

Mrs. L. A. Brodie, Chicago.

2 coffee cups sugar. 2 coffee cups flour. ½ cup cold water. Whites 4 eggs. Yolks 5 eggs. 2 teaspoons baking powder. Beat yolks and sugar together; add flour and baking powder and water, and lastly the beaten whites. Then take the juice (except one tablespoon) and grated rind of one large orange and stir in the batter. Bake in layers. Make frosting of whites 2 eggs, tablespoon orange juice and 6 tablespoons sugar. Spread on the layers.

BELVIDERE CREAM CAKE.

Lilla E. Miller.

½ cup of butter.
1 cup of sugar.
2 eggs.
½ cup of sweet milk.
½ teaspoon of soda.
1 teaspoon of cream of tartar.
1¾ cups of flour.

Cream for the above layers—

½ pint of milk.
1 egg.
¼ cup of flour, or large tablespoon of corn starch.
½ cup of sugar. Pinch of salt.

Mix egg, flour and sugar with part of the milk. Stir into the remainder of the milk when scalding hot. Flavor after it is cooked.

COOKIES.

CHRISTMAS COOKIES.

Mrs. F. W. Van B., Oak Park, Ill.

4 eggs and 1 pound of sugar stirred together for one hour. Add $\frac{1}{2}$ teaspoon pulverized hartshorn; then enough flour to make a stiff dough. Roll out and cut. Keep in a warm room all night. Then bake in a slow oven. Sprinkle the pans with annis seed before putting cookies in. Make as stiff as you can roll out. (Splendid.)

[As "Christmas comes but once a year," we may afford the time taken for these delightful cookies. Ed.]

GERMAN COOKIES.

Mrs. J. Engel.

1 pound of flour, with 2 teaspoons of baking powder, 3 eggs, $\frac{1}{2}$ pound of sugar, $\frac{1}{4}$ pound of butter, lemon and mace. Stir butter to a cream, put in sugar and yolks of eggs, then the beaten whites, and flour. Roll, spread on with a brush a beaten egg and sprinkle with cinnamon and sugar. Bake quickly.

GARFIELD COOKIES.

12 cups of flour, 3 cups of butter, 5 cups of sugar, 1 teaspoon of soda, 1 tablespoon of caraway seed. Large coffee cup of water. Rub the butter and sugar into the flour.

ARTHUR COOKIES.

1 cup of butter, 1 cup of sour cream, $2\frac{1}{2}$ cups of sugar, 2 eggs, 1 teaspoon of soda, nutmeg. Flour to roll out soft and thin.

BLAINE COOKIES.

3 eggs, 2 cups of sugar, 1 cup of butter, 1 tablespoon of sweet cream, 1 teaspoon of soda, same of cream of tartar.

WINDOM COOKIES.

1 cup of butter, 2 cups of sugar, $\frac{2}{3}$ cup of water, 2 eggs, 3 teaspoons of baking powder, nutmeg. Soft and thin.

LINCOLN COOKIES.

1 cup of sugar, $\frac{1}{2}$ cup of butter, $\frac{1}{2}$ cup of buttermilk, 1 teaspoon of soda, nutmeg. Roll soft and thin.

HUNT COOKIES.

3 eggs, 2 cups of sugar, 1 cup of butter, 1 cup of milk or water, ½ teaspoon of soda. Rub butter and sugar to a cream. Beat eggs to a froth; add them and stir; then add a pint of flour, then the soda dissolved in the milk, then the rest of the flour. Mix soft and roll thin.

MACVEAGH COOKIES.

1 cup of butter, 2 cups of sugar, ⅓ cup of sour milk, 3 eggs, 1 teaspoon of soda, 1 nutmeg or cinnamon. Roll soft and thin.

KIRKWOOD COOKIES.

Mrs. M. A. S.

1 cup of sour cream, 1 cup of sugar, 1 egg, ½ cup of butter, teaspoon of soda, nutmeg. Flour to roll thin.

JAMES COOKIES.

Mrs. L. S. H.

1 coffee cup of sugar, ⅔ cup of butter, 2 eggs, ½ teaspoon of soda dissolved in two tablespoons of milk. Roll soft and thin.

SEA FOAM.

Whites of 10 eggs beaten to a stiff froth, one and a half cups of sifted sugar, one cup of sifted flour, one teaspoon of cream of tartar. Put into rings and bake quick.

MOLASSES COOKIES.
Mrs. E. B. B.

1 cup of butter, 2 cups of molasses, 1 teaspoon of cloves, 1 tablespoon of ginger. Flour to make a stiff batter. Mould with the hand into small cakes, and bake in a steady rather than quick oven, as they are apt to burn. (Good.)

MOLASSES COOKIES.
Mrs. F. W. Van B.

1 pint of molasses, 1 coffee cup of butter and lard. Put on stove and boil two minutes. When nearly cold, add 3 tablespoons of boiling water, and 1 tablespoon of soda. Stir until it foams. Put in plenty of salt, and 1 tablespoon of ginger. Flour to roll. (Splendid.)

GINGER COOKIES.
Kittie Bradford, Sidney Plains, N. Y.

1 cup of butter, (or half drippings will answer,)

1 cup of sugar, 1 cup of molasses, 1 egg, 1 tablespoon of soda, 1 tablespoon of ginger. Mix not very stiff. Sprinkle with sugar before baking. These cookies took the premium at a State Fair.

GINGER COOKIES.

Mrs. Julia B. De Lon.

1 cup of sugar, 1 cup of molasses, 1 cup of butter, 1 cup of boiling water, tablespoon of ginger, same of soda. Mix not very stiff.

GINGER COOKIES

Mrs. A. C. H.

2 cups of molasses, $\frac{1}{2}$ cup of sugar, 1 cup of butter or lard, 1 cup of hot water, 2 teaspoons of alum, 4 teaspoons of soda; the alum and soda in the hot water. Heaping tablespoon of ginger. Flour to roll.

GINGER COOKIES.

Mrs. William Morrison, Spencer, Iowa.

1 cup of shortening, 1 cup of molasses, 1 cup of sugar, 3 teaspoons of soda, 3 teaspoons of ginger Sour milk to dissolve soda in. Flour to roll.

GINGER COOKIES.

Mrs. E. J. Wilber.

2½ cups of molasses, 1 cup of shortening, 2 tablespoons of soda dissolved in 1 cup of hot water, 1 tablespoon of ginger. Flour to roll out.

GINGER SNAPS.

Mrs. H., Niles, Mich.

1 cup of New Orleans molasses, 1 cup of brown sugar, 1 cup of butter or lard. Boil 20 minutes; then add 1 teaspoon of soda, one well beaten egg, and flour to make it very stiff. After it is well kneaded, cut off a small piece to roll out, and put the balance where it will keep warm until needed. It should be so stiff that it will be necessary to keep it quite warm in order to roll out smoothly.

GINGER SNAPS.

1 cup of butter, 1 cup of sugar, 1½ cups of molasses, ½ cup of water, 1 teaspoon of soda, 1 tablespoon of ginger. Flour to stiffen. Put the sugar into the flour, then add the butter and rub it in.

GINGER JUMBLES.

Mrs. M. A. S.

1 cup of butter, 1 cup of brown sugar, 2 cups of

molasses, 4½ cups of flour, 2 eggs, 1 teaspoon of soda. Drop on buttered tins.

DOUGHNUTS

RAISED DOUGHNUTS.

Set sponge for them the middle of the afternoon. Fry the next forenoon. 1 quart of water, 1 cake of yeast. Let rise till very light (about 5 hours). Add 1 coffee cup of lard, 2 cups of white sugar, 3 large mashed potatoes, or 2 eggs (the potatoes are nicer) and a small nutmeg. Let rise again, until very light. Either roll it and cut, or break off bits for frying. Lay enough for one frying on a floured plate and set in the oven to warm. When they are put in to fry, set some more in the oven. This improves fried-cakes very much. It takes longer to cook raised doughnuts, than those made with baking powder.

DOUGHNUTS

Mrs. E. B. B.

1 cup of sugar, 1 cup of cream, 1 cup of sour milk, 1 egg, 1 teaspoon of soda, nutmeg. Flour to roll.

DOUGHNUTS.
Mrs. Dr. B. M. Baker.

⅓ cup of butter, 2 cups of sugar, 2 cups of milk, 3 eggs, pinch of salt, nutmeg, 1 heaping teaspoon of baking powder to every pint of flour used to make them stiff enough to roll out. This will make 100 cakes.

LAZY DOUGHNUTS.
Mrs. Nellie Roe.

½ cup of sugar, 2 eggs, 1 cup of sour milk, 2 tablespoons of melted lard, ½ teaspoon of soda. Stir as stiff as possible, with flour. Drop from a teaspoon in hot lard and fry brown. Dip spoon in lard after each time, and they will not stick to the spoon.

FRIED CAKES.
Mrs. M. A. S.

1 teacup of sugar, 1 teacup of buttermilk, 1 egg, 2 tablespoons of melted lard, 1 teaspoon of soda. Cut in any shape desired, and fry in boiling lard.

AMALGAMATION DOUGHNUTS.

1 cup of yellow corn-meal, 2 cups of flour, 3 teaspoons of baking powder, 1 teaspoon of salt and 1 of nutmeg, 1 cup of sugar, and enough milk to roll well. Then fry in hot lard.

ANDOVER WONDERS.
M. S. M.

3 eggs, 1½ cups of sugar, 1½ cups of milk, 1 tablespoon of lard or butter, 1 teaspoon of soda, two teaspoons of cream of tartar, spice to taste, cut in rounds, boil in hot lard, like doughnuts.

SPANISH RUFFS.

Put into a saucepan a teacup of water, a tablespoon of powdered sugar, ½ a teaspoon of salt, and 2 ounces of butter. While boiling, add sufficient flour for it to leave the saucepan; stir in, one by one, the yolks of 4 eggs. Drop a teaspoon at a time into boiling lard, and fry a light brown.

RISSOLES.

Roll out nice pie paste, and put bits of jelly or preserves in a row along the edge, about two inches apart. Then turn the whole row over on to the layer of paste and cut down through the two layers with a cake or biscuit cutter, enclosing the bit of preserves in the cutting. Either fry in hot fat or bake in the oven. Stick the edges together with a little water.

FRIED CAKES WITHOUT SHORTENING.
Mrs O. Blackman, Chicago.

2 eggs, 1 cup sugar, beaten thoroughly together; add 1 cup sweet milk and a little more than 1 quart flour; 3 teaspoons baking powder. Mix as soft as can be rolled.

GINGER CAKES.

NOTE.—Water may be substituted for milk in any of the following recipes.

OLD-FASHIONED GINGER BREAD.

1 pint of molasses, 6 tablespoons of butter, 2 tablespoons of ginger, 2 teaspoons of saleratus, 1 teaspoon of alum. Dissolve the alum and saleratus separately in plenty of water, making in all one cup full; mix as soft as can be rolled; bake ten or fifteen minutes in a quick oven.

GINGER BREAD.

1 cup of molasses, 1 cup of sour milk, 2 eggs, 4 teaspoons of soda, 2 teaspoons of cream of tartar, 1 cup of brown sugar, $\frac{1}{2}$ cup of butter, 1 tablespoon of ginger. Mix stiff enough to roll out. Bake in a large dripping-pan and mark off.

GINGER BREAD.
Anna P.

1 cup of sugar, 1 cup of New Orleans molasses, 1 cup of sour milk, 1 cup of butter, 4 cups of flour, 1 teaspoon each of saleratus and cinnamon, and 2 of ginger. Bake in a steady oven.

GINGER BREAD.

Mrs. E. B. B.

2 or 3 eggs, 1 cup of molasses, 1 cup of sugar, 1 cup of butter, 3 cups of flour, 1 cup of milk, sour or sweet; and of soda, ginger, cinnamon, cloves, nutmeg and allspice, about a teaspoon each. Stir hard, and bake slowly.

TRAINING-DAY GINGER BREAD.

4 quarts of sifted flour, 1 quart of molasses, 1 scant tablespoon of soda dissolved in a little water, 1 tablespoon of good ginger, 1 pound of butter, 1 tablespoon of alum dissolved in $\frac{1}{2}$ teacup of boiling water. Make as soft as you can roll out; cut in cards, and bake in a rather quick oven.

SOFT GINGER BREAD.

1 cup of New Orleans molasses, 1 cup of sugar, 3 cups of flour, 1 cup of sweet milk, $\frac{1}{2}$ cup of butter, 1 teaspoon of soda, 2 teaspoons of ginger.

SOFT GINGER BREAD.

Mrs. M. A. W.

1 cup of molasses. Stir just as much flour in it

as it will take. 1 cup of boiling water, with a teaspoon of soda dissolved in. 1 tablespoon of lard, pinch of salt, 2 teaspoons of ginger. Pour into a square cake pan and bake in a moderate oven.

GINGER DROPS.
Mrs. Fidelia Evett, Chicago.

½ cup sugar. 1 cup molasses. ½ tablespoon ginger.
5 tablespoons melted butter.
1 teaspoon soda in ½ cup boiling water. Stir rather thick; bake in a drippingpan and eat warm.

SOFT MOLASSES CAKE.

1 tablespoon butter.
1 cup molasses.
½ cup warm water.
2½ cups sifted flour.
1 egg.
½ teaspoon soda.
1 teaspoon ginger. Pinch of salt.

SPICE CAKE.
Mrs. O. Blackman, Chicago.

1 cup sugar.   1 cup sour milk.
1 cup molasses.   1 teaspoon nutmeg.
1 small teaspoon soda.   ⅔ cup butter.
3 cups flour.   ½ teaspoon cinnamon.
3 eggs. Pinch of salt.   ½ teaspoon cloves.
Bake in patty pans or muffin rings.

MISCELLANEOUS.

DROP SPONGE CAKE.

Mrs. E. B. B.

½ pound of pulverized sugar, ¼ pound of flour, 4 eggs beaten separately, whites and yolks, 1 lemon, all of the juice, and half the peel. Drop on buttered paper, not too near together. Try one, and if it runs, beat in a trifle more flour, beating hard. Bake in a quick oven a delicate brown.

WARM TEA CAKES.

Mrs. E. B. B.

½ cup of butter, 1 cup of sugar, ½ cup of sweet milk, 2 cups of flour, 2 eggs, nutmeg, 1 heaping teaspoon of baking powder. Stir quickly and bake immediately.

TEA CAKES.

Mrs. J. B. De Lon.

2 cups of sugar, 1 cup of butter, 1 cup of sour milk, 2 eggs, 5 cups of flour, 1 teaspoon of saleratus.

MOLASSES TEA CAKES.
Mrs. J. B. De Lon.

2 cups of sugar, 1½ cups of molasses, 1 cup of boiling water, heaping cup of shortening, heaping teaspoon of saleratus.

WIDOW'S CAKE.

2 cups of Indian meal, 3 cups of wheat flour, 1 pint of buttermilk, 4 tablespoons of molasses, 2 teaspoons of saleratus. To be eaten hot, with butter, for tea or breakfast.

GERMAN COFFEE CAKE.
Mrs. J. Engel.

Take ½ cake of compressed yeast, (or teacup of home-made,) put it in a pint of warm milk. Stir this in the middle of a pan of flour. When light, add ½ pound of butter, ½ pound of sugar, some raisins, lemon, nutmeg, cinnamon and flour. Put in dripping-pans like ginger bread, or a shortcake. Let it rise, for baking. Then, with a cake-brush, rub over the top a beaten egg, and sprinkle on some sugar and cinnamon. Bake.

CREAM CAKE.
TO BE EATEN HOT WITH BUTTER.
Mrs. Dr. C. H. Evans.

1 cup of sour cream, 1 small cup of butter, 2 eggs,

small spoon of soda, very little ginger. Flour like ordinary cake.

KNICKERBOCKER CRULLERS.

½ cup of butter, 2 cups of sugar, 4 eggs, ½ teaspoon of soda, little salt and nutmeg, small cup of milk. Flour to make stiff. Roll very thin. Cut in cakes three inches square, and then make slits in each cake nearly the whole width, like a comb with the teeth half an inch wide. Fry in hot lard. The success in these lies very greatly in the cutting out.

VANITIES.

Beat 2 eggs very light, add teaspoon of salt and flour to roll. Take a piece of dough as large as a hickory-nut, roll as thin as paper and fry in hot lard. They will be done in a few seconds.

RAGAMUFFINS.

Take biscuit-dough, roll out, spread with butter, sugar and cinnamon; roll up like a jelly roll, cut from the end, and bake quickly. (Very nice.)

CHOCOLATE COMFITS.

Whites of 6 eggs, ½ pound of grated chocolate, ½ pound of sugar, (1½ cups,) 5 ounces of flour (1 cup full and one lacking half an inch of being full, after sifting). Beat the whites stiff. Stir in the sugar, chocolate, and lastly, the flour lightly. Drop from a spoon on a buttered dripping-pan, and bake in a moderate oven. This quantity of chocolate makes it very strongly flavored.

COCOANUT COMFITS.
Mrs. E. B. B.

Whites of 6 eggs, $\frac{1}{2}$ pound of grated cocoanut, $\frac{1}{2}$ pound of sugar. Drop the size of hickory-nuts, separately, on buttered paper laid on tins, and bake in a moderately hot oven.

SEED CAKES.
Mrs. E. B. B.

1 cup of butter, 2 cups of sugar, $\frac{1}{2}$ cup of sourish cream, 2 whites of eggs, $\frac{1}{2}$ teaspoon of soda. Stir like cake, then mix stiff with flour and roll thin as pie-crust, with caraway seeds sprinkled in. Then roll with fluted roller, and cut in square cakes. (Excellent.)

HERMIT CAKES.
Mrs. Nellie Roe.

$1\frac{1}{2}$ cups of brown sugar, 1 cup of currants, $\frac{1}{2}$ teaspoon of salt, $\frac{1}{2}$ cup of butter, 2 eggs, 1 teaspoon of soda in 2 tablespoons of milk, 1 teaspoon each of all kinds of spices; mix stiff with flour. Roll thin; cut in squares, like soda crackers.

CREAM PUFFS.

Melt $\frac{1}{2}$ cup of butter in 1 cup of hot water, and while boiling, beat in 1 cup of flour. Then remove from stove, and when cool, stir in 3 eggs, one at a time, without beating. Drop on tins quickly, and bake about twenty-five minutes in a moderate oven. For the cream, $\frac{1}{2}$ pint of milk, 1 egg, 3 tablespoons of sugar, 2 large tablespoons of flour. Boil and flavor with lemon. When puffs are done, open the side with a sharp knife and fill with the cream.

VARIETIES.

Mrs. E. B. B.

2 eggs beaten separately, 1 teaspoon of salt. Flour to roll thin as a wafer. Cut in strips an inch wide and four long, and wind around the finger; slip off and fry in hot lard.

FLORENTINES.

Roll puff paste to the thickness of the eighth of an inch, and lay it on a thin baking-tin. Spread over it a layer of green gage or any other preserve or jam, and bake it in a moderate oven. Take it out, and when partially cool, having whipped some whites of eggs with sugar, put the whip over the preserve, and strew some minced almonds all over the surface, finishing with sifted sugar. Put it once more into the oven until the whip is quite stiff. The florentines should be of a pale color, and a few minutes after the paste is finally removed from the oven, it should be cut into diamonds and served up.

MACCAROONS.

1 cup of hickory-nut meats, pounded in a mortar; 1 cup of sugar, 1½ eggs, 2 tablespoons of flour. Bake on a greased paper; put very little in a place.

LEMON MACCAROONS.

1 pound of powdered sugar, 4 eggs, whipped very light and long; juice of 3 lemons and peel of 1; 1 heaping cup of prepared flour, ½ teaspoon of nutmeg. Butter your hands lightly; take up small lumps of the mixture; make into balls about as large as a walnut, and lay them upon a sheet of buttered paper, more than two inches apart. Bake in a brisk oven.

EDINBORO' CHEESE.

Take 2 tablespoons of raspberry jelly, 2 tablespoons of pounded loaf sugar and the whites of two eggs; beat well together till it is perfectly mixed and forms a stiff paste; then turn it into a dish, and it is ready for use. This is most delicious, and is still further improved by mixing currant jelly with the raspberry. It can also be made with any kind of jelly. Care should be taken to beat it well.

SUGAR KISSES.

Whites of 5 eggs beaten to a stiff froth; add 1 pound of pulverized sugar, and 1 teaspoon of lemon extract. Drop on white paper and bake about twenty minutes in a moderate oven.

WELSH RAREBIT,

OR RABBIT AS IT IS FAMILIARLY CALLED.

Cut a piece of bread $\frac{3}{4}$ of an inch thick. Remove the crust. Toast nicely on each side. Lay cheese over the toast and set in the oven. When the cheese is sufficiently melted to penetrate the toasted bread, serve immediately.

FONDU.

A FAMOUS CANADA RELISH.

Scribner's Monthly.

2 ounces of butter, 4 ounces of bread crumbs, 8 ounces of cheese, 1 cup of sweet milk, 3 eggs. Cut the butter and cheese into small pieces and place them in a large bowl with the bread; on this, pour scalding milk, after which add the yolks well beaten, and

also a little salt; mix well together, cover, and place on the back of the range, stirring occasionally until all is dissolved, when add the whites beaten to a stiff froth; place in a buttered pie plate, and bake in a quick oven for about twenty minutes; serve the moment it is taken from the oven. Many eat mustard on this.

SCALLOPED CHEESE.

Soak one cup of dry crumbs of bread in new or fresh milk. Beat into this 3 well beaten eggs. Add a tablespoon of melted butter and $\frac{1}{2}$ a pound of grated cheese. Sprinkle the top with sifted bread crumbs and bake in the oven a delicate brown. A delicious relish to eat with thin bread and butter.

THIN BREAD AND BUTTER.

Cut off the end crust from a loaf of bread. Butter the bread on the loaf, and cut off the slice very thin with a sharp knife. Butter the next slice on the loaf and cut it off thin as before, until the plate is full, one upon another evenly. Then cut down through the middle of the slices, serving each one with a half slice. Thin bread and butter is nice for an impromptu lunch, or a Sunday tea. It is an old English dish.

GRAPE FRITTERS.

Juliet Corson.

1 cup of flour, yolks of two eggs, 2 tablespoons of salad oil, pinch of spice, salt also, enough cold water to make a batter about like sponge cake. When mixed smoothly, add the whites of the eggs beaten to a stiff froth. Dip little clusters of grapes in the batter and fry in smoking hot fat. Take up and lay on brown paper for a minute, to free them from fat. Dust with powdered sugar, and serve either hot or cold, as a dessert.

BANANA FRITTERS.

1 cup of flour, yolks of 2 eggs, pinch of salt, 2 tablespoons of melted lard or butter, water to make a batter like griddle cakes. Add the whites beaten to a stiff froth, and stir in lightly 2 or 3 bananas cut in thin strips. Dip with a spoon into smoking hot fat and fry like doughnuts. Dust with powdered sugar. The above will make a dessert for a family of eight persons.

PLAIN FRITTERS.

Make a batter like the above. Fry and eat with a sauce; or stir in chopped apple or any fruit desired.

CUSTARDS, ICES, and CREAMS.

When floating island or ice cream through neglect or by accident has been cooked too long and curdles, take a bowl full at a time and beat with a patent egg-beater, and you will never know it had been curdled.

ICE CREAM.

Mrs. P.

1 quart of milk, 2 eggs, heaping tablespoon of corn-starch. Sweeten to taste; also, flavor. We prefer flour to corn-starch. Put milk in a Farina kettle; or, in lieu of that, put it in a tin pail, and set pail in boiling water. Put in flour or starch mixed in cold milk, and cook thoroughly, having sweetened before. Then lift out of the boiling water, and put in the well beaten eggs. Cool, and flavor just before freezing.

ICE CREAM.

Mrs. E. B. B.

1 quart of cream. 1 pint of milk, 2 cups of sugar, 1 egg, well beaten, 1 dessert spoon of vanilla, 1 des-

sert spoon of corn-starch. Heat sugar, milk, cornstarch and egg, as for custard. When cool, beat in the cream, and freeze. (Excellent.)

CHOCOLATE ICE CREAM.

Allow 1 tablespoon of grated chocolate dissolved in warm milk to every quart of cream. Put in when partly frozen.

COFFEE CREAM.

6 eggs, 2 cups of sugar, 1 coffee cup of strong coffee. Beat the yolks of the eggs and the sugar together; add a little cold milk. Then add one quart of boiling milk and the coffee, stirring the same way till it begins to thicken, but don't let it boil. Pour into a large glass dish and add the whites of the eggs beaten stiff, for a frosting.

VANILLA CREAM.

$\frac{1}{2}$ box of gelatine soaked in 1 quart of milk one hour. Set on the fire, add the yolks of 3 eggs, beaten with 1 cup of sugar. Heat to boiling, flavor with vanilla and turn into a mould.

ORANGE CREAM.

Take $\frac{1}{2}$ a dozen oranges, grate the peel into a pint and a half of hot water, and beat up with it four eggs; sweeten the liquid, pass it through a strainer, then simmer it until it becomes of the consistence of cream, and pour it into glasses.

STRAWBERRY CREAM.

Mash the fruit gently; drain it on a sieve; when well drained (without being pressed), add sugar and cream to the juice, and if too thick, a little milk; whisk it in a bowl, and as the froth rises lay it on a sieve: when no more will rise, put the cream in a dish and lay the froth upon it.

ORIENTAL CREAM.

Mrs. E. J. W.

Half a box of gelatine, dissolved in a pint of water. Add the juice of one lemon and a cup of sugar. When boiled thoroughly, pour into a mould or large glass dish. Make a boiled custard of one quart of milk, yolks of four eggs, and flavor with lemon. Pour over the jelly. Beat the whites to a stiff froth; spread over all. Heat a shovel and hold over to brown slightly. To be eaten cold.

BAVARIAN CREAM.

1 quart of milk or cream, 6 eggs, ½ box of gelatine, 1 coffee cup of sugar, 3 teaspoons of vanilla.

Make syrup of the sugar by boiling it in water enough to dissolve it. Dissolve the gelatine in water that will cover it. Boil the milk. Stir in the gelatine while on the stove. Take it off. Stir in the beaten yolks of eggs, the syrup, flavoring, and the whites beaten to a froth. Turn into a mould. Eat cold.

ROYAL FRENCH CREAM.

$\frac{1}{2}$ pound of sweet almonds, 2 ounces of bitter almonds, $\frac{3}{4}$ of a pound of sugar, eight eggs, $1\frac{1}{2}$ pints of milk. Blanch and dry the almonds thoroughly in a cloth, then pound them in a mortar until a smooth paste. Add the well beaten eggs, sugar and milk. Stir them all over the fire until they thicken, but do not boil. Then strain, and put the mixture in a freezer or tin pail. Surround with ice and freeze it. When quite frozen, fill a mould, place the lid on, and keep the pudding in ice until wanted for the table. Then turn it out on the dish, and garnish with any fruit prepared in fine syrup, pouring a little over the top of the pudding. Vanilla flavoring is liked by some.

FRUIT CREAMS.

Take $\frac{1}{2}$ an ounce of isinglass, dissolved in a little water, then put 1 pint of good cream, sweetened to the taste; boil it; when nearly cold, lay some apricot or raspberry jam on the bottom of a glass dish, and pour it over. (This is most excellent.)

ANGEL CREAM.
Mrs. L. C.

1 pint of milk, ½ cup of sugar, little salt, 3 even tablespoons of corn-starch. Cook the above over hot water, and at the last, stir in the beaten whites of 2 eggs. Take the yolks and make a boiled custard with not quite a pint of milk. Flavor. Set on ice.

OAK PARK CREAM.
Mrs. F. W. Van B.

Make a jelly of gelatine, putting 1 pint of water on ½ box of gelatine. Add juice of 2 small lemons and 1 cup of sugar. Strain when cool. Then slice six oranges thin, removing the seeds, and place on jelly, putting sugar over them as you slice them. Then whip ½ pint of cream, sweeten a little and flavor. Pour it on top when cold.

VELVET CREAM.

1 pint of sweet cream, 1 ounce of gelatine, 3 tablespoons of sugar. Dissolve the gelatine in warm water. Whip the cream to a stiff froth. Pour the gelatine in, while whipping. Sugar and flavoring, should be with the cream. Pour into a mould.

WHIPPED CREAM.

Take a pint of cream, 2 tablespoons of sugar, flavor with $\frac{1}{2}$ teaspoon of lemon extract, and whip with an egg-whip. Stop for a minute, and remove the froth with a spoon to a sieve. Repeat, and stop again, to remove the froth, until all has set that can be raised. Set the sieve in a cool place until the whipped cream is wanted. Use it for Charlotte Russe, or Vienna coffee.

TAPIOCA CREAM.
Mrs. A. S. J.

Swell one small teacup of tapioca in a little milk over night. Add beaten yolks of 3 eggs and boil in 1 quart of milk; add a little salt. When at boiling heat, sweeten and flavor. Then stir in the beaten whites of the eggs lightly. To be eaten cold.

APPLE CREAM.

Stew apples, leaving quarters whole. Skim them into a glass dish and whip with egg-beater, 1 cup of cream and 1 cup of sugar; pour over the apples. When cold, it makes a delicious dessert in warm weather.

CREAM CHARLOTTE.

Make a sponge cake in 3 layers from any plain recipe. Pour over it a boiled custard made of one quart of milk, 3 eggs, 3 tablespoons of sugar. Take ½ pint of good cream, whip to a froth, sweeten and flavor and spread smoothly over the whole. Set on ice.

A CHARTREUSE OF ORANGES.
Mrs. C. S. Jones.

Take two moulds, the one, one and a half inches larger than the other (in diameter). Make nice orange jelly of gelatine, pour a portion of it into the larger mould; pare, quarter, and free from every vestige of skin, a half a dozen oranges, carefully separate the quarters, into three or four pieces, and cover the jelly with a layer, two or three slices in depth, place on ice to set. When the jelly is firm, place on it the smaller mould, and fill the space between the two with sliced oranges, sugar and jelly, until level with the top. Whip one pint of cream, the whites of two eggs beaten stiff, and half an ounce of gelatine dissolved in a little cream with lump of sugar rubbed upon the orange skin until the zest has flavored it. When the jelly has set, pour warm water into the inner mould and remove it at once, turn the jelly out upon a glass or silver dish, and fill the other space with the whip. Strawberry, raspberry or peach jelly and fruit may be substituted if desired. With peaches flavor the cream with one-fourth of a drop of the oil, or a teaspoon of extract of bitter almonds, or peach.

CHARLOTTE RUSSE.

Mrs. E. B. B.

1 pint of cream whipped light, ½ ounce of gelatine dissolved in 1 gill of hot milk, 2 whites of eggs well beaten, 1 small cup of pulverized sugar. Flavor with bitter almond and vanilla. Mix the whipped cream, eggs and sugar, and let get quite cold before adding the gelatine and milk. Line a mould with slices of sponge cake, or lady-fingers, and fill with the mixture. Set upon the ice to cool.

ALMOND BLANC MANGE.

Mrs. M. W. Miller.

1 quart of milk, 3 eggs, 5 tablespoons of cornstarch, a pinch of salt, sugar to sweeten a little. Let the milk come to a boil slowly. Blanch half a pound of almonds. Pound in a mortar with loaf sugar, putting into the mortar two or three almonds and a lump of the sugar at a time. As soon as they are beaten as fine as possible, pour the paste into the milk, letting them warm gradually with the milk. Beat the yolks of the eggs with the corn starch, salt and sugar, and stir into the scalding milk. Flavor with vanilla strongly. Just before taking from the fire, stir in the whites beaten to a stiff froth. Pour into a mould and let get cold. Take fruit syrup as a sauce, pouring over the whole.

ISINGLASS BLANC MANGE.

Mrs. E. Judson.

One ounce of isinglass soaked for an hour in enough of the milk to cover it. The remainder of one quart of milk heated smoking hot, but not boiling, in a farina kettle. To this, add the soaked isinglass and stir constantly till it is dissolved. Add about one tablespoon of sugar, and when it is thoroughly dissolved, take off the fire, and allow it to cool. When cool, *not cold*, add one teaspoon of vanilla, or other flavoring. Then pour into moulds and set in a cool place to harden. Eat with cream or sugar.

FRUIT BLANC MANGE.

Anna R.

Use strawberries or raspberries, two-thirds juice and one-third water; boil this and stir into it sufficient corn-starch to thicken it. Put it in one large dish; when cool turn it over on a plate and stick long narrow slices of sweet almonds into it. This will make a very pretty effect.

SOUFFLE VANILLA.

Separate the whites and yolks of four eggs; mix two tablespoons of powdered sugar, a small pinch of salt, and a few drops of strong extract of vanilla with the yolks. Have the whites beaten a long time, even after they seem as light as possible. Heat and butter an earthern dish, and pour in two-thirds of the mixture. Put in a very hot oven, and, after a few minutes, open the oven door, and you will find that it has risen to a high pyramid. Break open the apex with a fork and pour the remainder of the uncooked portion into the opening. Work fast, and close the door as soon as possible. Leave the dish in a few minutes. Let it turn a golden brown, and try with a straw as you would cake. It will boil and bubble at the top, but this will not injure the looks or taste. Eat with sugar and lemon.

FLOATING ISLAND.

One quart of sweet milk put over hot water to heat. Whites of six eggs beaten stiff and laid on the milk until cooked. Remove to a platter. Beat the yolks with three tablespoons of sugar. Pour hot milk over them, instead of putting the eggs into the milk, and there will be no danger of the milk curdling. Flavor to suit. Stir till cooked through. Turn into custard dish. A silver spoon in the glass dish will prevent its breaking. Put the whites on top, and serve with a bit of jelly on each dish at table.

BAKED CUSTARD.

3 pints of milk, 6 eggs well beaten, pinch of salt, sugar and flavor to taste. Mix together and pour into cups and set in a baking pan of boiling water, to reach to the top of the custard, if possible. As soon as done, set cups in a pan of cold water. They will be firm and not watery. The custard may be baked in one large dish, if preferred.

[Custards are very nice set in a steamer and cooked in cups. Ed.]

PINE-APPLE CREAM.

Chop one can pine-apple; add cup sugar; cook till clear; put in a dish one ounce gelatine that has been dissolved in half cup warm water; add one quart milk; let come to a boil; sweeten to taste; flavor with **lemon**; strain slowly over the **pine-apple**.

LEMON HONEY.

Take 6 well beaten eggs, 3 lemons, grated rind, 1 pound of white sugar, 2 ounces of butter. Add juice of lemons, stir butter and sugar to a cream, then add all but the eggs, and simmer. When hot, turn in the eggs, stir quickly for five minutes and take from the fire, setting in a pan of cold water. **Very** nice for jelly cake or hubbs, and **will keep months**.

LEMON EXTRACT.

Mrs. A. C. Hastings.

Put the rind of three lemons in a glass jar and pour over it one pint of alcohol. Let it stand four days, pour off into a bottle and add one ounce of the oil of lemon, and you have a pint of lemon extract at less than one-fourth the usual price.

LEMON ICE.

Make a rich lemonade. Strain into the freezer. Then add the beaten whites of two eggs to a quart or little more of the lemonade. Freeze.

ORANGE ICE.

8 oranges, 1 pound of sugar, 1 lemon, 1 quart and a cup of water. Make a syrup of the sugar and water, skim it well, cool, add the juice of the oranges. Boil up the rinds and strain the water into the syrup, and add the juice and rind of a lemon same way. Freeze.

PINE-APPLE WATER ICE.

Peel and pound a pine-apple and put through a sieve. Add the juice of one or two lemons with half a cup of water and sugar to taste. Strain into the freezer.

PUDDINGS.

Pudding moulds or basins must be well buttered and the puddings put into boiling water and the water kept boiling all the time. Have the water come up as high as the pudding in the mould. Fill up with boiling water as fast as it evaporates. If a bag is used, wring it out of hot water, and flour it well; and when done, dip into cold water, and the pudding will come out easily. The same may be done with a mould. It takes as long again to boil or steam it, as it does to bake.

For corn-starch, desiccated cocoanut and snow-flake puddings, the recipes on the packages are perfectly reliable, and it is useless to take up the room in a cook book to re-print them.

We give a variety of both hard and liquid sauces. The taste of the person, and the character of the pudding, must determine which to use.

BEE-HIVE SAUCE.
Mrs. E. B. B.

Make a hard pudding sauce, and when beaten very light, set aside three or four tablespoons in a plate.

To the remainder, add cherry, currant or cranberry juice, or jelly, or chocolate. Beat the coloring matter in well, and shape in a conical form. Roll half sheet of stiff note-paper into a long narrow funnel. Tie a string around it to keep it in shape and fill with the uncolored sauce. Squeeze it out gently, commencing at the base of the cone and winding it about it to the top, leaving alternate light and dark stripes.

HARD SAUCE FOR PUDDINGS.
Mrs. A. S. J.

1 ounce of butter, 2 ounces of sugar, beaten till creamy. Stir in thoroughly the beaten yolk of an egg. Flavor to suit.

ANOTHER.

2 tablespoons of butter, 10 tablespoons of sugar. Beat to a cream. Nutmeg.

LIQUID SAUCE.

Yolks of 4 eggs, 4 tablespoons of sugar, 1 of flour, 2 cups of milk. Set on fire, and stir until it thickens. Flavor to taste.

ANOTHER.

1 cup of sugar, $\frac{1}{3}$ cup of butter beaten to a cream. Add the beaten white of one egg, flavor with lemon or nutmeg. Add one cup of boiling water just before serving.

ANOTHER.

1 cup of sugar, ½ cup of butter, 2 cups of water, large tablespoon of flour, flavoring. Mix and boil a long time on back of stove.

ANOTHER.

¾ of a cup of butter, 1½ cups of sugar, 1 egg, juice and grated rind of a lemon; all beaten well together. Just before serving, pour on the beaten mixture 1 pint of boiling water. This is good for all sorts of puddings.

VINEGAR SAUCE.

1 cup of brown sugar, 1 cup of water, tablespoon of butter, ½ teaspoon of salt, a few drops essence of lemon, a tablespoon of vinegar, a tablespoon of flour. Boil together enough to cook the flour.

JELLY SAUCE.
Mrs. E. B. B.

½ glass of currant jelly, 1 tablespoon of butter, 1 dessertspoon of corn-starch, juice of 1 lemon, 1 cup of boiling water. Sweeten to taste. Beat the sugar and butter together and corn-starch dissolved in a little cold water. Then add jelly, a little at a time; next, the boiling water, and let it just boil up. Flavor.

JELLY SAUCE—PLAINER.
Juliet Corson.

2 tablespoons of sugar, 1 tablespoon of jelly, 1 teaspoon of corn-starch, 1 pint of water. Cook just enough to incorporate together and leave no raw taste of the starch. Nice to serve with Cabinet Pudding.

CREAM SAUCE.
Juliet Corson.

1 tablespoon of butter melted with 1 tablespoon of flour over the fire, in a saucepan; add 4 tablespoons of sugar, and a pint of hot water. Boil 2 minutes. If wanted very nice, remove from the fire, and stir in the beaten white of an egg.

BARONESS PUDDINGS.
Juliet Corson.

One-half pound of suet, same of raisins chopped, same of stale bread broken in crumbs, (cracker will not answer,) $\frac{1}{4}$ pound of sugar, 1 pint of milk. Flour a pudding-cloth thickly after dipping in hot water. Boil 4 hours. Spice may be added. If wished, it may be made into smaller puddings and boiled in small cloths. Tie rather closely, as it will not swell much. A grated rind and juice of orange in place of part of the milk, is nice. Serve with sauce or powdered sugar, as preferred.

APPLE PUDDING.
Mrs. E. B. B.

5 apples pared and quartered and sprinkled with sugar, 1 tablespoon of butter, ½ cup of sugar, ½ cup of milk, 1 egg, 1 heaping teaspoon of baking powder, and flour to make a thick batter. Pour over the apples and bake slowly.

APPLE FRUIT PUDDING.
Mrs. M.

5 large apples (chopped), 1 cup of raisins, 1 cup of sugar, 1 cup of sweet milk, 1 cup of flour, ½ cup of butter, 2 eggs, little salt, butter and sugar worked together; bake 1 hour; eat with sauce. Take 1 teacup of sugar, ½ teacup of butter; stir together until light; flavor with wine or essence of lemon; smooth the top with a knife, and grate nutmeg over it.

APPLE TAPIOCA PUDDING.
Mrs. C. B.

1 cup of tapioca soaked several hours in 6 cups of water. Add 6 chopped apples and 1 cup of sugar. Bake 4 hours slowly. Eat warm or cold, with cream.

APPLE SAGO PUDDING.
American Home.

For a 2-quart pudding dish, take a cup of sago, (tapioca if preferred) put it in a pan of cold water, let heat and cook gradually, adding hot water; if required, add a little salt. In the meantime, pare and core apples enough to fill the dish. Fill the holes with sugar and season with nutmeg. Put a little water in the dish and partly bake them, then take the dish out, pour the sago over, return and bake till apples are done. Eat with sugar and cream. Better to be done half an hour before meal time. One of my best puddings.

BAKING-DAY PUDDING.
Grandma Graves.

On baking day, take $1\frac{1}{2}$ cups of dough, work in a little shortening, place in a basin. Let it get light and steam for 1 hour. If the basin has no tube, put an inverted cup in the center. Eat with sauce made of 1 large cup of sugar, $\frac{1}{2}$ cup of butter, 1 pint of water. Boil 1 hour, thicken slightly with flour and flavor with vanilla or nutmeg. (Splendid.)

BATTER PUDDING.
Mrs. J. B. DeLon.

7 eggs, 11 heaping tablespoons of flour, 1 quart of milk, teaspoon of salt.

BIRD'S NEST PUDDING.
Mrs. E. B. B.

3 pints of boiling milk, 6 crackers rolled, 1 cup of

raisins; when cool, add 4 well beaten eggs and 1 cup of sugar. Pour the mixture over 4 apples pared and cored with corer. Bake $\frac{3}{4}$ of an hour. Serve with sauce.

BIRD'S NEST.

Anna P.

Pare and cut up good cooking apples till a 2-quart basin is $\frac{2}{3}$ full. Sprinkle with sugar, and pour over a little water. Make a batter of $1\frac{1}{2}$ cups of milk, 2 eggs, 1 tablespoon of butter, $1\frac{1}{2}$ tablespoons of sugar, 2 teaspoons of baking powder and flour to thicken like muffins. Pour over and bake slowly in a steady oven. Serve with sugar and cream.

CASSEL PUDDINGS.

Juliet Corson.

For 6 cups, take 4 ounces of butter, same of sugar, beat to a cream, add the grated rind of a lemon, 4 ounces of flour, yolks of 2 eggs, and lastly, the beaten whites. Bake them in buttered cups from 20 to 30 minutes. Test them with a broom straw. Eat with following sauce: Squeeze the juice of a lemon till you get a tablespoon, 4 heaping tablespoons of sugar, and 2 of butter. Beat well together.

BAKED SUET PUDDING.

Mrs. L. D. Rankin, Mendham, N. J.

1 quart of milk, scald all except a teacup, pour hot milk on 5 tablespoons of corn-meal, ½ teaspoon of salt, 1 teaspoon of ginger, ½ nutmeg, 1 cup of molasses, ½ cup of chopped suet. Butter a pudding dish, pour in the cup of cold milk, then the mixture, and bake 2 hours.

BAKED INDIAN PUDDING.

Mrs. E. B. Baldwin.

1 cup of corn-meal stirred slowly into 1 quart of boiling milk and water, 1 tablespoon of butter, 1 cup of sugar, ½ cup of flour, 5 eggs, cinnamon and cloves. A ½ cup or more of cold milk may be added. Bake 3 or 4 hours.

BAKED INDIAN PUDDING.

1 quart of sweet milk boiled, 2 eggs, added well beaten with 3 tablespoons of meal and 1 of flour, little salt. Bake 45 minutes. Serve with sugar.

ANOTHER.

Marrion Clinton, Menasha, Wis.

3 pints of milk. When scalding hot, stir in ⅔ cup of corn-meal and sugar to taste. When cooked, take

off, cool, add 1 beaten egg, cup of raisins, butter size of an egg, and bake till it wheys. Add spice, if liked.

BOILED INDIAN SUET PUDDING.

Author's Recipe.

$\frac{1}{2}$ a pound of beef suet chopped fine, $1\frac{1}{2}$ cups of corn-meal, $1\frac{1}{2}$ cups of hot water, 2 large iron spoons of flour, 1 cup of brown sugar, $\frac{1}{2}$ teaspoon of saleratus, $\frac{1}{2}$ teaspoon of salt. Steam 4 hours, or longer. Eat with sugar and cream. (Very nice.)

BOILED INDIAN PUDDING.

Mrs. M. A. Smith.

1 pint of sweet milk, 1 teaspoon of salt, 1 tablespoon of wheat flour, 10 tablespoons of corn-meal, 1 tablespoon of butter, 2 tablespoons of brown sugar, 1 tablespoon of molasses, 4 tablespoons of dried berries, 1 teaspoon of soda. Boil 3 hours, or longer if a larger pudding is made.

BOILED INDIAN PUDDING.

2 cups Indian meal, 2 cups of flour, 1 egg, $\frac{1}{2}$ cup of molasses, one teaspoon of soda, 2 teaspoons of cream of tartar. Wet with milk till about as thick as cake. Steam 3 hours.

BOILED BREAD PUDDING.

Take pieces of dry bread, about a quart, soak in warm water till soft. Add 3 beaten eggs, 1 cup of sugar, 1 cup of raisins. Mix well. Boil in a bag or pudding mould an hour or two. Eat with following sauce: 3 tablespoons of butter, 1 cup of sugar, 1 tablespoon of flour, 1 pint of boiling water. Flavor with lemon.

BUCKEYE PUDDING.

Mrs. Oliver P. Arnold, White Pigeon, Mich.

1 cup of raisins, 1½ cups of molasses, 1 cup of warm water, 2½ cups of flour, dessert-spoon of soda, yolks of 2 eggs. Steam 2 hours. Sauce: 1 cup of pulverized sugar, ½ cup of butter, beat well, 1 teaspoon of warm water, whites of two eggs beaten stiff and put in last.

CABINET PUDDING.

Juliet Corson.

Use a smooth plain mould with straight sides. Butter it thickly with cold butter. Stick all around it, on the sides and bottom, small slices of French candied fruit if wished very fine, or raisins and currants for a plainer pudding. They may be put on in rings, stars, or any fancy shapes. Half a pound is sufficient for a three pint mould. Place slices of cake, sponge is best, on the layers of fruit; then fill the mould with alternate layers of fruit and cake. Pour over all a simple custard made of six eggs, a pint of milk and four tablespoons of sugar. Steam the pudding, either in a kettle of water over the fire, allowing the water to come half way up the side, or in a pan of water set in the oven. Cook about three-quarters of an hour; but test it, by running a knife down the center. If no liquid adheres, it is done. Bread may be used instead of cake. Serve either with powdered sugar dusted over, or with sauce.

CASSAVA PUDDING.

Mrs. E. B. B.

1 pint of milk. Stir in ½ cup of cassava, ½ cup of cocoanut, either fresh or desiccated, 2 eggs, 1 tablespoon of butter; salt, sugar and vanilla to taste. Cook like boiled custard. When done, put it in the dish in which it is to be served, and beat the white of one egg to a stiff froth and lay over the top smoothly, and brown in the oven. Some prefer a tablespoon pulverized sugar added to the frosting. Eat warm or cold, with jelly.

COCOANUT PUDDING.

Mrs. E. B. B.

1 quart of milk, 4 eggs, 1 cup of grated breadcrumbs, 1 cup of sugar, 1 grated cocoanut, salt and flour. Bake half an hour.

COTTAGE PUDDING.

Mrs. A. S. J.

1 cup of milk, 2 cups of flour, 2 or 3 eggs well beaten, a little salt, 1 teaspoon of soda, 2 of cream of tartar. Bake quickly and eat hot with rich sauce.

CREAM TAPIOCA PUDDING.

Mrs. Samuel Packard, Oak Park, Ill.

Soak 3 tablespoons of tapioca in water over night. Put it in a quart of boiling milk. Cook half an hour. Beat yolks of 4 eggs, with 1 cup of sugar, add 3 tablespoons of prepared cocoanut; stir in and boil ten minutes longer. Pour into pudding dish. Beat the whites of eggs to a stiff froth, with 3 tablespoons of sugar added. Pour this over the top. Then sprinkle cocoanut over all. Set in oven and brown. (Very nice.)

CURREY PUDDING.

Mrs. L. Currey.

1 quart of bread crumbs softened in boiling water. 1 cup of chopped suet, 1 cup of currants or any other fruit, ½ cup of molasses, 2 eggs, pinch of salt. Bake in a hot oven about half an hour. Serve with any kind of sauce.

HEN'S NEST.

Author's Recipe.

Use plain blanc mange recipe on corn starch package. Take half a dozen or a dozen egg shells and fill with the blanc mange while warm. When cold, break the shell off and put them in a glass dish. Cut small strips of lemon peel and boil in a clear syrup till tender. Place them around the egg-forms, and make a boiled custard and pour over all. (Very pretty and very good.)

KISS PUDDING.

Mrs. E. B. B.

1 quart of sweet milk, 3 tablespoons of corn-starch, 1 cup of sugar, 5 yolks of eggs, salt, flavor. Boil the milk, and stir in the starch wet with cold milk; add the sugar and eggs, and let it boil a few minutes. Make a frosting of the whites, with a little more sugar, and brown in the oven.

MINUTE PUDDING.

Put some milk over the fire, with a bit of lemon-peel or essence of lemon; let it boil; then having made a large cup of flour into a smooth paste with a little cold milk, stir it, by degrees, into the boiling milk; let it boil, stirring it all the time until it is thick; then dip a bowl in cold water, pour the pudding in, and let it cool a little before turning it out. Eat with butter and sugar sauce. The juice of a lemon is an improvement.

MY FAVORITE PUDDING.

Mrs. M. A. S.

1 pint of milk. When scalding hot, stir in ½ pint of Indian meal and a teaspoon of salt. Take 6 medium sized sweet apples, pare and cut in pieces, and stir in this mixture. Bake 3 hours. Sweetened cream with nutmeg, for sauce.

OLD ENGLISH PLUM PUDDING.

1 pound of suet chopped fine, ¾ pound of bread crumbs, 1 pound of sugar, nearly 1 pound of flour, 1 pound of currants, 1 pound of raisins stoned, 1 pound of candied lemon, orange and citron mixed, 6 eggs, 1 quart of milk. Have the bread dry, and rub the inside of the loaf through a colander. Weigh

it after it is rubbed through. Mix the suet, bread and sugar together; add the flour, fruit, and peel shredded up fine. The beaten eggs and milk mixed together, and added last. I fill several small basins, tie a cloth over the top and boil them in a wash boiler for 10 hours. In England, I am told, they often cook them longer still. Any puddings left over may be boiled again, and are as good as new the next fourth of July.

ORANGE PUDDING.

6 oranges, peeled, sliced thin and sprinkled with sugar. Make a boiled custard of 1 pint of milk, yolks of 3 eggs, pinch of salt, 1 tablespoon of cornstarch, and 3 tablespoons of sugar. When cool, pour it over the oranges. Whip the whites of eggs to a stiff froth; add ½ cup of sugar and put on the top. Set the dish in a pan of water and put in a hot oven a few seconds till the frosting is browned. To be eaten cold. (Very delicious.)

ORANGE PUDDING—COOKED.

2 oranges, juice of both and grated peel of 1; juice of 1 lemon; ½ pound lady's fingers, stale and crumbed, 2 cups of milk, 4 eggs, ½ cup of sugar, 1 tablespoon of corn-starch wet with water, 1 tablespoon of butter, melted. Soak the crumbs in the milk (raw), whip up light and add the eggs and sugar,

already beaten to a cream with the batter. Next the corn-starch, and when the mould is buttered and water boiling hard, stir in the juice and peel of the fruit. Do this quickly, and plunge the mould directly into the hot water. Boil one hour; turn out and eat with rich sauce.

PINE APPLE PUDDING.
Author's Recipe.

Take 1 fresh pine apple, or a two-pound can, cut into small pieces in a pudding dish, strew plentifully with sugar and let stand several hours. Take 1 quart of milk, put the greater part of it in a pail and set into boiling water. Use the remainder of the quart to wet up 6 tablespoons of loose sifted flour. Mix it with the beaten yolks of 6 eggs, $\frac{1}{2}$ cup of sugar and $\frac{1}{2}$ a saltspoon of salt. Stir into the scalding milk. When cooked, remove, and when cool, or nearly so, pour over the fruit. Make a frosting of beaten whites of eggs, with 3 tablespoons of sugar. Put over the top and brown in a quick oven.

PLUM DUFF.
Mrs. E. B. B.

1 cup of butter, $1\frac{1}{2}$ cups of sugar, 1 cup of milk, 1 large cup of raisins, 3 eggs, 2 teaspoons of baking powder. Flour to make stiff batter. Steam 3 or 4 hours.

PUFF PUDDING.

Mrs. Dr. Baker.

1 quart of milk, 6 eggs, 6 tablespoons of flour, salt. Bake 20 minutes, or half an hour. Serve with liquid sauce, flavored with lemon.

QUEEN OF PUDDINGS.

1 pint of fine grated bread crumbs. 1 quart of milk, 1 cup of sugar, the yolks of four eggs beaten, the grated rind of a lemon, a piece of butter the size of an egg. Bake until done, but not watery. Whip the whites of the eggs stiff, beat in a teacup of sugar, in which has been strained the juice of lemon. Spread over the pudding a layer of jelly; pour the whites of the eggs over this; replace in the oven; brown slightly. To be eaten cold, with cream if preferred. (Decidedly the best of all puddings.)

RICE HANDY-ANDY.

Take a cup of raw rice and a cup of raisins; put together in a bag, tie securely, leaving plenty of room to swell. Boil about two hours in water salted a little. To be sliced and eaten with cream and sugar.

RICE PUDDING WITHOUT EGGS.

½ cup of rice, 3 pints of milk, ½ cup of sugar, teaspoon of butter, pinch of salt. Stir frequently, while baking. It should be of the consistence of cream when done. Bake two or three hours. Raisins may be used, if liked.

RICH TAPIOCA PUDDING.

Mrs. A. S. J.

Put 1 cup of tapioca in 1 quart of milk for 2 hours. Then add $\frac{1}{2}$ cup of sugar, 1 cup of raisins, yolks of 3 eggs well beaten, and a little salt. Bake slowly 1 hour. Take whites, beat to a stiff froth; add 2 tablespoons of sugar; lemon flavor. Spread over and brown.

ROLLED PUDDING.

1 pint of flour, 2 small teaspoons of baking powder, salt, milk to make soft enough to handle. Roll thin; spread all over it fresh cranberries, candied cherries, or any sauce. Roll up like a jelly roll. Lay in a steamer and steam one hour. Serve with sauce.

SAGO PUDDING.

Mrs. E. B. Baldwin.

4 tablespoons of sago soaked in water all night, $1\frac{1}{2}$ pints of milk, 4 eggs, pinch of salt, 1 small cup of sugar. Lemon-peel, cinnamon, nutmeg, either, or all. Bake slowly.

SALLY LUNN.

Mrs. Dr. B. M. Baker

1 cup of sugar well beaten with 3 eggs, 1 teaspoon of cream of tartar added to 1 cup of milk and mixed with sugar and eggs. Then stir in flour to a thin batter, and add ½ teaspoon of soda, little salt, and stir briskly, and put in a buttered pan and bake in a quick oven. Sauce for the above: ⅔ pint of water, 1 cup of sugar, 1 tablespoon of butter, nutmeg. A little vinegar or lemon-juice.

SNOW BALLS.

Mould simple boiled rice in teacups. When turned out, serve with cream and sugar, or boiled custard. A pretty effect is obtained by using red sugar-sand to sweeten the rice before moulding. Call it "Red Rice."

SNOW PUDDING.

½ a box of gelatine, whites of 3 eggs, 2 teacups of sugar, pint of hot water, juice of 1 lemon. Dissolve gelatine in the water; then add lemon-juice and sugar; mix well, and strain through flannel into a large mixing bowl. When cool enough to begin to thicken stir in the whites of the eggs beaten to a stiff froth with egg beater, and beat until it is thick and snow-white all through. It will take a half hour or longer, and the colder the better. Turn into moulds which have been dipped in cold water, or pile in pyramid form in the center of a glass dish, leaving a space all around. Keep on ice till the next day. Make a soft custard with a pint of milk, yolks of the 3 eggs, pinch of salt, 4 tablespoons of sugar, little grated lemon rind. The custard should be very cold, and if the pudding is in a pyramid, pour the custard around it (not over it). If it is in a mould, serve the custard from a pitcher. (Very delicious.)

SUET PUDDING.

Author's Recipe.

1 cup of fine chopped suet, 1 cup of brown sugar, 1 cup of hot water, 1 cup of raisins chopped, salt, 2 teaspoons of baking powder, teaspoon each of cinnamon, cloves and nutmeg. Flour to make stiff batter. Steam from 2 to 5 hours. The longer the better. To be eaten with liquid sauce.

SUET PUDDING.

Mrs. M. A. Smith.

1 cup of chopped suet, 1 cup of molasses, 1 cup of raisins, 1 cup of sour milk, 3 cups of flour, 1 teaspoon of soda, salt. Steam 3 hours.

SUET PUDDING.
Mrs. M. A. S.

1 pound of beef suet chopped fine, 1 pint of sour milk, 1 egg. ½ cup of molasses. 1 teaspoon each of soda, cinnamon, cloves, nutmeg and salt, 1 cup of raisins, ½ cup of currants. Steam 4 hours. Flour to thicken like cake. Sauce: 1 pint of hot water, 1 cup of sugar, 2 tablespoons of flour, ½ cup of butter. Flavor to taste.

SUET PUDDING.
Mrs. M. A. Woodworth.

1 cup of chopped suet, 1 cup of raisins or currants, 1 cup of chopped apples, dried or green, 1 cup of sugar, 1 cup of sour milk, 2 cups of flour, spices; no soda. Steam. Eat with sauce.

THICKENED RICE.
Lizzie Hill, Maysville, Ky.

1 cup of rice boiled in water until soft. Add a pint of milk, little salt, 2 eggs well beaten, ½ cup of sugar, tablespoon of flour in some cold milk; flavoring. Boil up. Eat cold or warm. It does not require sauce, and is much nicer than one would think.

WASHDAY PUDDING.

Put a layer of bread crumbs in a pudding dish,

with little lumps of butter over them. Then a layer of chopped apple with sugar and cinnamon. Another layer of crumbs and another of apple. So on, until the dish is full. Pour over a cup of water, and bake till the apple is done. Eat with cream and sugar

FAMILY BEVERAGES.

TEA.

"Except the water boiling be,
Filling the tea-pot spoils the tea."

After scalding the tea-pot put in a teaspoon of tea for one person, but of course a less proportionate amount if for many persons. Pour less than a cup of actually boiling and freshly boiled water on. Let steep on the back of the stove a short time, and fill up the required amount with boiling water. Japan tea is better for families whose meals are kept waiting. Its flavor is not injured by long standing as much as many other teas. If tea boils, the tannic acid is extracted, and acts with very bad effects on the coats of the stomach.

COFFEE.

A tablespoon of ground coffee for one person, 3 tablespoons are sufficient for 4 persons. Take egg enough to moisten the coffee, put in a pinch of salt. Pour on a cup of cold water. Set on the hot stove. When it comes to a boil fill with boiling water and set back where it can not boil. If it is necessary to use cold water to settle coffee, take a little in a cup at a considerable height above the coffee-pot and pour it in from there. A little salt is always an improvement to coffee. If coffee is allowed to boil the tannic acid is extracted and it will be bitter and unhealthy. By combining with the milk an indigestible substance is formed in the stomach.

COFFEE.

Put the coffee in the coffee-pot and fill up with cold water at first. Let boil up once and set back. If any cold remains after breakfast strain it and keep it to wet up the next batch. Wash the coffee boiler clean every day. If the bottom gets sticky boil up some cooking soda in it until it is cleansed.

The coffee we prefer in our family is equal parts of Old Government Java and Mocha. But Rio and Java make a very pleasant drink. It is all a matter of taste.

A very popular mixture of coffee for boarding-houses is one-fourth Java, one-fourth Chicory, and one-half Rio, mixed and ground together.

COFFEE FOR FESTIVALS.

Put the ground coffee into flannel bags each holding half a pound, and sew up tightly. When the first coffee is wanted put as much water in a wash boiler as will be required; when it boils throw in a couple of the bags and steep long enough to extract the strength. Then take them out. Add boiling water when necessary and throw in another bag, letting it remain as before. In this way, by removing the old and adding the new, the beverage will be kept aromatic as well as strong, and the bitterness of long boiled coffee be prevented.

VIENNA COFFEE.

Make your coffee in your usual way. Put one quart of cream into an oatmeal cooker, or if you have none, into a pitcher in a kettle of boiling water. Keep the water boiling. Beat the white of an egg to a froth, put with it 3 tablespoons cold milk, mix well and add to the cream after removing from the fire. Stir briskly for a minute and serve in the coffee cups with the coffee.

ICED TEA.

It is better to put the tea in cold water and set in the ice box the morning of the day it is to be used for supper. The flavor is better than if steeped in hot water.

PREMIUM CHOCOLATE.

Scrape fine about one square of a cake, add it to an equal quantity of sugar; put these into a pint of boiling milk and water (half and half) and stir constantly for two or three minutes. Some prefer boiling ten minutes.

EGG CHOCOLATE.

Allow about 1 egg to 2 cups. Prepare this chocolate as above, and the last thing stir in briskly the well-beaten yolks of the eggs, and at the same time have the whites beaten to a stiff froth and put a little on top of each cup (very hot) and serve. (Very fine.)

BREAKFAST COCOA.

Put a teaspoon of the powder into a breakfast cup, add a tablespoon of boiling water and mix thoroughly. Then add equal parts of boiling water and boiled milk, and sweeten to taste. Let it boil a couple of minutes.

COCOA SHELLS.

Take about two ounces of the shells and pour 3 pints of boiling water over them. Boil rapidly half an hour. Serve like coffee.

BOTTLED SODA-WATER.

1 quart water, 2 pounds white sugar, 1 ounce tartaric acid, ½ ounce essence, 2 lemons, 2 eggs beaten, 1 tablespoon flour. Strain, bottle, and shake every day for a week. When you wish a glass of soda-water, take one-third cream, two-thirds water, and add ½ teaspoon soda; stir and drink immediately. You can use sassafras, wintergreen, or any other essence you wish. Some prefer to flavor it to taste when preparing it to drink. Be sure to use bicarbonate of soda, and buy it of a druggist. The soda we procure at groceries is apt to contain sulphate of soda and is unhealthy.

RASPBERRY NECTAR.

Pour over 2 quarts of ripe raspberries 1 quart of vinegar. Let it stand till the fruit ferments; strain and to every pint of juice, add ¾ of a pound of loaf sugar. Simmer 20 minutes.

IMPERIAL.

2 ounces of cream of tartar, juice and rind of 2

lemons; put into a stone jar, pour over it 7 quarts of boiling water, stir and cover closely; when cold, sweeten to taste, strain and bottle.

CREAM BEER.

Mrs. Hattie A. Harris, Clinton, Iowa.

It is an effervescent drink and much pleasanter, I think, than soda-water. 2 ounces tartaric acid, 2 pounds white sugar, the juice of 1 lemon, 3 pints of water; boil together five minutes; when nearly cold add, after being beaten together, the whites of 3 eggs, $\frac{1}{2}$ cup flour, and $\frac{1}{2}$ ounce of essence of wintergreen. Some other essence may be used if preferred. After being well mixed, bottle and keep in a cool place. For a drink of this, take 2 tablespoons of the syrup to 1 tumbler of water, and add $\frac{1}{4}$ of a teaspoon of soda. Drink quickly.

SUGAR BEER.

2 pounds loaf sugar, 3 pints water, juice of half a lemon, 2 ounces tartaric acid. Boil all 5 minutes. When nearly cool add the whites of 3 eggs well beaten and $\frac{1}{2}$ cup of flour.

CORN BEER.

Cold water, 5 gallons; sound, nice corn, 1 quart; molasses, 2 quarts; put all into a keg of this size;

shake well, and in two or three days a fermentation will have been brought on as nicely as with yeast. Keep it bunged tight. It may be flavored with oils of spruce or lemon, if desired, by pouring on to the oils 1 or 2 quarts of the water boiling hot. The corn will last five or six makings. If it gets too sour, add more molasses and water in the same proportions. It is cheap, healthy, and no bother with yeast.

GINGER POP.

Water, $5\frac{1}{2}$ gallons; ginger root, bruised, $\frac{1}{4}$ pound; tartaric acid, $\frac{1}{2}$ ounce; white sugar, $2\frac{1}{2}$ pounds; whites of 3 eggs, well beaten; lemon oil, 1 teaspoon; yeast, 1 gill. Boil the root for 30 minutes in 1 gallon of the water, strain off and put the oil in while hot; mix. Make over night, and in the morning skim and bottle, keeping out sediments.

SPRUCE BEER.

Mrs. E. B. B.

3 gallons warm water, 1 quart molasses, 1 large spoon essence of spruce, 1 large spoon essence of wintergreen, 1 pint good yeast. Let it remain over night in a warm place and bottle in the morning.

LEMON BEER.

Mrs. E. B. B.

10 gallons water, 6 peeled lemons sliced, ¼ pound ginger, ¼ pound cream of tartar, 3 grated nutmegs. Boil all together. When cool enough add the beaten whites of 6 eggs and ½ pint yeast, and let it ferment 12 hours. Strain and bottle. It is better after standing a day or two.

HOME BREWED BEER.

10 gallons water, 1 pint loose hops, 1 gallon molasses, 2 ounces essence of spruce, 1 ounce ginger, 1 ounce cream of tartar. Boil 10 minutes; when cool enough add ½ pint of yeast. Let it ferment 12 hours, then bottle up or put it into casks.

CREAM SODA.

3 ounces tartaric acid, 4 pounds sugar, 5 pints water, whites of 3 eggs beaten to a froth. Boil 4 minutes after adding the eggs, stirring constantly. Cool, flavor with ½ ounce of vanilla. Cork tight. Use 2 tablespoons to a glass of ice water, stirring in a pinch of soda.

SHAM CHAMPAGNE.

1 ounce tartaric acid, $\frac{1}{2}$ ounce ginger root, 4 ounces brewer's yeast, $1\frac{1}{2}$ pounds white sugar, 1 good-sized lemon. Slice the lemon, bruise the ginger, mix all together except the yeast. Boil $2\frac{1}{2}$ gallons water and pour it on the mixture. Let it cool to blood heat, add the yeast, let it stand all day in the sun, and at night bottle. It may be used in two days.

STRAWBERRY SHERBET.

1 quart of strawberries, 3 pints of water, 1 lemon —the juice only, 1 tablespoon orange-flower water, $\frac{3}{4}$ pound white sugar. The strawberries should be fresh and ripe. Crush to a smooth paste, add the rest of the ingredients (except the sugar) and let it stand 3 hours. Strain over the sugar, squeezing the cloth hard; stir until the sugar is dissolved, strain again and set in ice for two hours or more before you use it.

PORTABLE LEMONADE.

Press your hand on the lemon and roll it back and forth briskly on the table, to make it squeeze more easily; then press the juice into a bowl or tumbler— never into a tin, strain out all the seeds as they give a bad taste. Remove all the pulps from the peels and boil in water—a pint to a dozen pulps—to extract the acid. A few minutes boiling is enough, then strain the water with the juice of the lemons; put a pound of white sugar to a pint of the juice, boil 10 minutes, bottle it, and your lemonade is ready. Put a teaspoon or two of this lemon syrup in a glass of water, and you have a cooling, healthful drink.

PINE APPLE SYRUP.

Pare and cut the pine apples in pieces and add a quart of water to 3 pounds. Boil till very soft. Mash and strain. To a pint of this juice add a pound of sugar. Boil to a rich syrup, and cork tightly.

ORANGE SYRUP.

Take fully ripe fruit, and thin skinned if you can get them. Squeeze juice through a sieve and add a pound of sugar to every pint. Boil slowly for ten minutes. Skim carefully. Bottle when cold. Two or three spoons of this in a glass of ice water in summer is refreshing. It may also be used with melted butter for pudding sauce.

CURRANT WINE.

Mrs. E. B. B.

Mash and strain the currants, which should be very

ripe. 1 quart of juice, 1 pound sugar, ½ pint water. Put in a cask or jar and cover with mosquito-net and let it ferment four or five weeks. Then drain off and bottle close.

RHUBARB WINE.

Mrs. E. B. B.

Peel and slice as for pies. Put a small quantity of water with it and boil gently. Strain and add an equal quantity of water. To each gallon of this add 5 pounds sugar and ferment like currant wine.

BLACKBERRY WINE.

The following is said to be an excellent recipe for the manufacture of a superior wine from blackberries: Measure your berries and bruise them. To every gallon add 1 quart of boiling water. Let the mixture stand twenty-four hours, stirring occasionally, then strain off the liquor into a cask; to every gallon add 2 pounds of sugar; cork tight and let stand till the following October.

ELDERBERRY WINE.

1 quart of juice, 1 quart water, 1½ pounds brown sugar. Mix and put in jug or keg. Keep full to the top by filling morning and evening with some of

the mixture reserved for that purpose, until the pulp of the berry has worked off, which takes about a week in a moderately warm place. It will then commence to froth. In a week cork tight and put in a cool place. Bottle in February.

GINGER WINE.

10 gallons water, 15 pounds loaf sugar, whites of 6 eggs well beaten and strained; mix all together, then boil and skim. Put in ½ pound of ginger, boil twenty minutes. When cool, put in the juice and rind of four or five lemons, also 2 tablespoons of good yeast, stir well together, bottle and cork tight.

CREAM NECTAR.

3 pounds of white sugar, 2 ounces of tartaric acid put into a quart of soft water over night. Then stir in the well-beaten whites of 3 eggs. Use any flavoring desired. Bottle and keep in a cool place. Three tablespoons of it to one glass ice water. Soda enough to make it effervesce. After one trial you can determine the amount of soda. The soda should be put into the water first.

PRESERVES AND JELLIES.

To prevent jams, preserves, etc., from graining, a teaspoon of cream of tartar must be added to every gallon.

To preserve fruit jellies from mould, cover the surface one-fourth of an inch deep with fine sugar.

Earthern milk crocks unglazed are best adapted for stewing apple-sauce, boiling jelly, rice, and many other things, as tin or iron injures the delicate flavor and color of fruits, and porcelain kettles are expensive and scorch easily. I have used these earthen crocks for years with but one accident. Let water gradually heat several times in them on the back of the stove when new, and you will prefer them to anything else for cooking certain things.

JAM.

¾ pound of sugar to a pound of fruit, either stawberry, blackberry or raspberry. Mash well, and boil half an hour. Seal up.

FRUIT.

When canning in glass jars, either put a **silver** spoon in the jar while pouring in the hot fruit, or set the can on a wet towel. Either way will insure it against breakage.

When the top of a glass jar refuses to yield to all efforts at unscrewing, hold a hot cloth around it, and it will soon succumb.

TO CAN STRAWBERRIES, RASPBERRIES, BLACKBERRIES, PLUMS, CHERRIES, OR ANY SMALL FRUIT.

Mrs. F. McKercher.

Look over carefully, and fill your cans, as many as will stand in your wash boiler. Put sugar enough in each can to sweeten for the table. Pack the **jars full**, and screw the covers on, but do not put on the rubber bands. Put cold water in the boiler, nearly to the top of the jars. It is safer to stand them on something in the boiler. Pieces of berry boxes answer every purpose. Let the water boil twenty minutes. Then remove a couple of the jars. Take off the covers. The fruit will have settled down some. Fill one up from the other. Put on the rubber band and seal up. Then take another from the boiler and fill it up from the same jar. If you fill thirteen to start with, it will take about three of them to fill up the other ten that have settled. After canned fruit stands all night, it is safer to use a little wrench to give an extra turn to the cover before putting away for good. (I should include peaches in this list. Ed.)

LEMON BUTTER.

Mrs. J. W. Smith.

2 pints of white sugar, $1\frac{1}{2}$ pints of water, 3 eggs well beaten, lump of butter size of a hickory-nut, 2 tablespoons of corn-starch, juice of 2 lemons, rind of 1. Cook in a dish set over boiling water. Stir often to keep it smooth. Use as sauce, filling for tarts, or as jelly for layer cake.

APPLE PRESERVE.

Peel, halve and core 6 large apples, selecting those of the same size; make a syrup of 1 pound of granulated sugar and a pint of water; when it boils, drop in the apples with the rind and juice of a lemon. As soon as they are tender, care must be taken that they do not fall in pieces, take the halves out one by one, and arrange, concave side uppermost, in a glass dish. Drop a bit of currant jelly into each piece; boil down the syrup, and when cool, pour around the apples. This makes a very nice preserve for tea.

APPLE BUTTER.

Take 9 gallons of cider, boil down to 3 gallons; then add to the boiling cider about 3 gallons of apples that have been pared and quartered; boil rapidly for about two hours without ceasing, to prevent the apples from sinking. By this time they are well reduced, and will begin to sink; thus far, no stirring has been done, but must be commenced as soon as the apples begin to sink, or they will scorch. Spice to suit taste. Stir without ceasing until it is reduced to a thick smooth pulp, which will take about half an hour. Apple butter made in this way has been kept perfectly good over two years, without sealing, and is as good, if not a better article than that made in the usual way.

COOKING APPLES.

Owaissa.

Here is a nice recipe for cooking apples for present use. I tried it, and like it very much: Take about 20 nice snow or other good cooking apples, wipe them clean, and place them in a preserving-kettle, with water enough to about half cover them; then add 2 cups of sugar, $\frac{1}{2}$ a cup of vinegar, and a dessertspoon of ground cinnamon. Let them simmer over a slow fire until soft. Use them cold. While cooking, keep the kettle covered tightly.

APPLE JELLY.

Take tart apples and cut them up; put to them a little water, and let them boil until it becomes glutinous and reduced; then strain it; put $\frac{3}{4}$ pound of white sugar to each pint of juice; flavor with lemon essence and boil until it is a fine, clear jelly; then strain it into moulds.

MICHIGAN FRUIT JELLIES, AND ALSO APPLE BUTTER.

SUCH AS ARE SOLD IN STORES.

For jellies, take 6 pounds of dried apples, and 6 gallons of cold water, and let them soak twelve hours; then strain through a flannel bag; add to each pint of the juice 1 pound of the gluco or grape sugar, and 1 ounce of Cooper's sheet gelatine; boil twenty-five minutes, and flavor to taste.

For apple butter, take 4 pounds of dried apples, 2 pounds of dried pumpkin; soak them twelve hours, then add 1 gallon of gluco, 1 quart of boiled cider, 1 quart of golden syrup, 6 pounds of New Orleans sugar, a $\frac{1}{4}$ pound of Cooper's gelatine, a little mixed spice to suit the taste; boil gently for 1 hour, stirring all the time.

COMPOTE OF APPLES—BAKED.

Take a wide jar with a cover; put into it golden pippins, or any small apples of similar appearance, pared and cored. Cut very thin a small fresh rind of lemon for 2 quarts of apples and strew among them, and ½ pound of sugar thrown over the top. Tie the cover on and set in a slow oven for several hours. Serve hot or cold.

JELLIED APPLES

Slice fresh apples and put in pudding dish with alternate layers of sugar. Cover with a plate and put a weight on it. Bake in a slow oven 3 hours. A delicious dessert of slices of apples embedded in jelly will be the result when turned out cold. Better cooked the day before it is wanted.

BAKED SWEET APPLES,

TO EAT IN MILK.

Quarter and core without paring; fill a dish rounding full, with no water. Set in a kettle of water or steamer, and steam till nearly soft, then in the oven, with a plate over them. Let them bake till the juice is nearly cooked out. Much nicer than cooked with the cores in.

BOILED APPLES.

Place fair smooth apples in a saucepan with just enough water to cook them, and boil until tender, but not to break them. Put in sufficient sugar to sweeten well and let cook until apples are thoroughly penetrated. Skim apples out, cook syrup longer and pour over.

APPLE CROUTES.

Juliet Corson.

Take slices of stale bread. Trim off the crusts and shape them prettily to suit the size of the apple. Spread with a little butter, and a sprinkling of sugar. On each slice lay half an apple peeled and cored, flat side down, a bit of butter, more sugar on the apples, spice, if liked. Bake in a slow oven and dust with powdered sugar before serving.

APPLE MERINGUE.

Juliet Corson.

Peel some nice smooth apples, cut in halves, lay them on a dish that is suitable to serve on the table. Dust with sugar. Cook in oven until tender. Take the whites of eggs, one for each apple, beat to a stiff froth; add a heaping tablespoon of powdered sugar for each one. Put over them when done, and brown in the oven.

FRIED APPLES.

Juliet Corson.

Remove the cores with an apple-corer. Cut the slices round, one-quarter of an inch thick. Put half a cup of drippings or butter in a frying-pan. When smoking hot, put in slices enough to cover the bottom of the pan. Fry brown on both sides. Do not let them break. As fast as done, take them up in little even piles, four or five together. Keep hot, and dust a little sugar over and serve.

CRAB APPLE PRESERVES.

Core the crab apples with a sharp pen-knife, leaving the stems on. Allow pound for pound of sugar. Put in just water enough to help dissolve the sugar. Let it boil up and skim. Put in the apples and boil till they look clear and tender. Skim out. Boil the syrup down and pour over the fruit.

STRAWBERRY PRESERVES.

Put the berries and sugar, pound for pound, into a preserving kettle, and heat slowly till the sugar is melted. Then boil rapidly for 20 minutes, and seal up hot.

GRAPE PRESERVES.

Press the pulp from the fruit. Put the pulp over to boil in a little water. Then press through a colander to remove the seeds. Then put juice, pulp and skins together; add a pound of sugar to a pint, and boil down thick.

GRAPE JELLY.

Grapes green or half ripe, are much nicer for jelly, than when fully ripe. Stem them, cook them. Strain the water, and allow half or three-quarters of a pound of sugar to each pint of juice.

CITRON PRESERVES.

Pare, slice, and cut in fancy shapes. Take some ginger-root, an ounce to 8 or 10 pounds of fruit; boil in sufficient water to extract the flavor. Throw the root away. Put the sugar into this water and make a rich syrup. For citron preserves, allow one pound and a quarter of sugar for each pound of citron. Skim very thoroughly. Put in the citron, and boil until transparent. Skim out. If the juice is not thick enough, cook still longer. Pour over, and then slice in some lemons. One lemon to every two pounds of citron is about right.

PRESERVED WATERMELON RINDS.

Peel and cut the rinds into the sizes and shapes desired. Put in a steamer and steam till a straw will pierce them easily. Prepare a syrup of one and one-fourth pounds of sugar to each pound of rinds, with a very little water. Boil up and skim. Cook the rinds in the syrup until clear. Use one lemon to every two pounds of rinds.

QUINCE PRESERVES.

Take an equal quantity of smooth sweet apples, pound sweets are best, and put with the quinces. Even double the quantity may be used. Pare and quarter and core them. Steam in a steamer until a straw will pierce them readily. Make a syrup of an equal weight of sugar. Put in the steamed fruit and boil until of a rich red color. Skim frequently. Lay them out on flat dishes. Boil the syrup down until it begins to jelly at the side of the kettle. The syrup is nicer if strained through a sieve. Pour it over the quinces. Use the parings and cores for jelly. Boil till very tender, and proceed as in other jellies.

APPLE MARMALADE.

12 pounds of apples, 3 pounds of brown sugar, 3 lemons. Boil slowly. Mash well.

PEACH MARMALADE.

To a pound of fruit put $\frac{3}{4}$ of a pound of sugar. Boil the pits in water until the water is well flavored. Peel and quarter the peaches and add to the water after the pits are removed. In half an hour add the sugar. Stir constantly. Boil an hour after the sugar is added.

QUINCE MARMALADE.

Pare and core the quinces, and cut up small. Boil the parings and cores in water that covers them. When soft, strain through a cloth. Add the quinces and sugar ($\frac{1}{2}$ a pound to each pound of fruit). Boil all together over a clear fire until smooth and thick. Stir and watch almost constantly. When cold, put in glass jars.

PLUM BUTTER.

1 peck of plums, $\frac{1}{2}$ bushel of sweet apples. Cook in separate kettles until quite soft, with just enough water to prevent sticking to the bottom. When soft, put through a colander into the same kettle, and to each pound add $\frac{3}{4}$ pound of white sugar. Let cook a short time. Seal up.

WILD PLUM PRESERVES.

In order to make the skins tender and prevent that strong, rank taste, scald in saleratus water, allowing a tablespoon to 4 or 5 gallons of plums. As soon as the skins commence to break, pour off the water, and drain the fruit. Then take out the pits, and weigh, allowing pound for pound of sugar. Put the sugar over, with a little water. Let boil up and skim. Put in the plums, cook till tender, skim out, boil the syrup down till it is of the consistence of molasses, and pour over. They require no sealing.

[I lived once upon a time in a country where the scarcity of fruit kept us all on the alert for the best modes of utilizing the little we did have. We made delicious plum jelly and marmalade as follows:]

WILD PLUM JELLY.

Cover the fruit with water and boil until the pulp is well broken. Then strain through a cloth or jelly bag without squeezing. Procced with the juice, as with other jellies. It is not necessary to use pound for pound of sugar. Less will answer every purpose.

WILD PLUM MARMALADE.

Take the plums that remain in the jelly bag and rub through a sieve. To this, take a pound of sugar to each pint, and cook thoroughly. Watch and stir almost constantly. Try it in a dish, and when it will harden like jelly, it is done.

PRESERVED ORANGE PEEL.

Weigh oranges whole, and allow pound for pound of sugar. Peel the oranges neatly and cut the rind into narrow shreds. Boil until tender, changing the water twice, and replenishing with hot from the kettle. Squeeze the strained juice of the oranges over the sugar; let this heat to a boil; put in the shreds and boil twenty minutes. Lemon peel can be preserved in the same way, allowing more sugar. (Very nice.)

PRESERVED CHERRIES.

Stone the cherries, preserving every drop of juice. Weigh the fruit, allowing pound for pound of sugar. Put a layer of fruit for one of sugar until all is used up; pour over the juice and boil gently until the syrup begins to thicken. The short stem red cherries or the Morellas are best for preserves. Sweet cherries are not good.

CRANBERRY PRESERVES.

Author's Recipe.

Weigh the berries, and an equal amount of sugar. Put over to cook together, with just water enough to dissolve the sugar. Boil till the fruit is well cooked. This will be found a very delicious preserve.

PEAR PRESERVES.

Preserve as directed for quinces. Flavor with sliced lemon and ginger root.

PEACH PRESERVES.

Pare, and remove pits. Boil the pits in water to

extract the flavor. Add the sugar to this water, after the pits are taken out. Boil up, skim. When clear, put in the peaches, a few at a time, and cook gently till they are done, not over 15 minutes. When all are cooked, boil the syrup till thicker than molasses. Pour over. Seal up.

DAMSON PLUM PRESERVES.

Weigh the fruit and sugar pound for pound, and put in layers in a stone crock. Set in the oven, moderately heated, and cook for three hours. The result is a very rich flavor and the fruit but little broken.

PLUM OR EGG-TOMATO PRESERVES.

Make same as above, except using 3 lbs. sugar to 4 of tomatoes. Add two sliced lemons to each gallon. When lemons are used in preserves, always add them after the fruit is cold.

CRAB APPLE JELLY.

Wash and quarter the apples and cover with water. Stew until well broken. Pour into a jelly bag, drain without squeezing. Allow $\frac{1}{2}$ lb. sugar to 1 pint juice. Boil the juice alone for ten or fifteen minutes. Heat the sugar, meanwhile, and add slowly, stirring constantly. Sometimes it will "jelly" by the time the sugar is all dissolved. It will require but very little boiling, if any. Stick cinnamon boiled with the juice improves the flavor. Remove it before adding sugar.

The pulp of the apples is good for **marmalade**, as in wild plums.

CURRANT JELLY.

Arts.

Put stems and currants into a jar. Set into hot water, cover, and boil 15 minutes. Now press out the juice, put into a preserve kettle, boil 10 minutes, put in the same quantity of sugar you have of juice, and 5 minutes finishes it.

[If the sugar is heated through and through in the oven, it is simply necessary to add it and mix well, and the jelly is done. Ed.]

CURRANT JELLY.

After straining and squeezing the currants, usual way, I measure the juice, and to every pint I put a pound of sugar, in a crock large enough to hold all when I am ready. Then place juice on stove, and let boil hard twenty minutes. Then throw it over the sugar in the crock, and stir until sugar is dissolved. Your jelly is made. You can leave in same dish, or put in tumblers. I keep mine in crock. To make white-currant jelly and not change color, use pure white cloth to strain, and have hands free from any soil; place juice in a crock and stir two hours and a half constantly; then put in granulated sugar, and stir half an hour; don't mash your currants, but stem them. Seal in glass tumblers, and in a couple of months your jelly will be hard, and clear as water. My red currant jelly is as thick as can be now. I know any one trying this will be delighted with the result.

GELATINE JELLY.

Mrs. M. A. S.

To a package of gelatine add a pint of cold water, the juice of 3 lemons and rind of one. Let stand an hour, then add 3 pints of boiling hot water, 3 gills of wine, 2 pounds white sugar. Boil 15 minutes and turn into moulds.

DRIED APPLE JELLY.

Mrs. M. A. S.

2 quarts dried apples put in a pan with water to cover. Boil 2 or 3 hours. Strain the juice and to every pint add $\frac{3}{4}$ of a pound of sugar and the juice of 2 lemons.

APPLE JELLY.

FOR LAYER CAKE.

2 large apples grated, juice and grated rind of 1 lemon, 1 cup sugar. Boil about 5 minutes, cool, then spread.

CANNED PUMPKIN.

Cut the pumpkin, remove the inside, leave the peel on and bake until done. It will peel out of the shell easily. Then mash it and can hot and seal up the same as fruit. It cannot be told from fresh.

TO KEEP GRAPES FRESH FOR WINTER.

Pick off full clusters, removing every bruised one. Dip the end of the stem in sealing wax, then wrap each bunch in tissue paper and pack in boxes in layers, with paper between. Close up the box and keep in a cool, dry room and you are sure of success.

DRIED APPLE SAUCE.

Mrs. Dr. Evans.

2 pounds dried apples, 1 pound raisins. Put in a crock with plenty of water and set on the back of the stove. Let boil slowly all day When almost done add 1 lemon sliced very thin and 2 pounds of sugar. (A good breakfast sauce.)

CRANBERRIES.

A pint of water to a quart. Boil till soft, put through a coarse sieve or colander, return to the kettle, put in a pint of sugar, boil up and take off. Less sugar may be used if desired very tart.

[Note.—If boiling water is poured over cranberries and allowed to stay till nearly cool and then poured off, they will require considerably less sugar.]

PICKLES.

Do not use metal vessels. If vinegar has to be boiled use a porcelain kettle or a stone crock. For a few years past I have pickled and spiced a good share of my cucumbers when first procured, and sealed them up hot in glass jars for winter use, the same as fruit. Glass cans are cheap and it has proved economy in my case, for the reason that I suffered severely at the hands of the vinegar seller. One year we paid fifty cents per gallon for "pure cider vinegar," and one lot of pickles I had to "do up" three different times to keep them from spoiling. But sealed up hot they are always ready, just the right flavor, and no further source of anxiety. This need not apply to those who are sure of the Simon pure article of vinegar, although it is the least work in the long run. The following recipes have been procured from different ladies who excelled in pickling:

CUCUMBER PICKLES.

Mrs. Hodge.

When you are ready to lay them down for winter, pour boiling water over them and drain well. Then pack in salt. When wanted for pickling, place in a jar as many as you want to freshen and cover with boiling water. When cool drain off and pour over another kettle boiling hot. Let this cool and drain off and pour on one kettle more. Then when cool and drained heat vinegar to a scalding point, flavor with red pepper, cloves, or anything preferred and pour over.

[This is the easiest way we have ever found to pickle cucumbers that are in brine. It does away with the trouble of having them around a day or two freshening. Ed.]

CUCUMBER PICKLES.

Mrs. Bass.

Get small ones of uniform size. Place in a stone crock. Pour on boiling water to cover. Put in a large handful of salt. Let stand over night. Drain off in the morning. Pour on more boiling water and same quantity of salt. Let stand till the next morning. Drain off the water, wash the pickles in clear water, dry with a towel. Put in a crock and pour on boiling cider vinegar. Then put in small horse-radish roots. These pickles will keep in a common stone crock all winter.

CUCUMBER PICKLES.

Mrs. Witherel, Hudson, Mich.

1 gallon water, 1 teacup salt, alum size of a walnut. Put on boiling hot, having skimmed, three mornings in succession. Drain off and soak in clear cold water half a day. Put on vinegar cold, with pieces of horse-radish to prevent mould.

STRING BEANS.

Author's Recipe.

Boil in water a little salt till just a trifle tender. Drain very carefully. Put into glass cans, and after filling them stand them upside down to be sure and get out all the water. Then cover with hot vinegar flavored as you please. Seal up hot, and you will have one of the most palatable pickles you ever ate in midwinter. They may be steamed instead of boiled. It is not strictly necessary to salt them.

PICKLED WALNUTS.

Mrs. E. F. S.

Take white walnuts fresh and tender; put them in salt and water for three days, then put in the sun till they turn black. Take ½ pound of mustard seed, 2 ounces of pepper, ½ ounce of cloves, ½ ounce of mace, ½ ounce of nutmeg, and a good stalk of horse-radish, boiled in 1 gallon of vinegar. Cover the walnuts closely and let them remain three or four weeks. Pour off the liquid for catsup if desired, and bottle it, covering the walnuts again with cold vinegar.

PICKLED CHERRIES.

Fill a glass jar two-thirds full of large ripe cherries on the stems. Fill up with best cold vinegar. Do not cook.

SILVER SKIN ONIONS.

Pour scalding brine (weak) on them every day for nine days—new brine every other day; then throw them in cold spiced vinegar, and they will be ready to eat in a few days, and good, too.

NASTURTIONS.

They require no seasoning. Gather before they fall apart; pick clean of all bits of flowers, leaving about a half-inch of stem; drop them into some good cider vinegar, not over strong, and keep them well covered. Do not take too much vinegar to begin with, as more can be added if required. When frost comes so that you will have no more seeds to put in, pour off the vinegar and use it on the table. You will find it much better than pepper-sauce. Put the pickles into a bottle or glass jar just large enough to hold them, and fill up with good vinegar. You will now save the fresh picked ones in the bottom, and the top ones will be ready for use, but if kept covered they will keep until eaten, I presume, though I never had an opportunity to test their keeping qualities, over eight or nine months.

PICKLED CAULIFLOWER.

Cook the cauliflower till tender, then put it in jars and pour over it vinegar and ground mustard-seed, previously scalded together.

PICKLED RED CABBAGE.

Slice fine; pack in jar; pour over boiling spiced vinegar; use tablespoon brown sugar to one head; when cold tie down; fit for use in about ten days.

PICKLED TOMATOES.

Sliced green, they make splendid pickles if a pint of molasses is poured over 2 gallons; press down with plate and remove white scum as it appears; brown sugar is preferred by some.

GREEN TOMATO PICKLES.
Mrs. Judge Sherman.

1 peck green tomatoes sliced thin. Sprinkle with salt and let stand over night. Slice 12 onions, put with the tomatoes in layers with the following spices: 4 ounces white mustard seed, 4 ounces ground mustard, 1 ounce each of cloves, allspice, ginger, pepper and cinnamon, ½ ounce turmeric, 1 tablespoon salt, ½ pound brown sugar. Boil in vinegar to cover for two hours.

JACKSON PICKLES.
Grandma Owens.

Take firm, smooth, green tomatoes, slice and sprinkle with salt over night. In the morning pour clean water over and drain immediately. Be very particular about getting the water all out so as not to weaken the vinegar. Then pack in jars in layers with white mustard seed, plenty of horse-radish cut up fine, small bits of green pepper, allowing about 6 to each peck of tomatoes. Cover with cold vinegar. Tie cloth over. (Splendid.)

[I have never lost any pickles made in this way, and have put them up every year for a long time. Ed.]

HIGDOM.
Hattie A. H., Clinton, Iowa.

1 bushel green tomatoes, chopped fine and packed

in jars with salt. Let stand twenty-four hours, then drain well, then add 1 dozen green peppers, 2 large heads of cabbage, chopped fine; then scald in vinegar, then drain again; add 3 large spoons of black pepper (ground), 4 of cinnamon, 3 of allspice, 7 of cloves, 1 teacup of unground mustard; mix well with tomatoes and put in jars. Take 5 pounds brown sugar and mix with vinegar enough to cover; scald the sugar and vinegar and pour over while hot.

PICCALILLI.

Mrs. L. S. H.

1 bushel green tomatoes, $\frac{1}{2}$ peck green peppers, 12 onions, all chopped fine, 1 teacup grated horse-radish, 1 teacup ground mustard seed, $\frac{1}{2}$ ounce whole cloves, $\frac{1}{2}$ ounce ground cinnamon. Cabbage and celery added to suit. Sprinkle the chopped articles with salt and let them stand over night. Drain. Add vinegar enough to moisten, and scald until tender. Drain again. Add the spices, mix, pack in jars and cover with scalding vinegar.

MANGOES

Take young, tender, green musk-melons or nutmegs; soak them in strong brine for a week. Then scrape them, cut out a section an inch square, take out the seeds. Soak another day, then wash in clean water and wipe dry with a cloth. Then fill the cavity with finely-chopped cabbage, horse-radish, onion, green tomatoes, cucumbers, radish pods, nasturtion seeds, celery seed, young, tender string beans, cauliflower buds, peppers, mustard and whole cloves, with some stick cinnamon. Before putting in, wet this mixture with vinegar. Replace the cut piece, tie up well, pack in crocks, fill with cold vinegar, and in about a month they will be ready for use.

CHOW CHOW.

BETTER THAN THE IMPORTED.

Mrs. Nellie Roe.

1 large cauliflower, 1 quart green cucumbers sliced lengthwise, or watermelon rind will do. 3 dozen small cucumbers, 2 dozen small onions. Soak cucumbers in brine for two or three days, scald the rest in strong salt and water. Add pepper and whole cloves, allspice and stick cinnamon as you choose. Scald the following, stirring constantly, and when well mixed pour over your pickles: $2\frac{1}{2}$ quarts vinegar, $2\frac{1}{2}$ cups brown sugar, $\frac{1}{2}$ cup flour, 6 tablespoons ground mustard. Bottle in wide-mouthed bottles or glass cans. Seal. (A most delicious pickle.)

MIXED PICKLES.
Mrs. M. A. S.

300 small cucumbers, 4 large green peppers sliced fine, 2 large heads cauliflower, 3 heads white cabbage shredded fine, 9 large onions, sliced, or 2 quarts small ones, 1 quart or more small string beans cut in inch pieces, 1 quart small, green tomatoes, sliced. Put this all in a pretty strong brine 24 hours. Drain 3 hours, then sprinkle in $\frac{1}{4}$ pound black and $\frac{1}{4}$ pound white mustard seed, 1 tablespoon black ground pepper. Let the whole come to a boil in just enough vinegar to cover, with a little alum put in. Drain, and when cold mix a pint of ground mustard as for table use and put in. Cover the whole with good cider vinegar.

SWEET TOMATO PICKLE.
Mrs. R. R. Austin, Vermilion, Dakota.

15 pounds sliced green tomatoes; let stand over night, with a little salt sprinkled over; drain. 5 pounds sugar, 1 quart best vinegar, 1 ounce cloves, 2 ounces cinnamon. Boil 15 or 20 minutes, skim out and boil the syrup till thicker, if preferred, but it is not necessary. [The best I ever tasted. Ed.]

SWEET CUCUMBER PICKLES.
Mrs. L. S. H.

Take ripe cucumbers, cut them lengthwise, take

out seeds, soak in salt and water 24 hours. Then soak in vinegar and water 24 hours. Drain. Then make a syrup of 1 quart of vinegar, 1 pound sugar, cinnamon and cloves. Boil till tender.

SWEET CUCUMBER PICKLES.

Mrs. M. A. S.

Take ripe cucumbers. Peel and cut as above. Steam till tender. 1 gallon vinegar, 2 pounds sugar, 1 red pepper, 1 ounce cassia buds. Scald all together and pour hot over the pickles in a jar.

RIPE CUCUMBER PICKLES.

Pare and cut in strips. Remove the seeds. Put in weak brine for 12 hours; pour off and scald in alum water till clear. Wash in cold water and drain well. $3\frac{1}{2}$ pounds sugar, 1 gallon vinegar, some stick cinnamon, nutmeg and mace. Boil the cucumbers in this till a straw will pierce them. Put in glass jars.

WATERMELON RINDS.

Mrs. T. A. P.

Pare and cut in fancy shapes. Take weak alum water and pour it over hot. Let it stand 24 hours. Then soak till well cleansed, and boil in clear water till tender. Make a syrup of equal measures of vinegar and sugar, some stick cinnamon and race ginger. Boil the rinds in this till clear. Put in a jar, cover, seal and put away.

PICKLED PLUMS, GRAPES OR PEACHES.

7 pounds fruit, 4 pounds sugar, 1 pint vinegar, mace, cinnamon, cloves. Boil the fruit in this syrup till it is tender. Skim out and boil syrup thick. Pour over. It is better to seal up. Then it is sure to keep.

SWEET CRAB APPLES.

Put half a bushel of crab apples in a kettle with vinegar enough to cover them, and cook until tender; then take out and put in jars. Measure the vinegar and add a pint more than will cover the fruit, and to each pint add 1½ pints brown sugar, 2 sticks of cinnamon, 3 tablespoons cloves, 2 tablespoons mace. Tie spices in a bag and boil half an hour in the syrup. Then pour over the fruit.

WHOLE PEARS PICKLED.

Take 8 pounds pears; peel and cut out the ends, leaving stems in; put into a preserving kettle with 1 quart of water, and boil until they are easily pierced by a fork. Then lay out on a dish. Add to the juice 1½ pounds sugar, 1 pint vinegar, some stick cinnamon, whole cloves and race ginger. Boil all five minutes and skim. Put pears in and boil until the syrup thickens. Take out, put in jars, boil syrup five minutes longer, pour over.

VINEGAR.

HONEY VINEGAR.

To 1 quart of clear honey, put 8 quarts of warm water; mix it well together; when it has passed through the ascetous fermentation, a white vinegar will be formed, in many respects better than the ordinary vinegar.

CLOVER BLOOM VINEGAR.

This vinegar does not die on pickles: To ½ bushel of the bloom (pick the bloom clean of leaves) in a tub, put 6 pounds of brown sugar, pour on that 4 pounds of molasses, then pour 9 gallons of boiling water over all. When cool, add 3 pints of hop yeast; lay a folded sheet over the tub to make tight, and let it stand 14 days. Strain and rack off in a keg. You will have a better vinegar than you can buy. Keep in a shady place while making.

APPLE VINEGAR.

Save all parings and cores of apples when used for cooking purposes; put them in a jar; cover with cold water; add about a pint molasses to 3 or 4 gallons; tie mosquito netting over jar; add more apple parings as you have them, and all the cold tea left in teapot. Makes the very best vinegar.

POTATO VINEGAR.

2 gallons of water that a quantity of potatoes have been boiled in, 1 pound of brown sugar, a cup of hop yeast. In 3 or 4 weeks you will have most excellent vinegar. Cucumbers cut fresh from the vines without salt, will keep in this vinegar.

CURRANT VINEGAR.

1 quart of currant juice strained as for jelly, 3 quarts of rain water, 1 pound of sugar. Keep warm.

CONFECTIONERY.

MOLASSES CANDY

Mrs. M. A. S.

1 pint of molasses, 1 cup of sugar. Boil and stir every minute. When partly cooked, put in butter the size of a walnut. When it will break like glass, in cold water, it is done. Put in ½ a teaspoon of cream of tartar with the butter, and just before you turn it out, put in a spoon even full of soda.

MOLASSES CANDY.

Heat a kettle hot and butter it, then pour in a quart of molasses and a cup of sugar. Boil steadily for 20 minutes, stirring to prevent burning and boiling over. Try it by dropping a little in cold water; if it hardens immediately it is done, otherwise it must be boiled longer. Stir in a teaspoon of pulverized soda before turning out. Walnut, hickory-nut, or hazel-nut meats may be added to this candy, and a little of it saved to make pop-corn balls. Use just as little candy as possible in these balls, and let none of it get on the outside, where they should look perfectly white.

MAPLE CARAMELS.

Mrs. A. S. J.

1 pound of maple sugar. Melt in a teacup of sweet milk and a tablespoon of butter. Cook till almost brittle in cold water. Turn on to a buttered plate. Mark in squares, when cool enough.

CHOCOLATE CARAMELS.

7 tablespoons of chocolate, 3 tablespoons of milk, 6 tablespoons of sugar, 3 tablespoons of butter, 6 tablespoons of molasses. Boil till it hardens by dropping on a plate.

CHOCOLATE CARAMELS.

All that is needed is **1 cup** of sweet milk, 1 cup of molasses, ½ cup of sugar, ½ cup of grated chocolate, a piece of butter the size of a walnut; stir continually, and let it boil until it is thick, then turn it out into buttered plates; when it begins to stiffen mark it in squares, so that it will break readily when cold.

COCOANUT CARAMELS

Are made of 2 cups of grated cocoanut, 1 cup of sugar, 2 tablespoons of flour, the whites of 3 eggs beaten stiff. Bake on a buttered paper in a quick oven.

SNOW CANDY.

Nice white candy is easily made. Take 1 quart of granulated sugar, 1 pint of water, 2 tablespoons of vinegar; boil just as you do molasses candy, but do not stir it; you can tell when it is done by trying it in cold water. Pull it as if it were molasses candy; have a dish near by with some vanilla in it, and work in enough to flavor it as you pull; put it in a cold room, and the next day you will have delicious candy.

CREAM CANDY.

Frankie, Denver, Col.

2 cups of white sugar, vinegar enough to dissolve it. Boil until it will pull.

BUTTER SCOTCH.

4 cups of brown sugar, 2 cups of butter, 2 tablespoons of water, vinegar to taste. A little soda. Boil $\frac{1}{2}$ an hour. Drop a little in hot water. If crisp, it is done.

ANOTHER.

3 cups of sugar, 1½ cups of butter. Flavoring. Boil as above.

MOCK NONGAT.

Mrs. A. L. B.

To 1 quart of good molasses, add 1 pound of brown sugar and 1 ounce of butter. Put it on the fire and stir now and then to prevent scorching. After it has boiled 1 hour, stir in a teacup of walnut kernels, all particles of shell adhering having been carefully removed. Let it boil a short time longer, or until candied, which may be ascertained by dropping a little in cold water; if it does not discolor the water, and has a stringy appearance, it is done; continue to boil until this is the case. Grease a large dish, pour out the candy, and let it stand until cold, when it may be cut into squares or strips; or if preferred, the candy may be pulled as soon as cold enough to bear handling. (Very nice.)

FRUIT CANDY.

A delicious fruit candy is made by adding chopped raisins and figs to a syrup made by stewing 2 pounds of sugar with the juice of two lemons, or, if lemons are not at hand, with a cup of vinegar flavored with essence of lemon. Dried cherries and any firm preserves may be used instead of raisins and figs.

CHOCOLATE CREAM CANDY.

Puss.

1 cup each of sugar, molasses and milk; piece of butter size of an egg, boil this about 25 minutes, but do not stir it only to keep it from burning; just before taking it up add a pinch of soda and two grated squares of chocolate (notice that a cake of chocolate is divided into squares); try in water, and when brittle, it is done; then turn into a buttered pan and when the candy is cool mark it off into squares.

LEMON TAFFY.

N. A. D.

2 cups of white sugar, 1 cup of boiling water, ½ cup of butter, ¼ cup of vinegar. Flavor with lemon. When cooked sufficiently, pour it on buttered plates to cool.

DELICIOUS TOMATO FIGS.

Mrs. A. S. Johnston, Leavenworth, Kan.

8 pounds of sugar to 8 pounds of tomatoes. Take round ripe ones; peel and boil whole in the sugar

until it penetrates them, but do not boil to pieces. Then lay on flat dishes to dry. Boil syrup until quite thick and pour over them from time to time. When dry, pack in boxes in layers, with sugar sprinkled over each layer.

ICED CURRANTS.

Dip whole stems of currants into beaten whites of eggs. Sift white sugar over them.

PEACH PAPER.

Take very ripe peaches. Peel, stone and mash fine. Spread on a smooth surface, a platter, marble slab or board, and keep in the sun. When dry, sprinkle with white sugar and roll up. Good in winter.

CHOCOLATE CREAM DROPS.

1 pint granulated sugar. $\frac{2}{3}$ cup milk.
$\frac{1}{3}$ cup water.   1 teaspoon vanilla.
1 scant teaspoon butter. 3 squares chocolate.

Boil the sugar, milk, water, and butter for 20 minutes. Add the vanilla last. Remove from the stove and stir pretty constantly until cool enough to handle. Grate the chocolate and put in a dish over a kettle of hot water to melt. Form the candy into little balls the size of a thimble. When cold, roll them in the melted chocolate. Put on a greased plate or paper to harden.

PIC-NICS.

A few suggestions for pic-nic dishes, or lunches for a journey: Veal loaf, boiled ham, pressed veal, pressed chicken, fried chicken, chicken salad, plain hard boiled eggs, sausages, sardines, stuffed eggs, Saratoga potatoes, radishes, pickled string-beans (the white wax-beans are nicest, and spice them a little). For the egg stuffing, boil the eggs hard, take out the yolk by cutting off a piece from one end. Chop some ham or veal very fine, season it high, mix with a little of the yolk made smooth, and fill the egg. Replace the cut white part and you have a very palatable lunch dish; or, boneless sardine, minced very fine, with the skin removed, is a good stuffing. Ham minced fine, and mixed with mustard and pepper and chopped pickles, and spread on slices of bread makes a good sandwich. Potted meats that can be procured at the grocery stores are quite nice. Bottled pickles are rather in favor. Carry butter in a jelly glass or other covered dish. Take bread in a whole loaf instead of in slices. If slices are preferred, wrap each two in tissue paper. Biscuit are always nice. Ginger cookies will be relished more than rich cake. If Saratoga potatoes are used, fry them only a few at a time, in boiling hot lard, and take them in fancy papers. Jelly and preserves in glasses. Cakes and pies to suit one's taste. Tea may be put into a bottle in cold water, and will make a good beverage. Portable lemonade is handy, but lemons should always be carried if they can be had.

THE LAUNDRY.

I give here two different recipes for washing preparations, both of which I know to be just what they are represented to be. The second one I have used for several years past. It does no better service than the fluid, which I also used for some time, but I like a soap rather better than a fluid. A prejudice exists in many housekeepers against boiling clothes in the dirt. But if you will throw your prejudice to the winds, and try this way for one month, you will never go back to the old way. The question is asked: Does it rot the clothes? Emphatically, it does not. It rather saves them. More clothes are worn out on the washboard than on the back. As my family increased in size, I adopted this method with the Patent Magic Washing Soap. I put them to soak over night in two tubs—the fine ones together and the coarse together—and sometimes, if I have a large bed washing, put the sheets and pillow-cases in a third tub. I use the soap according to directions: a teacup to a pail of water. Cover all closely. In the morning I rub lightly on a board out of the water they are **soaking in, and put on to** boil. Rinse and hang out.

I do this, in order to have cleaner suds for my large washings of calico clothes. In doing this, you do not have to wait to heat water, and can easily get one boiler full done before breakfast. They look whiter, and wash so much easier than the old way, that it is a very great labor-saver. To make sure of having the water warm, you may turn a kettle of hot water over the clothes after they are well put to soak. Every one knows the whitening powers of lime and borax. I have done a washing in this way, and finished at noon, when it would have taken a washerwoman all day, the old way, if she had worked constantly and faithfully.

A RECIPE WORTH ONE THOUSAND DOLLARS.

Take 1 pound of salsoda and ¼ pound of unslaked lime, put them in a gallon of water, and boil twenty minutes; let it stand till cool, then drain off, and put it in a stone jar or jug. Soak your dirty clothes over night, or until they are well wet through, then wring them out and rub on plenty of soap, and to one boiler of clothes well covered with water, add ½ teacup of washing fluid. Boil half an hour briskly, then wash them thoroughly through one suds and rinse well with water, and your clothes will look better than the old way of washing twice before boiling. This is an invaluable recipe, and I do want every poor tired woman to try it.

The second method is called

PATENT WASHING SOAP.

To 5 gallons water (if hard, cleanse it,) add 5 pounds of common bar soap; cut up into small pieces and dissolve over a moderate fire, then add 12 ounces of borax and 16 ounces of salsoda; stir frequently while dissolving, and when thoroughly incorporated pour into a convenient vessel to cool; stir frequently while cooling, and it is done. Should you wish to use good, soft soap, from 10 to 15 pounds will be required, according to the thickness of the soap, with from $2\frac{1}{2}$ to $3\frac{1}{2}$ gallons of water; the thicker the soap the less, but more water; the thinner the soap the more of it, but less water, with 12 ounces each of borax and salsoda; in the case of soft soap, dissolve the borax and salsoda first in water and then add the soap. To use, heat as much soft water as will just cover the white clothing; a little more than blood warm. To each pailful of water add 1 teacup of the patent soap; dissolve well; moisten the dirty streaks of your clothes, rub on a little soap, and spread them in your tub, push down under the water and spread a thick cloth over your tub to keep in the warmth as much as possible; in about five minutes catch the clothes by one edge, raise them up and down once or twice, then turn them over entirely; repeat the same operation two or three times; soak from 20 to 30 minutes, as you please; in the meantime have your boiling suds ready, by adding half a teacup of soap to each pail of water needed; now wring your clothes moderately from the soaking water, overhaul them, rub some soap on the dirty streaks or places, if any remain; roll them up and put them to boil or simmer, stirring and turning occasionally for 15 minutes (no longer, remember), rinse in two waters and hang up to dry: no bleaching or washboards are needed. The above method of washing positively will not injure the clothes. Now use your boiling suds for washing your colored clothes and save by it. Be sure your soap, borax and salsoda are thoroughly dissolved.

LIQUID BLUEING FOR CLOTHES.

Take best Prussian Blue, pulverized, 1 ounce; oxalic acid, also pulverized, ½ ounce; soft water, 1 quart; mix. The acid dissolves the blue and holds it evenly in the water so that specking will never take place. One or two tablespoons of it is sufficient for a tub of water, according to the size of the wash. This is far preferable to the blueing sold in stores, and is much cheaper.

BRITISH ENAMEL FOR SHIRT BOSOMS.

Melt together with a gentle heat, 1 ounce of white wax, and 2 ounces of spermaceti. Prepare in the usual way a sufficient quantity of starch for a dozen bosoms,—put into it a piece of British Enamel the size of a large pea, and in proportion for a larger ironing. It will give your clothes a beautiful polish.

HOW TO WASH BLANKETS.

Cousin Bess.

The process for washing blankets which I recommend, and have thoroughly tested, is so simple and easy, that the formidable task, which is the dread of every housewife, is not nearly as laborious **as to wash** and iron a few muslins:

For one pair of blankets dissolve one-half bar of soap; when thoroughly melted add 1 tablespoon of borax and 2 of ammonia. Add the mixture to a sufficient quantity of water (already softened with 1 tablespoon of borax) to cover two blankets. Let the blankets remain in the suds 1 hour, without rubbing. Rinse thoroughly and hang up, without wringing. The absence of rubbing and wringing prevents the **hardness and shrinking of the old process.**

TO WASH TOWELS WITH COLORED BORDERS.

Mollie.

To set the colors, let the towels soak in a pail of cold water containing 1 teaspoon of sugar of lead; let them remain ten minutes before washing. To make the colors look clear and bright, use pulverized borax in the wash-water, very little soap, and no soda.

OX-GALL SOAP.

Mrs. H. W. Beecher, in Christian Union.

Ox-gall soap is an excellent article to use in cleansing woolens, silks, or fine prints liable to fade. To make it, take 1 pint of gall, cut into it 2 pounds of common bar soap very fine, and add 1 quart boiling soft water. Boil slowly, stirring occasionally until well mixed, then pour into a flat vessel, and when cold cut into pieces to dry. When using, make a suds of it, but do not rub it on the article to be washed.

TO WASH CALICO.

Mrs. Simmons.

If you have dark calico to wash that you fear will fade or the colors run, put it in a pail and pour boiling water on. Let stand till cool enough to wring out. Then wash like any other. It is better to wash such a garment before it gets very badly soiled, or the hot water might set the dirt.

Use glue instead of starch for stiffening black dresses. It makes them shine like new and leaves no white spots as starch does. Or common flour starch colored with cold coffee answers very nicely.

TO REMOVE MILDEW OR TO BLEACH.
Mrs. A. S. J.

Dissolve a heaping tablespoon of chloride of lime in a pail of water. Dip in the goods and spread out to dry in the hot sun, without wringing. When dry repeat the process. This will take out the worst case of mildew and many other stains. The lime must be well dissolved.

TO RENEW BLACK WOOLEN GOODS OF ANY DESCRIPTION.
Mrs. A. S. J.

Have the articles well cleansed, then dip in a very strong blueing water. Hang up to dry without wringing. When nearly dry press on the side intended for the wrong side, and you will be astonished at the renovation that has taken place.

Lemon juice and salt mixed together and put on iron rust will take it out. Keep it in the sun. If one application does not do it try another.

A solution of oxalic acid in water will remove iron rust.

TO CLEAN LACES.

Mrs. N. W. Hammond, Clear Lake, Iowa.

Spread on a clean cloth a mixture of dry magnesia and baking powder. Lay the lace flat on it. Cover with the mixture. Roll up for a few days. Then take a dry, soft nail or tooth brush and brush well, especially the soiled spots. Shake out and the result will be more than you anticipate. White Shetland shawls may be "dry" rubbed in flour and cleaned beautifully.

TO WASH LACE MITTS.

May Owens.

If you want to color white lace mitts cream, wash the mitts with toilet soap, put them into a cup of cold coffee and let them stay about half a day. Do not iron them but put them on your hands and wear till they are dry.

Rub clear ammonia on silk that is discolored from perspiration. It will also restore the color of goods, particularly black, when the color has been destroyed by lemon-juice.

Any shade of blue can be made fast color by dipping the dress or fabric into enough soft water to saturate the material, in which a heaping teaspoon of sugar of lead has been dissolved. Then wash the fabric as usual.

TO WASH LINEN SUITS.

Fill a pail with old, dry hay; put scalding water on it and let it stand until the water is colored; then wash the linen in it, and it will look as nice as new.

TO REMOVE GREASE SPOTS.

Put half a teaspoon of hartshorn to half a teaspoon of alcohol; wet a bit of woolen cloth or soft sponge in it and rub and soak the spot with it, and the grease, if freshly dropped, will disappear. If the spot is of long standing, it may require several applications. In woolen or cotton, the spot may be rubbed when the liquid is applied, and also in black silk, though not hard. But with light or colored silk, wet the spot with the cloth or sponge with which the hartshorn is put on, patting it lightly. Rubbing silk, particularly colored silk, is apt to leave a whitish spot, almost as disagreeable as the grease spot.

Cloth may be bleached beautifully by hanging on a line when the sun shines and snow is on the ground. Snow bleaches more rapidly than grass.

To keep wash tubs a long time, do not put water inside the tub when the washing is done, but turn it bottom side up and cover the bottom with water. It will be found that it prevents the staves spreading apart at the top.

As soon as the ironing is done for the day the flat-irons should be taken off the stove. To leave them on without using takes the temper out of them.

HOW TO STARCH SHIRTS.

WITH COLD STARCH.

Allow a teaspoon of starch for each shirt. Use only enough water to wet the bosom, wristbands and neckband well. Dip in, squeeze out, roll up and iron in fifteen minutes, or let it lie longer if desired.

WITH HOT STARCH.

Dissolve two tablespoons of raw starch in a little cold water. Pour on boiling water till of the consistence of paste. Cook several minutes. Many laundresses make their starch early and leave it to cook slowly on the back of the stove for two hours or more. Others just merely cook it through. Put in a piece of enamel according to directions, or a few shavings from a sperm candle. In the absence of these use a tablespoon of kerosene to two quarts of starch. If the clothes are dry make the starch quite thin. Bear in mind that the hotter it is, the better the garment will iron and the stiffer it will be. Dip the bosom in and rub the starch through and through with the fingers. Pat it hard with the hand and be sure that every thread is wet with it. Treat the neck band and wristbands the same way. Let dry thoroughly. Then take a teaspoon of raw starch in a quart of cold water. When well dissolved dip the starched parts in quickly, squeeze out, lay smoothly and roll up hard. They may be ironed in an hour or two. Some shirt ironers dip in clear cold water, and some, again, in clear hot water, and all with equally good results. This can only be determined by experimenting.

HOW TO IRON A SHIRT.

First iron the back, then the shoulder pieces, then the neck band. Be very sure to iron the band on both sides equally smooth, that it may not irritate the neck of the wearer. Next, iron the sleeves. Then lay the wristbands out flat, rub with a clean white cloth, slightly dampened, and iron smoothly both sides, finishing with the right side. Next, iron the front. If you take a flat-iron that is just the right heat for the bosom, iron that before you do the plain front. Stretch the bosom on the shirt-board. Be very particular to pull it crosswise as well as lengthwise, to prevent wrinkles at the neck. Rub with a cloth to get off bits of starch that may stick to it. Iron carefully with a moderately heated iron.

If little blisters appear, dip the finger in water and dampen clear through. It will then come out on being ironed over, provided the starch has been rubbed entirely through. If it has not, then the blister will remain and there is no remedy for it. If a smooch or spot from a rusty or greasy iron appears on a polished bosom, do not give up and throw the garment into the wash, but immerse the bosom quickly in hot water, squeeze dry, stretch on the board, rub over with a clean dry cloth and iron again. But first take the iron and rub well in salt on a brown paper—especially the point and edges—and then with a little beeswax, wiping with a dry cloth. A polishing iron should be wrapped in fine paper and put away carefully after each ironing.

TO FOLD A SHIRT.

First roll the wristbands around so they will shape themselves to the wrist. It is much nicer than to leave them open and flat. Then lay the shirt on the table, bosom side down. Fold a pleat the whole length of the back, where the opening is in the back, in order to make the back and front the same width. Then fold one sleeve over from the shoulder, lap that side of the shirt the whole length from the edge of the bosom over towards the back. Do the other sleeve and side the same way. Iron the folds to make it look more neatly. Then double the bottom of the shirt up to the neck, folding just below the bosom, and with the bosom outside. Iron the fold and it is done. A quick drying by the fire will make the bosom stiffer.

TO RENOVATE BLACK SILK.

Brush and wipe off thoroughly with a cloth; lay flat on a table and sponge with hot coffee strained through muslin. Sponge it on the side intended for the right side; then pin to a sheet stretched on the carpet until it dries. Do not touch with an iron.

COMFORTER SHAMS.
Mrs. Orlena S. Matteson.

Fold a breadth of prints or muslin as long as the width of the comforter over the end next the face, fastening the edges with safety pins or a running baste. When soiled it is easily taken off and washed.

SICK-ROOM & NURSERY.

SIMPLE REMEDY FOR EXPELLING SUBSTANCES FROM THE NOSE.

Children frequently get beans, grains of corn, buttons or other substances up their noses. In such a case, have the child open its mouth, apply your mouth to it and blow rather hard. The obstacle will be expelled from the nostril.

EXCELLENT REMEDY FOR A CUT OR BRUISE OF ANY KIND.

Immerse the part in as hot water as can be borne until the pain and inflammation are relieved. Even in cases where amputation seems necessary from the terribly lacerated condition of a cut or bruised hand, it may be saved by keeping it in a basin of hot water for a few hours. Keep the water hot and do not give up until the inflammation has subsided.

TO REMOVE MOLES.

Tribune Home Department.

Apply nitric acid with a pointed stick three times,

letting a day elapse after each application. Then let it heal, and if not entirely gone try once more and success is assured.

EASIEST WAY TO CLEANSE A NURSING BOTTLE.

Buy five cents' worth of shot and put into the bottle with a little water and shake it well. Every bit of sour milk or curd will come off readily. Pour out the shot, rinse the bottle and keep the shot in a dish on the stove shelf or near the stove to dry, and it is ready for use the next time.

TO STOP EARACHE.

Turn the little sufferer on the side and from a height of a foot or more pour into the affected ear a small stream of water just as hot as you dare use. It will cause a momentary screaming but the pain will cease. I have tried this with a child two years old who was suffering intensely from earache, and the entire face and head seemed inflamed. It was not fifteen minutes before he fell asleep, and that was the last of the earache.

If the eyes are weak and it is troublesome to thread a needle, it may be helped by holding the needle over something white and then threading it.

SIMPLE TREATMENT FOR CROUP

As soon as the wheezing is heard apply the coldest water you can get to the neck and chest. Pound up some ice in a napkin and feed the child a little at a time with a teaspoon. Keep the cold compress on the throat and chest, and if persisted in for a short time relief will be almost certain to follow. At any rate, even if a physician is sent for, use these precautions, and nine times out of ten the disease will be checked at once. The chief difficulty in croup is in letting it get full headway. There is not an instant to lose.

STRANGE CURE FOR INFLAMMATORY RHEUMATISM.

A gentleman writes to a Pittsburgh paper that he was completely cured by handling doves. He procured a number and would stroke and play with them daily, and the result was a cure for him, but death to the doves. This distressing malady is so obstinate that one afflicted with it will resort to almost anything suggested.

A CURE FOR HYDROPHOBIA.

Jane Grey Swisshelm.

Take three ounces of the root of elecampane, stew it in a pint of new milk and give it, milk and all, to the patient in the morning while the stomach is empty; have him fast six hours after taking it; repeat the dose three times in three successive mornings, and the cure is complete. Several persons have written to say that it had been tried, on my recommendation, and with success. One man who had two children, and, I think, twenty hogs and cows bitten by a dog furiously rabid, had administered it to all, and six months after wrote to say that none of them had had any symptoms of hydrophobia. Elecampane is generally known as a powerful medicinal plant, and, as it has been successful, and doctors are powerless before this disease, I hope it will be promptly tried and if it fails I should like to know it.

CURE FOR NEURALGIA.

Mrs. Dr. Alma S. Bennett, Elk Point, Dakota.

1 drachm sal ammonia, 4 ounces camphor water. Take a teaspoon once in five minutes until relieved. This has proved a great boon to a large number of sufferers.

CURE FOR TOOTHACHE.

Procure a little plantago from a Homœopathic Pharmacy and take a dose every ten minutes if instantaneous relief does not follow.

LATEST REMEDY FOR BURNS.

Dampen some bi-carbonate of soda or common saleratus with water, and apply to the whole burnt surface. Cover with a cloth and keep it moistened. This is effectual in every case.

Twenty minutes in the smoke of wool or woolen cloth will take the pain out of the worst case of inflammation arising from any wound. All danger from lock-jaw will be removed if this remedy is resorted to.

HOW TO CURE FROZEN FEET.

Get some lumps of fresh lime and make a foot-tub full of strong whitewash mixture, and immerse the feet in it as hot as may be borne. This remedy is to cure that disagreeable itching that troubles one after having frozen the feet. This itching will come on night after night and season after season. The relief will be instantaneous. Let them remain half an hour in the whitewash. They will be shriveled up, but free from pain. Rub them briskly and great rolls of dead cuticle will peel off. Anoint with mutton tallow, put on some cotton stockings and go to bed. Repeat the application if necessary, but it will not require but two or three to effect a cure.

SMALL-POX AND SCARLET-FEVER CURE.

Sulphate of zinc, 1 grain; foxglove, (digitalis) 1 grain, half a teaspoon of sugar. Mix with 2 tablespoons of water. When thoroughly mixed add 4 ounces of water. Take a teaspoon every hour. Either disease, it is claimed, will disappear in twelve hours. Give a child a smaller dose. This cure has been the rounds of the press from the Atlantic to the Pacific and thousands of cures ascribed to it.

LIME WATER AND MILK.

1 wine-glass of lime water, 1 goblet of milk. Can be retained in the stomach when it rejects everything else. It may be taken as often as desired.

EGG LEMONADE.
A. B. S.

The white of 1 fresh egg, juice of 1 lemon, a teaspoon of sugar beat into a glass of water. Is a pleasant and nourishing drink in low fevers, dysentery, inflammation of stomach, pneumonia, etc.

BAKED MILK.

Put half a gallon of milk in a jar and tie it down with writing paper. Let it stand in a moderate oven 8 or 10 hours. It will then be like cream and is good for consumptives and invalids generally.

If necessary to use hops on a sick person, make two bags and fill with them, and heat in a steamer over hot water. This saves many a burnt hand and bad stain. Keep one heating while the other is in use.

A high London authority recommends for sleeplessness a breakfast cup of hot beef tea, made from half a teaspoon of Leibig's extract. It allays brain excitement. (Worth trying.)

For any female weakness or bearing down, the greatest relief may be afforded by an injection of water as hot as can be borne. This is a far better remedy than any manipulation can afford.

The practice of inserting cotton in an affected ear is a very pernicious one. A well known army surgeon in a western city suffered much while in the army from earache, and kept putting in cotton to exclude the air. He finally became deaf and suffered from various nervous ailments for years. A friend, also a physician, finally examined his ear, and took out over half a finger length of thick wads of cotton. His deafness disappeared and his nervous system was restored to health. This case is perfectly authentic. A high medical authority said that nothing smaller than the elbow should be put into the ear.

It is claimed by good authority that milk, eggs and tomatoes must be omitted in the diet of those suffering with piles. **In which event no medicine will be necessary.**

Pork is considered unwholesome by nearly all medical authorities, and especially so for women. The less they eat of it the better for their physical and mental good. Poultry is the best substitute, with good fresh fish—pike, perch or bass, once or twice a week.

COUGH SYRUP.

Mrs. L. S. H.

One pint of the best vinegar. Break into it an egg and leave in shell and all, over night. In the morning it will all be eaten except the white skin which must be taken out. Then add one pound of loaf sugar and take a tablespoon three times a day, for an adult. This is a most excellent remedy for a cough in any stage.

WHOOPING COUGH CURE.

Geo. Butler, Waukegan, Ill.

Olive oil 2 ounces, Jamaica rum 2 ounces, brown sugar 2 ounces, laudanum $\frac{1}{8}$ ounce. Melt the sugar in a little water and add the other ingredients. Give a teaspoon after every paroxysm. This is recommended by many families who have used it.

If poison of almost any kind has been swallowed it may be rendered harmless by swallowing immediately half a pint of sweet oil.

To make a mustard poultice that will draw and not blister, mix the mustard with white of egg.

TO STOP NOSE BLEED.

Excite a vigorous motion of the jaws by chewing something—either gum or paper. This is said to be effectual. It is certainly worth trying.

TO CURE WARTS.

Get from a Homœopathic Pharmacy a small vial of causticum. Give half a dozen pellets three times a day for three weeks and the warts will disappear.

[This I could not credit had I not tried it in my own family. The child's hands were literally covered with these excrescences and more were coming all the time. But this remedy effected a cure in less than a month. Ed.]

MILK FOR BABIES.

When milk has been set aside for the baby, use the

upper third. The curd or cheesy part falls to the bottom. The upper is more easily digested.

Let me persuade mothers to discard the tubes that come with nursing bottles. They are a fruitful source of infantile troubles. Many a baby has gone to its grave through their use. No matter how particularly they are cleansed, particles of sour milk will adhere to some parts of the rubber. Our best physicians are now advising against them. This is so serious a matter that it can not be argued too strongly. A rubber nipple placed over the mouth of the bottle is very convenient and comparatively safe. It should be kept in cold water when not in use, and the bottle filled with water.

I wish to urge upon every young mother the plan of putting babies to bed without rocking them. If there were but one child in the family and it were known to a certainty that it would be the last of that line, there might be sufficient excuse to devote one's time to rocking it to sleep. But when the first steps aside for the second, and the second is followed by the third and so on, the mother's time is too valuable to spend two or three hours a day in forming a habit which will be but an injury to the little one afterwards. If it has been put to sleep at the breast during the period of nursing, then let the plan be formed when it is weaned. Feed it, and when it is time for its nap fondle and kiss it as much as you like, but lay it down, cover it up, turn and leave it. It will sob and cry, and perhaps sit bolt upright or slide out of bed, but put it back, if for twenty times. It will not take very many of these persistencies until the habit of going to sleep alone and quietly will be formed, and all parties to the proceeding will pronounce themselves the better for it. Pray do not think your child is an exception. Children are very much alike, after all. Of course, it takes longer to conquer some than it does others, and strong wills are very perceptible even in babies of a few months old. Our aim is not to break the will, only to bend it in a direction to benefit itself.

And now a parting word to mothers—those of you who do your own work. Women who keep servants may skip this chapter. Save yourself. *Save yourself.*

SAVE YOURSELF.

In the first place, sit all you can. Sit down to prepare the vegetables for dinner. Sit down to wipe the dishes. Sit down to scour the knives and rub up the silver. Sit down to take up the ashes. Sit down to the ironing board and smooth the plain pieces. And here, before I forget it, let me say, get your steel knives plated and save yourself about six hours time each month. Once plated, they will keep bright with ordinary washing and wiping three or four years. Nothing will spot them. Vinegar or acid of any kind has no effect. It is called Stannil Plating. The cost is one dollar per dozen knives. It is an investment that pays a very large interest.

Now, about ironing. If your husband's night-shirt is smoothed in front and folded artistically, who is to know whether the back has been ironed or not? I'll venture to say, that he will not, unless you tell him. The same with your own night-dresses; and the childrens' drawers! Little romps, they soil them in less time than it takes to do them up. Let the gathers go. Iron the bottoms of the legs smoothly, and that is enough. You can iron six or eight pairs in this way, while otherwise, you would be working at two pairs.

Learn to slight where it will do to slight. Aprons and dresses should be done the very best that one knows how.

Sheets may be folded smoothly and have a weight put upon them; or, take one at a time, and lay it under the ironing sheet and iron over it for awhile. Then fold and put away and take another, until all are done.

It is not absolutely necessary to iron skirts, except for twelve or fifteen inches above the bottom.

Bear in mind, these are hints to those only, who need them. But there is enough in life that has to be done, without vexing our souls and wearing out our bodies over work that is not essential either to the happiness or well-being of our fellows.

The latest cure for soft corns is this: Wash and dry the foot thoroughly, and put on a sprinkling of dry sulphur night and morning for several weeks, and a cure is assured.

STIMULATING SPONGE BATH.

Dr. J. E. Gilman.

1 cup water, 1 cup alcohol, 1 tablespoon salt, 1 oz. aromatic spirits of ammonia. Very agreeable and stimulating.

DIET FOR THE SICK.

CHICKEN JELLY.

Cut a large chicken into very small pieces, break the bones, put into a stone jar, water-tight; set the jar into a kettle of boiling water and boil three hours; strain off the liquid and put in a cold place. Season with loaf sugar, salt, pepper, mace and lemon-juice.

ARROW ROOT JELLY.

Mix three tablespoons of arrow root with water or milk until perfectly smooth; boil the peel of one lemon in a pint of water until reduced one-half; take out the peel and pour in the dissolved arrow root; sweeten it, and boil five minutes.

RICE JELLY.

One-quarter of a pound of rice, half a pound of loaf sugar, water sufficient to cover it, spice or lemon peel. Boil the rice until all dissolves; strain and season; set away until cold.

SAGO JELLY.

Teacup of sago, one quart of water or milk, rind of lemon, nutmeg. Wash the sago well, and soak for three hours; boil it in the same water until transparent.

TAPIOCA JELLY.

Wash a teacup of tapioca through several waters, soak all night, and boil until transparent; add sugar and lemon juice while boiling, and put it away to cool when done.

INDIAN MEAL GRUEL.

Mix half a cup of Indian meal with a very little water, stir until perfectly smooth; to a pint and a half of boiling water salted, add the meal, stirring it in slowly; let it boil half an hour; it can be retained on the stomach when almost everything else is rejected.

BEEF TEA.

One pound of lean beef, cut very small, put into a wide-mouthed bottle, corked closely; set the bottle into a pan of water, and keep it boiling for two hours; strain the liquid and season. Chicken can be used the same way.

TAMARIND WATER.

One tumbler of tamarinds, one pint of cold water. Turn the water over the tamarinds, and let it stand an hour; strain it before using. Currant jelly or cranberry jelly can be used similarly.

FLAXSEED LEMONADE.

Three tablespoons of whole flaxseed to a quart of boiling water; let it stand until very thick; then strain it over the juice of one lemon and powdered gum arabic; sweeten to taste.

BEATEN EGG.

Beat a fresh egg very light, add a little sugar, and stir into a tumbler of milk.

RENNET WHEY.

One quart of milk, almost boiling, two tablespoons of prepared rennet, or a piece of rennet which has been soaked in water. Sugar to taste. Stir the rennet into the hot milk; let it stand until cool, and strain it.

MRS. GARFIELD'S BEEF EXTRACT.

1 ℔. lean beef cut fine, put into 1 pint cold water, add 6 drops muriatic acid. Mix thoroughly, let stand 1 hour, strain and press until all the liquid is extracted.

USEFUL HINTS.

Be sure to keep a vessel of water on the stove in sitting or sleeping rooms. It will not only ward off headaches, but will prevent furniture coming apart. A dry heat unglues and is ruinous to furniture.

TO PRESERVE BOOT AND SHOE SOLES.

Warm the soles and apply a heavy coat of warm coal tar. Dry it in, and apply two more coats before wearing them at all. Smear the edges as long as they will absorb the tar. They will wear like horn, and once giving it a trial will convince the most skeptical of its value. The tar costs but a few cents at gas works. Warm it on the stove in a tin dish.

Those using copper vessels for cooking should have them re-tinned once a year.

It is economy to use individual butter dishes at table.

Do not put salt on meat, to keep it. It destroys all tenderness. Put on pepper instead.

To keep ink from getting thick, put two or three cloves in a bottle. Sure.

TO PURIFY WATER.

A tablespoon of powdered alum will purify a whole hogshead of water. It precipitates all impurities. A teaspoon will only be required for several gallons.

To cut butter in cold weather, heat the knife, and all crumbling is avoided.

The very best thing to clean Plaster of Paris statuary is common white calcimine. It gives them the look of the purest white marble.

Pack horse-radish in a box of earth and grate it as it is wanted in winter.

Grease may be removed from a white floor by making a common hasty pudding of corn-meal and laying it on the spot until cold.

TO REMOVE GREASE FROM WALL PAPER.

Pulverize a common clay pipe, mix it with water into a stiff paste, lay it on very carefully, letting it remain over night. Then lightly brush it off.

INK STAINS

Can be removed from a carpet by freely pouring milk on the place, and leaving it to soak in for a time, then rub it so as to remove all ink, and scoop up remaining milk with a spoon: repeat the process with more milk, if necessary; then wash it off completely with clean cold water, and wipe it dry with cloths. If this is done when the ink is wet, the milk takes all stain out of woolen material instantly; but when it has dried, a little time is required.

ANOTHER.

As soon as the ink is spilled, put on salt, and cover well. Remove as fast as it becomes colored, and put on fresh. Continue this till the salt is white, sweep well, and no trace of ink will remain. Corn-meal used similarly on coal oil spots on carpets, will remove every particle, even if a large quantity has been spilled.

If a canary-bird loses its voice, hang a small piece of salt pork in the cage, first soaking it in warm water and sprinkling it with cayenne pepper.

Clean paint brushes by soaking in turpentine, and then washing in hot soap suds.

HAIR BRUSHES.

A few drops of hartshorn in a little water will clean a hair brush better than anything else, and will do no harm. If very dirty, rub a little soap on. After cleaning, rinse in clear water, and hang up by the window to dry. Do not let the bristles rest on any hard substance while wet. Tie a string round the handle and hang up.

TO CLEAN WILLOW FURNITURE.

Take a coarse brush dipped in salt and water and wash the furniture well, and then dry; the salt keeps it from turning yellow.

TO CLEAN WHITE FUR.

Take a clean piece of flannel, and with some heated bran rub the fur well, when it will be quite renewed. The bran should be heated in a moderate oven, for a hot oven will scorch and brown the fur. Oatmeal with no husks is preferable to bran. Dried flour will also answer.

PASTE THAT WILL KEEP A YEAR.

Mrs. A. L. B.

Dissolve a teaspoon of alum in a quart of warm water. When cold, stir in flour to the consistency of thick cream, beating up all the lumps. Stir in powdered rosin, and throw in a half dozen cloves to give it a pleasant odor. Have on the fire a teacup of boiling water; pour the flour mixture into it, stirring well all the time. In a few moments it will be of the consistency of mush. Pour it into an earthen or china vessel; let it cool, lay a cover on, and put it in a cool place. When needed for use, take out a portion and soften it with boiling water. Paste thus made will last twelve months. It is better than gum, as it does not gloss the paper, and can be written on.

A CEMENT FOR RUBBER.

Rubber boots may be repaired by a cement made as follows: Cut gutta-percha in small pieces, and dissolve it in benzine to a thin mucilage. Clean the rubber free from grease with benzine and a sponge, and apply the patch covered with the gutta-percha cement. The cement should be warmed by putting the bottle in hot water before it is used.

WATER-PROOF BLACKING FOR BOOTS AND SHOES.

One-half pound gum-shellac; cover with alcohol, cork tightly, and let stand three days, shaking occasionally. Then add a piece of gum-camphor the size of an egg. Let stand as above, and add one ounce of lampblack.

To remove a glass stopple from a bottle, hold a lighted match or candle to the neck of the bottle, and the heat will cause the neck to expand so the stopple will loosen.

If you wish to cut rubber of any kind, wet the knife. It prevents sticking.

TO PREVENT RUSTING OF TIN.

When new, rub over with fresh lard, and put in a hot oven and heat thoroughly. Thus treated, it may be used indefinitely in water or out, and remain bright.

TO PREVENT HONEY FROM CANDYING.

After being taken from the comb put it into a kettle and over the fire; boil it gently and as the scum rises skim it off until it becomes clear, when it can be turned into the vessel you wish to keep it in, where it will keep clear and fresh without candying.

To prevent incrustation of kettles, keep a clean marble or oyster shell inside, which will attract the particles of sand.

FOR CLEANING SILVER.

One-half ounce of prepared chalk, two ounces of alcohol, two ounces of aqua ammonia. Apply with cotton flannel, and rub with chamois skin.

Wash silver in very hot, clear water, and wipe dry with a soft towel, and you will have no need for silver soap, or any other preparation.

INDELIBLE INK.

C. S. Johnston, Harford, Pa.

Dissolve a couple of drachms of nitrate of silver and half an ounce of gum-arabic in a gill of rain-water. Add aqua ammonia, a few drops at a time, till you get the color the right shade. After marking, dry the goods near the fire, or in the sun. Don't mark new cloth before the dressing is washed out, but starch and iron the garment, then mark, and all creation will not be likely to wash it out. Keep it dark.

Do not put milk in tin vessels that have the tin worn off. It will blacken the milk and cause a discoloring of tea in which it is used that is very unpleasantly perceptible.

MARKING INK.

Dissolve asphaltum in oil of naptha, and it will answer for marking parcels, drying quickly and not spreading.

INVISIBLE INK.

Make a solution of nitrate of chloride of cobalt. It is made visible by warming the paper written upon.

Notice the right and wrong side of cotton cloth, when making up. It will keep clean longer, and be smoother for it.

To get rid of red or black ants, sprinkle salt over your shelves.

Salt is also a dead sure preventive of moths in carpets if put around under the edges when tacked down.

VERMIN EXTERMINATOR.

Hot alum water is a recent suggestion as an insecticide. It will destroy red and black ants, cockroaches, chinch-bugs, and all the crawling pests which infest our houses. Take two pounds of alum and dissolve it in three or four quarts of boiling water;

let it stand on the fire till the alum disappears; then apply it with a brush, while nearly boiling hot, to every joint and crevice in your closets, bedsteads, pantry shelves and the like. Brush crevices in the floor of the mop-boards, if you suspect they harbor vermin. It may be applied with a common small oil can by wrapping the hand in a cloth to prevent burning.

For vermin in children's heads, use Indian berries in bay-rum. They may be procured of druggists.

Equal parts of borax and white sugar will drive away roaches or Croton bugs.

TO GILD A HORSE-SHOE.

Cover first with a solution of gum-arabic, then sift on the bronze dust, which can be procured from a painter; or, mix bronze with mucilage and apply with a brush

To stop a chimney burning, shut all the windows and doors, to prevent a current of air, and throw a handful or more of salt in the fire.

TO STOP FROTHING OF CREAM.

Mrs. A. L. Beaumont.

To stop the frothing of cream and make butter come quick, to two gallons of cream put in three pints of boiling water out of the teakettle; it will come in ten minutes.

TO KEEP UP SASH WINDOWS.

Bore three or four holes in the sides of the sash, into which insert common bottle-cork, projecting about the sixteenth part of an inch. These will press against the window frames along the usual groove and by their elasticity support the sash at any height which may be required.

Soak mackerel in a stone crock. Tin rusts badly.

Using soap on babies' heads is a fruitful cause of the hair falling off. Abstain from it, and the hair is much more likely to remain.

To make the hair stay in crimp, take two cents' worth of gum-arabic, and add to it just enough boiling water to dissolve it. When dissolved, add enough alcohol to make rather thin. Let this stand all night, and then bottle it to prevent the alcohol from evaporating. This put on the hair at night after it is done up in paper or pins will make it stay in crimp the hottest day, and is perfectly harmless.

One can have the hands in soap suds with soft soap without injury to the skin, if the hands are dipped in vinegar or lemon-juice immediately after. Indian meal and vinegar or lemon-juice used on hands when roughened by cold or labor will heal and soften them. Rub the hands in this; then wash off thoroughly and rub in glycerine. Those who suffer from chapped hands in the winter will find this comforting.

CAMPHOR ICE.
Mrs. M. A. S.

Six drachms of camphor gum, half an ounce of white wax, one and a half ounces of spermaceti, three tablespoons of olive oil. Melt together.

TO BEAUTIFY TEETH.

Dissolve two ounces of borax in three pints of boiling water. Before it is cold add one teaspoon of spirits of camphor. A tablespoon of this with an equal amount of tepid water will cleanse the teeth from all impurities. It is also a very excellent wash for the hair.

SCENT POWDER.

One ounce each of coriander, orris root, rose leaves and aromatic calamus, two ounces of lavender flowers, one-fourth drachm of rhodium wood, five grains of musk, mix and reduce to powder. This scent is as if all fragrant flowers were pressed together.

WAXED FLOORS.
Mrs. G. B. L.

One pound of beeswax, one quart of benzine—the beeswax melted soft, to which add the benzine; put them over a stove, the fire closely covered, as benzine is highly inflammable; stir together until well mixed. These are the proportions; the quantity must depend upon the space to be covered. Apply to the floor, first making it clean, and rub in thoroughly. It shows the grain of the wood and makes a permanent polish, growing better by use and rubbing in. It is free of dust and clean.

POLISHED FLOORS

Should not be scrubbed or scoured, but simply swept with a broom covered with flannel. Polish twice a year.

PAINT FOR KITCHEN FLOOR.

Three pints of oil, one pint of dryer, three pounds of white lead, five pounds of yellow ochre, add a little turpentine.

A HOME-MADE CARPET.
Exchange.

Paste the floor of the room over with newspapers. Over this, paste wall paper of a pattern to look like carpet or oil-cloth. Put down as smoothly as possible, match it nicely where the widths come together. Use good flour paste. Then size and varnish it. Dark glue and common furniture varnish may be used. Place a rug here and there, and your room is carpeted.

TO PREVENT STAIR CARPETS FROM WEARING.

Stair carpets should always have a slip of paper, or a padding made of cheap cotton batting tacked in a cheap muslin put under them, at and over the edge of every stair, which is the part where they wear first. The strips should be within an inch or two as long as the carpet is wide and about four or five inches in breadth. A piece of old carpet answers better than paper if you have it. This plan will keep a stair carpet in good condition for a much longer time than without it.

To remove putty that has become hardened, heat an iron and apply to it. It softens, and may be removed very readily without injury to the window sash.

Mutton tallow for sores is made better by adding a little spirits of camphor.

To mend broken china, glass, marble, or common crockery, mix fresh slaked lime with white of egg until it becomes a sticky paste. Apply to the edges, and in three days it will be as firm as when new.

To stop a tooth cavity from bleeding, fill the cavity with Plaster of Paris made into a soft putty with water.

MAKE YOUR OWN COURT PLASTER.

Tack a piece of silk on a small frame. Dissolve some isinglass in water. When well incorporated, apply with a brush to the silk, let it dry, repeat it, and when dry, cover it with a strong tincture of balsam of Peru.

COLOGNE WATER.

One pint of alcohol. Add thirty drops of oil of lemon and thirty of burgamot. Shake well; then add half a gill of water. Bottle for use.

Lemons may be kept fresh for a long time by keeping in water in a covered vessel. Change the water every day or two.

FIRE KINDLERS.

Mrs. A. S. J.

To one pound of resin, put from two to three ounces of tallow; melt very carefully together, and when hot, stir in fine sawdust, and make very thick.

Spread it immediately about one inch thick upon a board. Sprinkle fine sawdust over the board first, to prevent sticking When cold, break into lumps one inch square. If made for sale, take a thin board, grease the edge, and mark it off into squares, pressing it deep, while yet warm, so it will break in regular shapes. This may be sold at a good profit. It takes but very little to kindle a fire.

Flowers that are quite withered may be revived wonderfully by immersing the stems in hot water. Not boiling, but so hot that the hand cannot be borne in it.

Here is a list of a few articles not always provided for a young housekeeper: Spice boxes, nest of grocery boxes, butter pat, larding needle, trussing needle, jelly or blanc mange moulds, waffle iron, cake **box, dredging boxes for flour, sugar, and salt; Victor potato masher.**

DYES.

COCHINEAL RED.

One and a half ounces of cochineal, two ounces of **cream** of tartar, two ounces of muriate of tin, one pound of yarn or cloth. Put the cochineal into water sufficient for the goods, and set over the fire. When warm, add the cream of tartar. When scalding hot, put in the tin. Boil the goods in the dye half an hour. Rinse in warm water. Color in brass. If the muriate of tin cannot be procured, use muriatic acid and pour on pieces of tin and let it remain over night. The muriate of tin will be formed and can be used in the morning.

PURPLE.

Ten cents worth of cudbear tied in a bag, one pail of water. Heat scalding hot. Dip the cloth into warm suds, and then into the dye for fifteen or twenty minutes. Dry, then wash in clean soap and water and rinse.

YELLOW FOR COTTON.

Six pounds of goods in water, to wet through. Nine ounces sugar-of-lead dissolved in the same quantity of water. Six ounces bichromate of potash in the same quantity of water. Keep separate. Dip the goods first into the sugar-of-lead water, then into the potash water, then into the sugar-of-lead water again. Dry. Rinse in cold water and dry again.

ORANGE FOR COTTON

Prepare a strong lime water—the stronger the

deeper the color. Pour off the water and boil. While boiling, dip the goods previously colored yellow into it. All these solutions are to be cold except the lime water. Will not fade.

MADDER RED.

One pound of yarn or cloth, eight ounces of madder, three ounces of alum, one ounce of cream of tartar. Five gallons of soft water. Let it boil with the alum and cream of tartar. Put in the goods and boil two hours. Take out, air, rinse in clean water. Pour the liquor away and prepare the same quantity of water as before. Put in the madder, broken fine. Heat the water. Enter the goods. Stir constantly one hour; then let it boil five minutes. Take out, rinse in cold water; then wash through three suds.

GREEN.

Five pounds of fustic, ten pounds of goods. Put the fustic into water and almost boil for twelve hours. Then remove the chips and put in the yarn or goods and boil half an hour. Take it out and add two pounds of alum. Dip again for half an hour. Take out the goods and stir into the dye one tablespoon of composition and let it boil, stirring it well together. Then dip till the color suits.

COMPOSITION.

Three ounces of good indigo, ground and sifted, one pound oil of vitriol, mixed gradually. Let stand one hour.

For pale blue, take a little composition in boiling hot water. Very nice for little children's stockings.

ORANGE.

Two and a half pounds of camwood, one pound of fustic. Boil in a brass kettle half an hour. Boil five pounds of goods one hour; cool, and add one ounce of blue vitriol and two quarts of copperas water to the dye and boil five minutes; then let cool and put in your goods till the color suits.

ANNATO.

Mrs. E. B. B.

Five ounces annato in a bag, three pails of strong soap suds or weak lye. Dip the cloth in suds previously prepared. Then put into the dye and boil until it takes the strength of the dye.

BLACK.

For a dress with overskirt, three ounces extract of logwood, one and a half ounces of blue vitriol. Dissolve the vitriol in water and the logwood in another water. Wet the goods thoroughly in warm water before putting into the vitriol water. Put a piece of copperas the size of a walnut into the logwood dye, and when the dye is hot, put in the goods, stirring and airing it for about half an hour, then dry it. Then wash immediately in hot soap suds in several waters, so that it will not crock. In the last water put a little salt. Wring it dry, roll up and let remain several hours before pressing.

[This recipe may be relied upon fully. Ed.]

RED.

Mrs. Hollett.

Three ounces solution tin, four ounces powdered cochineal. Boil the latter in water enough to cover the goods for about six minutes, then add the tin. Put in goods and boil half an hour. Rinse in cold water, and dry in the shade.

SEAL BROWN FOR WOOLEN GOODS.

For ten pounds goods take one pound catechu, four ounces blue vitriol, four ounces bichromate of potash; dissolve each in separate water; heat the goods one hour in the catechu water; wring out; dip and wring out of the hot vitriol water; leave them fifteen minutes in the potash water; dry and wash them.

BILLS OF FARE.

I offer here a few suggestions as helps to the practical housewife in her everyday cooking, and some hints for a child's party. If large lunch, dinner, or tea parties are given in the city, a caterer may be employed. If given in the country, the season of the year and the articles obtainable must enter into the bill of fare served.

SUGGESTIONS FOR A BILL OF FARE IN A PRIVATE FAMILY FOR ONE WEEK.

SUNDAY.

BREAKFAST.

Oatmeal Mush. Codfish Balls. Saratoga Potatoes. Waffles.
Maple Syrup. Coffee.

DINNER.

Roast Beef with Yorkshire Pudding.
Potatoes, Celery, Canned Vegetables and Pickles.
Blanc Mange. Apple Pie. Coffee.

SUPPER.

Thin bread and Butter. Cold Baked Beans. Sauce.
Cake. Tea.

MONDAY.

BREAKFAST.

Cracked Wheat and Milk.   Ragout of cold Roast Beef.
Baked Eggs.   Baked Potatoes.   Coffee or Chocolate.

DINNER.

Boiled Dinner.   Suet Pudding.

SUPPER.

Mush and Milk.   Buttered Toast.   Cheese.   Sauce.
Cake.   Tea.

TUESDAY.

BREAKFAST.

Fried Mush.   Maple Syrup.   Corned Beef Hash.
Hot Rolls.   Coffee.

DINNER.

Roast Pork.   Fried Apples.   Boiled Potatoes.   Tomatoes.
Lemon Pie.

SUPPER.

Potato Salad.   Cold Roast Pork.   Milk Toast.
Jelly Cake.   Jam.   Tea.

WEDNESDAY.

BREAKFAST.

Oatmeal Mush.   Codfish Stew.   Baked Potatoes.   Muffins.
Coffee or Chocolate.

DINNER.

Boiled Mutton. Boiled Rice. Mashed Potatoes. Turnips.
Baked Indian Pudding.
(Leave enough Potatoes for Breakfast.)

SUPPER.

Cold Mutton, sliced with Lemon. Russian Salad. Hot Biscuit.
Lemon Butter. Soft Gingerbread. Tea.

THURSDAY

BREAKFAST.

Rice Croquettes. Broiled Beefsteak. Lyonnaise Potatoes.
Laplanders. Coffee or Chocolate.

DINNER.

Calves' Liver Larded. Potatoes. Cold Slaw. Corn.
Mince Pie. Cheese.

SUPPER.

Chipped Beef. Sweet Pickles. Buttered Toast.
Preserves and Cake. Tea.

FRIDAY.

BREAKFAST.

Hominy. Egg Omelet. Saratoga Potatoes. Graham Gems.
Doughnuts. Coffee or Chocolate.

DINNER.

Fished Baked, Boiled or Fried. Potatoes. Cauliflower.
Tomatoes. Rice Pudding.

SUPPER.

Sardines with slices of Lemon. Banana or other Fritters.
Bread and Butter. Floating Island.
Sponge Cake. Tea.

SATURDAY
BREAKFAST.

Macaroni. Mutton Chops. Potatoes a la creme.
Griddle Cakes. Coffee or Chocolate.

DINNER.

Oysters or Fowls. Seasonable Vegetables. Berry Pie.

SUPPER.

Boston Baked Beans and Brown Bread. Lettuce.
Welsh rarebit. Cranberry Sauce. Cake. Tea.

SUGGESTIONS FOR BREAKFASTS FOR ANOTHER WEEK.

1st—Veal Cutlets. Johnny cake.
2d.—Liver and Bacon. Wheat Cakes.
3d.—Scrambled Eggs. Graham Muffins.
4th.—Tenderloins. Corn-meal Rolls.
5th.—Salt Mackerel. Bread Pancakes.
6th.—Ham and Eggs. Popovers.
7th.—Fried Chicken. Corn Cakes.

SUGGESTIONS FOR DINNERS FOR ANOTHER WEEK.

1st.—Roast Turkey. Pumpkin Pie.
2d.—Boiled Ham. Roll Pudding.
3d.—Veal Pot Pie. Cranberry Pie.
4th.—Beef a la mode. Queen of Puddings.
5th.—Parsnip Stew. Pie plant Pie.
6th.—Fish. Boiled Indian Pudding.
7th.—Beef Soup with Vegetables. Snow Balls.

HINTS FOR A CHILD'S PARTY.

Sandwiches, Panned Oysters, Small Pickles, Jelly Tarts, Vanities, Kisses, Comfits, Birthday Cake, Patty-pans, frosted, Whistles, Jelly Roll, Variety Cake, Pyramid Paste, Raisins, Nuts, Popcorn Balls, Seasonable Fruits, Lemonade, Ice Cream, Chocolate.

Also, make a pyramid cake of four loaves, baked in a two-quart, three-pint and a pint basin and a muffin ring, all put together and heavily frosted.

Give each little guest a tiny lace bag of confectionery tied with a ribbon. Either make the bag square, or in the shape of a stocking. If you have no lace, use mosquito netting, and tie it with bright worsted.

Festoons of popcorn are pleasing, and a tiny bouquet for each one is just the thing. The bouquet should be placed by the plate at table.

PYRAMID PASTE.

Make a rich pie paste and cut three or four sizes, fitting one upon another. Cut a bit from each except the bottom. Bake on a buttered paper laid on tins. Then place one above another with a different kind of preserve or jam in each. On top place green gages, currants, grapes, or other fruit.

WHISTLES.

½ cup butter.

1 cup sugar.

6 eggs. Beat butter and sugar to a cream; add the beaten eggs, and flour to make a stiff batter; drop little pats on a buttered paper, 3 inches apart; spread thin; bake in a pan 5 minutes, or until a light brown; lay on a sugared moulding board while warm, and roll on a stick; when cold, fill with jelly.

AN OLD CITIZEN TO A YOUNG WIFE.

You have noticed the monotony of existence, of course. With your husband the round of life is by days. With you it is three times as short, or by meals. Having to prepare food three times a day, indefinitely, you find that there are only narrow lines of eatables which can be relied on implicitly. However fancifully you may cook certain things, there are certain other articles which can be simply gotten up, and which will give better satisfaction. You will find that, for a steady jog over the course of life, yourself and husband will rely largely on good bread, butter, coffee, potatoes, beef, and mutton. These, with the fruits which come along already cooked, make up a constant bill of fare which puts strength in the limbs and, I think I may say, nobility in the heart. Now, if I can give any little hint about these cardinal elements of vitality which will hurry on your own conclusions, then any excuse for having opened my mouth at all will be sufficient.

Now, about bread. The old-fashioned way of making "sponge" is the best. If your mother or your grandmother can tell you how to make the bag of corn-meal stuff and then the more fleeting jar of wet, sour, and uncomfortable mixture, you will have light bread. The compressed yeast of the grocer never yields the same results. Again, if you live in the city, the "Vienna bread" will give you a good deal for your money. The true "Vienna bake" has cracks in the roll, where the gas has escaped in heating. This bread averages better than you or any other person with a small oven can bake. It never palls on the taste.

If you have but two in the family, it is cheaper than home-made bakings of equal freshness.

Butter, since the introduction of grease into its manufacture, has become a problem. You cannot be sure that you are getting what you pay for, except during June. In June, butter is grass-sweet, and cannot be mistaken. If your grocer have butter at 20, 23, and 28 cents, pay him 28 cents. When it comes June, observe whether or not the first-class butter is grass-sweet. If not, your grocer is a rascal, and you must make a change, at all hazards. If the grocer be honest, he buys honestly. His best butter will have little or no grease in it. I am inclined to think this particular grease brings on the fearful winter cholera which has made its appearance simultaneously with the invention of oleomargarine. "Butter" set in a north window, exposed to the outside air, will often turn deathly white if there be grease in it, and by "grease" I, of course, mean the rendering fat of the slaughter-houses. Let your grocer understand that you resent grease in your butter; he will then make an effort to save you from that trial. Never hesitate in paying the highest price. The grocer deals with many who want "first-class" butter at a second-class price. They do not wish to be told they are not buying the best. Let him know that you are not a hypocrite in this matter. Good butter is the cheapest for *all* purposes, principally on account of your health.

A good cup of coffee is a "square meal" in itself. I can tell you just how to get it. Buy the best grades. If you choose roasted, have the grocer grind it before your eyes. Buy only one pound. Keep it in a tin canister. You need two-thirds of a pound of Java and one-third of a pound of Mocha. Go to the tinner's with a common, large coffee-pot. This ought to cost 35 cents. Have the tinner make an inside can something like a "plug hat," with a rim. On the inside of the pot, a little below the top, set out four tin shoulders to catch the rim of the inside can as it is set down into the pot. The bottom of the inside can should almost touch the bottom of the pot. This ought to cost about 60 cents more. Now, this inside can should hold the grounds and water for four cups of coffee. To make the coffee, use a "top-full" and a little more of coffee, and pour water to fill up the inside can. Then hang the can in about three inches of water in the big pot. This will cook the coffee as glue or oatmeal should be cooked. The aroma will be in the coffee, instead of up stairs in the parlor or bedroom. If your husband has to hurry to business in the morning, get an oil-stove without any "extras," two wicks, and the coffee will cook in twenty minutes. That is about all an oil-stove is good for—to hurry up a coal stove. The coffee is done when the grounds have sunk. Put absolutely nothing in it save cream and sugar. This coffee will make your husband love you. It is a love-philter of the strongest nature. He will famish when he goes elsewhere for a meal.

Your potatoes should be of the same size, peeled and cooked in cold water to start with. When they are fairly done, drain them excellently well, and keep the cover off them carefully. Do not let the steam strike in. Mash and mash and mash. Potatoes will stand a great lot of salt, and butter is thrown away on them, I am afraid. You can try that, however; what I am after is a dish of dry, mashed potatoes, as flaky as the snow in a blizzard. Some people's potatoes are as slushy as hop yeast. Bah! There are housewives who *never* have wet mashed potatoes, and I have given you their exact mode. If yours continue sloppy, simplify the proceeding; do not slice; be careful about the steam, and mash and mash.

If you live in the city, beef is your constant trouble. It is beef, beef, beef, until you sicken at the sound and turn paler still at the thing itself. Your reliance here must be on the Lord and in the butcher. It is the butcher's interest to sell you all his bad beef first, and you will find him singularly true to his interests. It is a good idea to change butchers once a month. Buy, however, at the centre of the city, if possible. The nearer the limits the poorer the meat, as a rule. Good meat *costs*, but it is all eatable and digestible. I have found it the safest rule to buy the fattest. The marbled appearance sometimes cor s from the sudden fattening on swill of a tough old cow. A good porterhouse steak is as long as a large platter, and is grateful to the taste, tail, fat, and all. This, broiled on a big bed of coals, turned often, and dressed with melted butter, pepper, salt, slices of lemon and bits of parsely tops, is the best eating in the world. It makes one hungry to think of it! Never fry meat in lard. But you can neither get nor afford this big porterhouse regularly. Do the best you can with your own butcher. His meat is not fit to eat. Tell him so. He knows it. But it is up to the demand. That is what he is after. When you go down town you get where they have to have better meat. Never buy mutton far from the centre of the city, under any circumstances. Have your husband go into a shop where the sides hang. You want a young wether with three inches of fat on the outside. You want no bucks. The buck is high over the shoulders—a regular hump. No real wether ever grows high there. You don't want any ewe, either. Cut from the ribs about as many as you can eat—a hungry man can eat two or three. The butcher will clip off an inch of the fat. You will have a time of broiling it, for it will burn like oil. But, on the table, it is the healthiest meat in the world. It comes close to being the best tasting. The bad popular idea of mutton comes from the fact that the lean bucks all go toward the limits of the city to be sold. After a meal of gilt-edged broiled mutton, your husband will think this is quite a good world to get along in.

As for yourself, you thrive best on poultry. Have it often. You are, probably, not a bad judge of a chicken. Twist the wing. See that the butcher has not already twisted it before you! Never, my dear friend, trust your stomach with the digestion of pork. It is a meat unfit for female food. Use lard about as much as you use calomel. Cake is not so dyspeptic as pies. I think the butter makes the difference. Avoid frying for weeks at a time; make your own experiments in this matter. Our fresh water fish are the very best. In little lakes they get bad in July. In cold lakes they keep good longer. Keep honey, dried peaches, and prunes on hand, to regulate your bowels. Some people can eat neither milk nor cheese, nor eggs (except in March). Experiment with them. I have great doubts about tomatoes being fit for anything, except flavoring for gravies. I do not like the way they "turn" a silver spoon. People with the piles must not eat tomatoes at all. For centuries they were considered poisonous, and I guess they are. Cider is a magnificent thing for bad livers, catarrh, and other troubles which come from or cause bad action of the bowels. You see I mix medicine with meals; it cuts down doctors' bills.

It may strike you that I have laid out a costly schedule. You must, therefore, be the more economical elsewhere. I have calculated on shaving off a little from physic and tonic, in order to put it on the porterhouse and mutton chops. Physic and tonic come high. Think how much longer your husband will live on first-class food! Waste of such materials can have no fitting apology.

JOHN McGOVERN.

RELATION OF WEIGHTS TO MEASURES.

Wheat Flour, - -	3 cups make -	1 pound.
Corn Meal, - -	3½ cups make -	1 pound.
Granulated Sugar, -	1 large coffee cup makes	½ pound.
Dry Brown Sugar, -	1 large coffee cup makes	½ pound.
Good Firm Butter, -	1½ cups pressed down,	1 pound.
Eggs, - -	10 make - -	1 pound.
Raisins, - -	1 cup makes about	½ pound.

4 large tablespoons equal 1	wine-glass.
8 large tablespoons equal 1	gill.
2 gills are - -	½ pint.
2 pints are - -	1 quart.

BLACKBERRY CORDIAL.
Mrs. Wm. F. Carroll.

To one quart of blackberry juice add one pound white sugar, one tablespoon each of cloves, allspice, cinnamon and nutmeg. Boil all together fifteen minutes, add one wineglass **brandy or whisky**. Bottle while hot, cork and seal.

GAME.

Soups, - - - - - - *359* *Winged Game,* - - *366*
Four-Footed Game, - *361* *Frogs and Terrapin,* *372*

PREFATORY REMARKS.

For convenience, I have inserted "Green Turtle Soup" and "Frogs and Terrapin" in this chapter, and have placed the recipes alphabetically under the above headings.

Of course, there is no absolute rule for cooking. I have selected, from many sources, what I consider will be best received by the generality of ladies. The best variety possible is presented in the space allotted to the subject, and I feel confident that my readers will regard as plain common sense the directions here given.

My correspondence, to gain all the information possible on this subject, has elicited various opinions from many excellent cooks.

For instance, one lady says: "I find it safe, generally, to parboil wild meat, with a small pinch of soda in the water."

Another one writes: "Of one thing I am certain, and that is, that game should *never* be parboiled."

Another lady says: "I think wild meat should be soaked a short time in weak saleratus water."

And still another one says: "If wild ducks and prairie chickens are skinned, the necessity for parboiling is removed, for the skin is the tough part."

Very many good cooks unite in this, that, whenever practicable, game should be cooked without washing. Wiping with a damp cloth is deemed sufficient. If found necessary to wash, they do it as quickly as possible, and wipe dry. Game should never remain in water a moment longer than is essential to perfect cleansing, according to their theory.

A free current of air is very advantageous. A damp atmosphere is destructive to animal food.

After poultry or birds are dressed, hang them up by the head, not in the sun, but in a cool place. A piece of charcoal put into each bird will guard against tainting for several days. This is especially the case in warm weather, and almost a necessity. Even if they become tainted, it said that they can be restored to sweetness by being kept in sweet milk twenty-four hours. I have never had occasion to test this. The flavor of game is heightened by keeping it several days before cooking.

When venison is hung up it should be looked at and wiped off whenever it has gathered moisture. A thorough dusting with black pepper will preserve it from flies. Ginger will answer the same purpose.

Bear and buffalo meats are cooked substantially the same as beef or venison.

Dark meat is usually served rare; light meat, well cooked.

To the Hon. MONROE HEATH, ex-Mayor of Chicago, I am deeply indebted. He knows from personal experience how to kill, dress, cook, and serve, in the daintiest manner, nearly everything treated of in this entire chapter, and has very kindly revised it for me.

SOUPS

GAME SOUP.

In the game season, a good soup may be prepared at very little expense, and by using the remnants of different dishes a very agreeable flavor will be imparted. Take the legs and bones, break up, and boil in some broth for an hour, putting in all the meat from the breasts of birds left over. Boil four or five turnips and mash them fine. Then pound the meat up fine and pass through a fine sieve. Put the broth a little at a time through the sieve. Heat it all up together in the soup-kettle. Do not boil. Mix the yolks of three or four eggs with half a pint of cream. Stir into the soup and remove just as it comes to a boil, as boiling curdles it.

GREEN TURTLE SOUP.

Chop the entrails (some cooks do not use the entrails), bones, and coarse parts of the turtle meat, and put into a gallon of water, with a bunch of sweet herbs, a couple of onions, pepper and salt. This must cook slowly but constantly for four hours. In the meantime simmer the fine parts of the turtle and the green fat for an hour in half a gallon of water. This must be added to the above soup after straining the latter, at the end of the four hours' boiling. Thicken slightly with browned flour, then simmer all together for another hour. If there are eggs in the turtle boil them alone in clear water for three or four hours and add to the soup before serving. If not, use force-meat balls. At the last add the juice of one lemon. For the force-meat balls, take the yolks of two hard boiled eggs, rubbed fine with six tablespoons of chopped turtle meat, a tablespoon of butter and, if you have it, a little liquor of oysters. Season with mace, a pinch of cayenne, half a teaspoon o white sugar. Bind together with a raw egg. Roll into small balls, dip into beaten egg, then rolled cracker, fry in butter, and drop into the soup as directed above.

BROWN RABBIT SOUP.

Cut at the joints, dip in flour and fry in butter until a nice brown. Add three onions, also fried brown. To two large rabbits allow fully three quarts of water. Pour it over boiling hot. Add a teaspoon of salt; skim frequently and carefully until it looks clear. Add a sprig of parsley, three or four carrots, and season with whole peppercorns. Boil gently for half a day. Season more highly if necessary. Strain, let cool, skim off the fat. Heat it afresh for serving, and send to the table with croutons—as described on page 8.

RABBIT SOUP.

Sometimes rabbits or hares will be found very tough. They can then be made into soup that is excellent. Crack the bones of two rabbits and boil with a pound of ham or salt pork, cut up small. Chop three small onions and put in, with a bunch of sweet herbs. Stew in three quarts of water slowly for three hours. Season and strain. Thicken slightly with browned flour, wet with cold water. Add tablespoon of catsup and teaspoon of Worcestershire or some other kind of sauce.

FOUR-FOOTED GAME.

HARE—JUGGED.

After casing the hare, wipe off all loose hairs carefully, cut at the joints and fry brown. Season well with salt, pepper, chopped parsley, mace, nutmeg, cloves, grated lemon peel, and a sprig of thyme. Put a layer of this into a bean-pot or a small-necked jar, alternately with a layer of thin slices of bacon, until all are used. Pour one cup of water over, cover closely and set in a kettle of water. Boil three hours, or longer if the hare is old and tough. Skim out when done and strain the liquor. Take one tablespoon of flour and one tablespoon of butter and mix in a saucepan over the fire, and add the strained liquor. Let boil up and pour over the hare in a deep dish.

OPOSSUM.

Clean like a pig—scrape, not skin it. Chop the liver fine, mix with bread crumbs, chopped onion, and parsely, with pepper and salt; bind with a beaten egg and stuff the body with it. Sew up, roast, baste with salt and water. In order to make it crisp, rub it with a rag dipped in its own grease. Serve with the gravy made of browned flour. Serve it whole on a platter, and put a baked apple in its mouth. It is very nice stuffed with apples peeled and sliced. Opossum may be made into a very palatable stew.

RABBIT BOILED—LIVER SAUCE.

Truss for boiling; cover with hot water and cook gently about forty-five minutes if of medium size. In another vessel, boil the liver for ten minutes, mince very fine and put it back into the water in which it was boiled, season with butter, pepper, and salt, and thicken with flour, and pour over the rabbit.

Onion sauce is preferred by some, in which case boil some onions (three or four) in a separate vessel; change the water once, and when done drain and chop them. Then put them in a saucepan, sprinkle with one tablespoon of flour, put in butter size of an egg, with one cup of milk. Let it boil up and pour it over the rabbit

RABBIT—FRIED.

After skinning, cleaning, and wiping dry, fry the same as chicken. Unless known to be young and tender, it is a surer way to parboil before frying.

RABBIT PIE.

After cleaning, cut up like chicken and stew until tender. Then put into a deep pan with sides lined with pie paste. Thicken the gravy and add butter, pepper, and salt. Pour over and cover with crust. Bake about twenty minutes.

RABBIT—ROASTED.

After skinning and cleaning, lay in salt water for an hour. Parboil the heart and liver, mince them with a slice of fat salt pork, and add thyme, onion, pepper, and salt, and bread crumbs moistened with the water in which the giblets were boiled. Mix with a beaten egg. Stuff the rabbit with this, sew up, rub the body with butter or tie over it a few slices of fat pork. Put a cup or more of water into the drippingpan. Baste often. An hour will generally suffice for cooking it. Dredge with flour before taking it from the oven, and pour melted butter over. When browned remove to a hot dish, and to the gravy add lemon juice, a bit of minced onion, and one tablespoon of flour made smooth with the same quantity of butter. Let boil up and serve in a gravy dish. Garnish the rabbit with slices of lemon and sprigs of green parsley.

RABBIT STEW.

Skin, clean, and cut in small pieces a couple of rabbits. Let stand in cold salted water for an hour. Then put on to cook, in enough cold water to cover them, and boil till tender. Season with pepper and salt, and stir one tablespoon of butter with two tablespoons of flour made smooth into the gravy. Lemon juice is an improvement. If onions are liked, they may be boiled in a dish by themselves and added to the gravy before dishing up. Serve rabbits and gravy together on a large platter.

RACCOONS—*See Woodchucks*.

SQUIRREL PIE.

Clean one pair of squirrels and cut into small pieces. Wipe off with a damp cloth. Put into a stewpan with two slices of salt pork, and water to nearly cover. Cook until half done. Season it well and thicken the gravy. Pour into a deep dish, cover with pie crust, and bake thirty minutes.

Squirrels may be fried, broiled, or stewed, like chickens or rabbits.

VENISON—ROAST.

The haunch is the choicest piece for roasting. Wipe off with a damp cloth. Rub over with butter or lard. Then cover the top and sides with a thick paste of flour and water half an inch deep. Lay a coarse paper over all and put to roast with one cup of water in the dripping pan. Keep the oven well heated. Baste every fifteen or twenty minutes with butter and water. Twenty minutes before serving remove the paste and paper, and dredge with flour, and baste with butter until of a light brown. Pour in one pint of water and make a thickened gravy as for roast beef or pork, adding a pinch of cloves, nutmeg, cayenne, and a few blades of mace. Strain before sending to table, and two tablespoons of currant jelly may be added if you have it. Have dishes very hot.

The shoulder is also a good roasting piece, but need not be covered with the paste as in the above directions.

VENISON SAUSAGE.

Take equal quantities of old salt pork and bits of raw venison. Chop fine. To each pound of chopped meat add 3 teaspoons of sage, 1½ of salt, and 1 of pepper. Make into flat cakes and fry with no other fat, as that in the sausage is sufficient.

VENISON STEAKS.

These take longer to cook than beef, but should be similarly broiled or fried. When done, place in a hot dish with a gravy made of butter the size of an egg for each pound of steak, mixed with a spoon of flour, and properly seasoned with pepper and salt. Jelly may be added if desired. Before serving, cover the platter and set in a hot oven for five minutes or less. Have the plates well heated, as venison cools quickly. At table, it is nice to place a bit of jelly on each piece served.

VENISON STEW.

Cut the meat into small pieces. Inferior cuts will make a very good stew. Boil for a couple of hours. Season to suit the taste. Add potatoes peeled, and if large, cut in two. When done, skim out, thicken the gravy and pour over.

WOODCHUCKS AND 'COONS.

Mrs. E. E. Bower, Erie, Pa.

In Pennsylvania, woodchucks are called groundhogs and esteemed a great delicacy, and really a fine fat one well roasted is not to be despised. To cook either ground-hogs or 'coons, parboil for thirty minutes, to take off the wild smell; then rub well with salt and pepper, and roast in a quick oven at first, allowing the fire to cool gradually. Thirty minutes to every pound is a safe rule. Young animals need no parboiling. Where fireplaces are used, people cook them on a spit over a drippingpan.

NOTE.—It is said that if a cup of vinegar be put on the stove while cooking onions, their smell will not be noticed.

It is the common custom of cooks to give claret as one of the adjuncts in cooking wild meat. It is a mere matter of taste. It can be made very palatable without it, and I prefer not to give it.

WINGED GAME.
CRANES AND HERONS.

May be broiled or stewed, like chickens. They make a very fine soup. Dress and joint five or six and put into a pot with an equal weight of beef cut small; slice one onion (or more); add a slice of salt pork; water to cover. When tender add, if you have them, about a pint of oysters with their liquor. Crabs cleaned and quartered may be substituted. Let simmer till done. Then just before serving stir in one or two tablespoons of gumbo.

DUCKS—CANVAS BACK—ROASTED.

Pluck, singe, draw, and wipe well. Do not wash; let the duck retain its own flavor as far as possible. Leave the head on to show its species. Roast without stuffing, twenty-five or thirty minutes, in a hot oven, after seasoning with pepper and salt. Baste with butter and water. A bit of cayenne and a tablespoon of currant jelly added to the gravy are an improvement. Thicken with browned flour.

DUCKS—WILD—ROASTED.

Prepare for roasting the same as any fowl. Parboil for fifteen minutes with an onion in the water, and the strong fishy flavor that is sometimes so disagreeable in wild ducks will have disappeared. A carrot will answer the same purpose. Stuff with bread crumbs, a minced onion, season with pepper, salt, and sage, and roast until tender. Use butter plentifully in basting. A half hour will suffice for young ducks.

DUCKS—WILD—STEWED.

Cut the ducks into joints; pepper, salt, and flour them; fry in butter in a stewpan. Then cover with a gravy made of the giblets and some bits of lean veal if you have it, all minced and stewed in water until tender. Add a minced onion or shallot, a bunch of sweet herbs, and salt and pepper, with a bit of lemon peel. Cover closely and let them stew until tender. About thirty minutes will suffice. Skim out the ducks; skim and strain the gravy, add a cup of cream or milk and a beaten egg, thicken with browned flour, and let boil up once and pour over the ducks. The juice of a lemon may be added, or lemon may be sliced and served on the ducks.

LARKS.

Clean, wipe dry, brush them over with the yolk of egg, roll in bread crumbs and roast in a quick oven for ten or fifteen minutes. Baste with butter and keep them covered with bread crumbs while roasting. Serve the crumbs under the birds and lay slices of lemon on them.

PARTRIDGE—BROILED.

Pick and draw; divide through the back and breast, and wipe with a damp cloth. Season highly with pepper, salt, a bit of cayenne, and broil over a clear, bright fire. It will broil in fifteen or twenty minutes. When done, rub over with butter. Serve with lemon.

PARTRIDGE PIE.

After dressing, divide in halves, rub with pepper, salt, and flour, sprinkle in parsley, thyme, and mushrooms if you happen to have them. Put a slice of ham and two pounds of veal cut up small at the bottom of the bakingdish. Then add the partridges and pour over them a pint of good broth or gravy. This is for about four birds. If you have no gravy, use water with a large spoon of butter. Cover with rich piepaste. Leave an opening in the center and bake about one hour.

PIGEON PIE.

Do not stuff pigeons, but cut them in four pieces; parboil and place in layers with egg and pork or bacon, as directed for quail pie. Use plenty of butter to make the gravy rich. Bake same as quail pie.

PIGEONS—POTTED.

Pluck and clean. Take a cracker, an egg, a piece of butter or chopped suet the size of an egg, and a pinch of sage or sweet marjoram. Make into small balls and put one with a thin slice of salt pork into each bird. Lay the birds close together in a pot. Dredge well with flour. Put in a good tablespoon of butter to six birds. Cover with water. Cover the pot and stew slowly for about an hour and a half. Less time if young and very tender, and longer if old. Serve on a large platter with the gravy. Other birds may be potted the same way.

PILAU OF BIRDS.

Boil two or three large birds or half a dozen small ones with a pound of bacon, in water enough to cover well. Season it with salt. When tender take them out with a little of the liquor. Into the remainder put two pounds of clean washed rice. Cook until done, keeping closely covered. Stir into it a cup of butter, and salt to taste. Put a layer of the rice in a deep dish. On this lay the birds with the bacon in the middle. Add the liquor. Then cover them all with the rice that is left. Smooth it and spread over it the beaten yolks of two eggs. Cover with a plate and bake fifteen or twenty minutes in a moderate oven.

PLOVER.

Clean and truss. Lay in a pan and season with salt and pepper. Rub over with butter and cook in a quick oven. A piece of fat bacon or salt pork laid on each one gives a good flavor. Toast some bread and put a piece under each bird before it is quite done. Baste with butter and water. Take up on a hot platter, a bird on each slice of toast, and serve together.

PRAIRIE CHICKENS.

Fry as directed for chickens, or broil like quail or partridge. Or cook as on page 51.

QUAIL—BROILED.

Clean and split down the back. Wipe carefully, season well with salt and pepper, and place on a gridiron over a clear, hot fire. Turn, and when done lay on a hot dish; butter well, and serve on buttered toast.

QUAIL PIE.

Clean, truss, and stuff the quail. Parboil for ten or fifteen minutes. Line the sides of a deep pan with rich piepaste. In the bottom put a couple of slices of salt pork or bacon cut into small pieces. Then some slices of hard boiled eggs, with butter and pepper. Then the quail with a sprinkling of minced parsley. The juice of a lemon is an improvement. Put bits of butter rolled in flour over the birds, then a layer of slices of egg and bits of pork. Pour in the water in which they were parboiled, and cover with the piepaste, leaving an opening in the center. Bake about an hour.

QUAIL—STEAMED.

Steam quail until nearly done, then roast in the oven to a nice brown, basting often with melted butter in water. Serve on buttered toast. Very nice.

REED BIRDS, RAIL BIRDS, AND SNIPE.

May be cooked precisely as plovers, or they may be broiled and served with toast the same as quail or partridge.

WOODCOCK.

Many excellent cooks do not draw them, asserting that the trail should be left in, even by those who do not like it, and removed after it is served. They claim that the flavor of the bird is much impaired if the trail is taken out before cooking. It looks rather plausible, as they are said to live by suction, have no crop, and a stomach only the size of a bullet. The trail, head, and neck are regarded as great delicacies by epicures. For my own eating, I could not cook them without drawing.

TO BAKE.

Divide down the back, put in a pan in the oven, salt and pepper them and baste with melted butter. Garnish with slices of lemon.

TO BROIL.

Split down the back, wipe with a damp cloth, and broil over a clear fire. Rub on butter, pepper and salt when done. Serve on a hot platter and help each person to half a bird.

TO ROAST.

Clean, draw, and stuff with simple bread crumbs well seasoned with pepper and salt and moistened with sweet cream or melted butter. Sew them up. Tie a small, thin slice of salt pork around the bird. Place in a drippingpan and baste with butter and water. Put slices of buttered toast under them before taking up, and serve with them.

GENERAL REMARKS.

If hares and rabbits are young, the ears tear easily and the claws are sharp and smooth. They will keep good a week or two in cold weather.

In venison the fat should be bright, clear, and thick; the cleft of the hoof close and smooth. The more fat there is, the better the quality of the meat.

Ducks with plump breasts and pliable feet are best.

Partridges with dark-colored bills and yellow legs are best, and if allowed to hang a few days are much finer in flavor, and more tender.

Pigeons to be good will not bear being kept, as the flavor leaves them. So they must be eaten fresh.

Plovers are scarcely fit for any cooking but roasting. They should feel hard at the vent, as that indicates their fatness. If very stale, the feet will be very dry, and they should be discarded.

FROGS AND TERRAPIN

FROGS.

Skin them as soon as possible. The hind legs are usually the only part used, although the back is good eating. Fry or broil the same as chickens — or fricassee them.

TERRAPIN OR TURTLE.

Plunge the turtle while yet alive into boiling water. When life is extinct, remove the outer skin and the toe nails. Then rinse well, and boil in salted water until perfectly tender. Then take off the shells, remove the gall and sand bag carefully, and clean the terrapin thoroughly. Next cut the meat and entrails into small pieces, saving all the juice, put into a saucepan without water and season to your taste with salt, cayenne and black pepper. Add for each terrapin, butter the size of an egg made smooth with a tablespoon of flour. A few tablespoons of cream should be added last. Many persons add the yolks of three or four hard boiled eggs just before serving. While cooking it should be stirred very often—and must be dished up and eaten very hot.

INDEX.

SOUP.

Croutons	8	Louisiana Plantation	12
German soup balls	8	Mock turtle	14
Noodles	8	Onion	11
To clarify soup	14	Oxtail	12-17
Soup stock	15	Pea	16
Bean soup	12	Pea hull	11
Brunoise	16	Potato	11
Brown fish	20	Pottage a la Reine	17
Chestnut	13	Puree of fish	18
Chicken	12	Puree of game	18
Cream of spinach	19	Rabbit	360
Confederate army	13	Rice	9
Economical	10	Tomato	10
Game	359	Turtle, green	359
Giblet	13	Very cheap	16
Gumbo	9	White	9
Julienne	20	Wrexham	19

FISH.

Baked fish	23-28	Fried smelts	28
Boiled fish	22	Fritters, clam	25
Boiled, Hollandaise sauce	29	Frogs and Terrapin	22, 372
Boiled Pike, egg sauce	27	Halibut	27
Broiled fish	31	Lobster salad	26
Chowder, fish	21	Mackerel, fresh	25
Chowder, clam	24	Mackerel, salt	25-26
Codfish balls	24	Pickled fish	26
Codfish stew	23	Potted fish	31
Croquettes, fish	29	Stuffing for fish	23
Eels	22	Shadroe, with oysters	28
Fried fish	22	Turbans of fish	30

OYSTERS.

Cream	35	Sauce, with Turkey	35
Fricassee	32	Soup	33
Fried	34	Steamed	34-35
New way of cooking	36	Scalloped	35
Omelet	38	Stew	34
Pickled	36	Stew, Virginia	33
Pie	38	Stewed with celery	37
Roast, Mobile	33	Stuffed	36

EGGS.

Baked 40	Omelet, orange 44
Boiled 39	Panned 41
Broiled ham and eggs.. 40	Pickled 44
Chowder 41	Poached 41
Fried 41	Proper way to cook..... 40
Fried ham and eggs.... 40	Salad, hot egg......... 42
Omelet 42-43	Scalloped 42
Omelet celestine....... 44	Scrambled 39
Omelet saccharine...... 43	To color for Easter..... 45
Omelet souffle 43	To keep.............. 44

FOWLS.

Boning, directions for... 52	Duck, curry of 53
Chicken, boned........ 52	Ducks, roast.......... 51
Chicken fricassee....... 50	German relish......... 51
Chicken, fried......... 50	Goose, roast 51
Chicken salad.......54-55	Poultry, roast......... 46
Chicken smothered..... 50	Prairie chicken......51-369
Chicken stew 48	Pressed veal or chicken.. 54
Chicken pate 54	Stuffing for ducks 51
Chicken pie........... 49	Suggestions........... 45
Chicken pot pie 49	Turkey, roast 48
Cutting up chicken..... 46	Winged Game 366

MEATS.

Beef *a la* mode....... 64	Dumplings Rhode Island 78
Beef, corned, pressed ... 79	Game 361
Beef, cure for 80	Ham, cold boiled 63
Beef, dried............ 77	Ham, cure for......... 80
Beef heart 66	Ham, to stuff a 62
Beef heart equal to tongue 66	Head cheese 78
Beef pickle 80	Kidneys, deviled....... 71
Beef pot roast 59	Kidneys stewed 71
Beef, pressed 62	Lamb and green peas... 61
Beef roast............ 63	Lamb, blanquette of.... 60
Beefsteak broiled....... 68	Lamb, leg of, roast..... 65
Beefsteak, fried........ 67	Liver 71-72
Beefsteak round........ 68	Mutton boiled......... 61
Beefsteak with onions.. 67	Mutton chops......... 70
Beef stew............. 66	Mutton macaroni...... 61
Beef tongue 69	Mutton roast......... 65
Beef, stuffed and pressed 62	Mock duck 67
Boiled dinner 58	Parsnip stew.......... 60
Calves' liver larded 72	Pigs' feet............. 79
Calves' liver stewed.... 72	Pig roast 69

MEATS—Continued.

Pork and liver	72	Spareribs	69
Pork roast	64	Souse	79
Pork tenderloin	70	Sweet breads	75 77
Pork, to keep fresh	78	Veal cake	76
Pork pie, English	65	Veal cutlets	70
Tripe fried	77	Veal loaf	76
Tripe curried	74	Veal marbled	76
Tripe potted	74	Veal roast	65
Sausages	78	Veal stuffed	76
Sausage, creole	73	Yorkshire pudding	63

HASH.

Beef patties	83	Minced mutton	85
Corned beef hash	82	Minced veal	83
Croquettes, chicken	84	Meat omelet	86
Croquettes, veal	83	Philadelphia scrapple	82
Fricassee of beef	85	Ragout	86
Meat dumplings	85	Union hash	83
Meat pies	84	Wonders	82

SAUCES, SALADS, AND CATSUPS.

Caper butter	91	Salad, potato	98
Caramel	86	Salad, Russian	97
Catsup, cucumber	92	Salmagundi	97
Catsup, currant	92	Sauce, asparagus	89
Catsup, gooseberry	93	Sauce, celery	83
Catsup, tomato	91-92	Sauce, Chili	90
Catsup, walnut	91	Sauce, drawn butter	83
Curry powder	87	Sauce, Dutch	83
Dressing for cabbage	94-5-6	Sauce, maitre d' hotel	96
Dressing for cold slaw	95	Sauce, mushroom	89
Dressing, lettuce	96	Sauce, plain white	96
Green tomato soy	94	Sauce, Queen of Oude	90
Mustard for table use	88	Sauce Robart	89
Salad dressing, French	94	Sauce, Tartar	96
Salad dressing, Mayonaise	94	Spiced currants	93
Salad, orange	97	Spiced peaches	93

VEGETABLES.

Artichokes, Jerusalem	112	Cabbage cream	111
Asparagus	114	Cabbage fried	110
Beans, Boston baked	108	Cabbage, with sour cream	111
Beans and pork, baked	108	Cabbage spiced	110
Beans, Lima	107	Carrots, spring	112
Beets	112-113	Cauliflower	109
Cabbage *a la* Cauliflower	111	Egg plant fried	115

VEGETABLES—Continued.

Egg plant stuffed	115	Potatoes cooked dry	100
Green corn	105	Potatoes Lyonnaise	102
Green corn baked	106	Potatoes mashed	100
Green corn patties	106	Potatoes Parisian	103
Green corn pudding	106	Potatoes quirled	100
Green corn, to can	106	Potatoes Saratoga	101
Greens	109	Potatoes scalloped	103
Green peas	114	Rice	105-112
Macaroni	113	Sauerkraut	110
Macaroni and cheese	113	Squash	116-117
Onions boiled	116	Succotash	107
Parsnips	114	String beans	107
Potato balls	102	Tomatoes baked	104
Potato croquettes	102	Tomatoes fried green	104
Potato pudding	101	Tomatoes scalloped	104
Potato puffs	102	Tomatoes stewed	103
Potatoes *a la* cream	101	Tomatoes and rice	105
Potatoes baked	101	Turnips	113
Potatoes boiled	99	Vegetable oyster	115

BREAD.

Bread, brown, Pauline's	124	Gems, Graham	132 133
Bread, brown, Pris'n Miss.	123	Hoe cake	132
Bread, brown, Vermont	124	Johnnycake	131-132
Bread, election	124	Laplanders	133
Bread, Graham	122	Muffins	134
Bread, Indian	123	Muffins, corn	135
Bread making, easy	120 121	Muffins, hominy	133
Bread, milk yeast	121	Muffins, mush	135
Bread, rye and Indian	123	Muffins, raised	134 135
Biscuit, baking powder	129	Mush	136
Biscuit, Graham	130	Mush, oatmeal	134
Biscuit, Kentucky	130	Pancakes, bread	127
Biscuit, Mobile	129	Popovers	137
Biscuit, raised	125	Puffs, French	137
Biscuit, soda	129	Rolls	125
Biscuit, sour milk	130	Rolls, corn-meal	126
Cakes, buckwheat	136	Rolls, flannel	127
Cakes, corn-meal	127	Rolls, Saratoga	126
Cakes, griddle	137	Rusk	124
Corn-meal cakes	128-131	Toast, French	128
Crumpets	137	Toast, milk	128
Fritters, rice	135	Waffles	130-131
Gems, corn	133	Yeast	118-119-120

PIES, DUMPLINGS, AND SHORTCAKES.

Pie crust	139--140	Huckleberry pie	150
Apple pie	144	Lemon pie	147--148
Apple custard pie	148	Lemon potato pie	147
Apple pot pie	153	Mince pie	140--141
Apple puffs	154	Mince pie, summer	142
Apple dumplings	153-154	Orange pie	146
Brother Jonathan	153	Peach pan dowdy	155
Berry pie	146	Peach pie	149
Cherry pie	150	Pumpkin pie	144
Cocoanut pie	145	Raisin pie	146
Cranberry pie	149	Rhubarb pie	143
Cream pie	145	Squash pie	145
Custard pie	149	Shortcake, hard winter	153
Currant pie	150	Shortcake, orange	152
Dewdrop apples	155	Shortcake, peach	152
Dried apple pie	143	Shortcake, strawberry	151
Emancipation pie	148	Sweet potato pie	145
English currant pie	144	Tomato pie	142--143
Fried pies	151	Wild grapes for pies	143

CAKE.

Relation of Weights to Measures, page 356.

Baking powder	157	Fruit cake	166--167
Frosting and icing	159--160	Fruit cake, English	166
Frosting, without eggs	159	Fruit cake, poverty	168
Glazing for cake	159	Fruit cake, village	169
1, 2, 3, 4, cake	182	Gold cake	173
Almond cake	186	Graham cake	187
American Home cake	178	Graham composition cake	188
Angels' food	161	Hollis cake	181
Birthday cake	180	Jenny Lind cake	183
Black cake	165	Lady cake	172
Buckeye cake	183	Lemon cake	180
Cake without eggs	186	Love cake	165
Chocolate cake	162--163	Marble cake	174
Coffee cake	160	My wedding cake	170
Corn starch cake	174	Plymouth cake	183
Cream cake	172	Porcupine cake	176
Cup cake, clove	171	Pound cake, Presidential	179
Cup cake, sister Julia's	184	Pound cake, prize	179
Dakota cake	185	Pound cake, Quaker	177
Delicate cake	181	Pound cake, soda	178
Everyday cake	161	Pound cake, white	178
Feather cake	175	Pork cake	170

CAKE—Continued.

Raisin cake 168	Surprise cake 176
Roll jelly cake 184	Walnut cake........... 182
Silver cake 173	Watermelon cake....... 176
Snowball cake.......... 177	White cake, Cora Bell's . 164
Spice cake 171	White citron cake 186
Sponge cake 173-184	White fruit cake........ 164
Sponge cake, molasses .. 185	White sponge cake 185

LAYER CAKE.

Almond nagout 188	Lemon jelly cake....... 195
Caramel cake 193	Pineapple cake......... 189
Chocolate cake......... 191	Orange cake 196
Confectioner's cake..... 194	Ribbon cake............ 193
Cream cake, Belvidere .. 196	Rocky mountain cake .. 191
Cream cake, cocoanut .. 190	Strawberry cake 191
Dolly Varden cake..... 189	Variety cake........... 195
Fig cake............... 191	White Lincoln jelly cake. 190
Gilt edge cake......... 194	White mountain ditto... 192
Ice cream cake......... 192	

COOKIES.

Christmas cookies...... 197	Windom cookies 198
German cookies........ 197	Lincoln cookies........ 198
Ginger cookies..... 200-1-2	Hunt cookies 199
Ginger jumbles 202	MacVeagh cookies..... 199
Ginger snaps 202	Kirkwood cookies...... 199
Garfield cookies........ 198	James cookies.......... 199
Arthur cookies......... 198	Molasses cookies 200
Blaine cookies.......... 198	Sea foam.............. 200

DOUGHNUTS.

Amalgamation 204	Lazy doughnuts 204
Andover wonders 205	Raised doughnuts 203
Doughnuts 203-204	Rissoles 205
Fried cakes............ 204	Spanish ruffs.......... 205
—— without shortening. 205	

GINGER CAKES.

Gingerbread 206-207	Soft molasses cake...... 208
Ginger drops........... 208	Spice cakes 208
Old-fashioned gingerbr'd 206	Training-day gingerbr'd 207
Soft gingerbread 207	

MISCELLANEOUS.

Chocolate comfits 211	Cream puffs............ 213
Cocoanut comfits 212	Drop sponge cake 209
Cream cake 210	Edinboro' cheese....... 214

MISCELLANEOUS—Continued.

Florentines 213	Scalloped cheese 216
Fondu 215	Seed cakes............212
Fritters 217	Sugar kisses..........215
German coffee cake.....210	Tea cakes.............209
Hermit cakes 212	Thin bread and butter ..216
Knickerbocker crullers..211	Vanities 211
Maccaroons............214	Varieties 213
Molasses tea cakes......210	Welsh rarebit..........215
Ragamuffins 211	Widows' cake..........210

CUSTARDS, ICES, AND CREAMS.

A chartreuse of oranges.224	Lemon honey..........228
Almond blanc mange ...225	Lemon ice.............229
Angel cream...........222	Oak Park cream.......222
Apple cream...........223	Orange cream 219
Baked custard.........228	Orange ice 229
Bavarian cream 220	Oriental cream........220
Chocolate ice cream 219	Pineapple cream.......228
Charlotte Russe........225	Pineapple water ice....229
Coffee cream 219	Royal French cream....221
Cream Charlotte 223	Souffle vanilla.........225
Floating island........227	Strawberry cream 220
Fruit blanc mange......226	Tapioca cream.........223
Fruit creams...........221	Vanilla cream..........219
Ice cream..............218	Velvet cream 222
Isinglass blanc mange...226	Whipped cream 223
Lemon extract.........229	

PUDDING SAUCES.

Beehive sauce..........230	Jelly sauce.........232-233
Cream sauce 233	Liquid sauce 231-232
Hard sauce 231	Vinegar sauce.........232

PUDDINGS.

Apple pudding.........234	Boiled Indian 238
Apple fruit 234	Buckeye 239
Apple tapioca..........234	Cabinet 239
Apple sago 234	Cassava 240
Baked Indian 237	Cassel................236
Baked suet 237	Cream tapioca 241
Baking-day 235	Cocoanut 241
Baroness 233	Cottage 241
Batter 235	Currey 242
Bird's nest.........235-236	Hen's nest 242
Boiled bread..........239	Kiss..................242

PUDDINGS—Continued.

Minute 243	Rich tapioca 247
My favorite........... 243	Rolled pudding 247
Old English Plum 243	Sago 247
Orange 244	Sally Lunn 248
Pineapple pudding..... 245	Snow Balls 248
Plum duff............. 245	Snow pudding.......... 248
Puff 246	Suet pudding...238-249-250
Queen of puddings 246	Thickened rice......... 250
Rice Handy Andy...... 246	Wash-day pudding 250
Rice, without eggs..... 246	

FAMILY BEVERAGES.

Blackberry wine 261	Iced tea............... 254
Bottled soda water..... 255	Imperial 255
Breakfast cocoa........ 254	Lemon beer............ 258
Cocoa shells 255	Orange syrup.......... 260
Coffee 252	Pineapple syrup........ 260
Coffee for festivals..... 253	Premium chocolate..... 254
Corn beer 256	Portable lemonade 259
Cream beer 256	Raspberry nectar 255
Cream nectar 262	Rhubarb wine 261
Cream soda........... 258	Sham champagne 259
Currant wine 260	Spruce beer 257
Egg chocolate 254	Strawberry sherbet..... 259
Elderberry wine........ 261	Sugar beer 256
Ginger pop 257	Tea 251
Ginger wine 262	Vienna coffee.......... 253
Home brewed beer 258	

PRESERVES AND JELLIES.

Apple butter........... 266	Crab apple jelly 276
Apple croutes.......... 269	Crab apple preserves.... 270
Apple jelly 267	Cranberry preserves 275
Apple jelly for layer cake 278	Cranberries 279
Apple marmalade 272	Currant jelly........... 277
Apple meringue 269	Damson plum preserves. 276
Apple preserve......... 265	Dried apple jelly....... 278
Baked sweet apples..... 268	Dried apple sauce...... 279
Boiled apples 268	Fried apples 269
Canned pumpkin 279	Gelatine jelly 278
Canned small fruits..... 264	Grape jelly 271
Canning in glass jars.... 264	Grape preserves........ 270
Citron preserves........ 271	Jam 263
Compote of apples, baked 267	Jellied apples 268
Cooking apples......... 266	Lemon butter.......... 265

PRESERVES AND JELLIES—Continued.

Michigan fruit jellies ...267	Preserved melon rinds ..271
Peach marmalade.......272	Quince marmalade 273
Peach preserves 275	Quince preserves.......272
Pear preserves 275	Strawberry preserves ...270
Plum butter............273	To keep grapes fresh ...279
Plum tomato preserves..276	Wild plum jelly 274
Preserved cherries......275	Wild plum marmalade ..274
Preserved orange peel...274	Wild plum preserves....273

PICKLES.

Cauliflower 284	Plums, grapes or peaches 290
Cherries 283	Red cabbage 284
Chow chow............287	Ripe cucumbers........289
Cucumbers........281-282	Silver skin onions......283
Green tomatoes....284-285	String beans 282
Higdom 285	Sweet crabapples 290
Jackson pickles 285	Sweet cucumbers...288-289
Mangoes...............286	Sweet tomatoes........288
Mixed pickles 288	Walnuts 283
Nasturtions 283	Watermelon rinds......289
Piccalilli 286	Whole pears..........290

VINEGAR.

Apple 292	Honey 291
Clover bloom 291	Potato 292
Currant 292	

CONFECTIONERY.

Butter scotch 295-296	Iced currants 298
Chocolate caramels.....294	Lemon taffy 297
Chocolate cream candy.297	Maple caramels 294
Chocolate cream drops..298	Mock Nongat..........296
Cocoanut caramels.....295	Molasses candy 293
Cream candy 295	Peach paper 298
Delicious tomato figs...297	Snow candy 295
Fruit candy 296	

PICNICS AND LUNCHES.

Suggestions 299

THE LAUNDRY.

A few plain truths......300	How to starch shirts...309
Ammonia for silk.......307	How to iron a shirt....310
A recipe worth $1,000..301	How to fold a shirt....311
British enamel for shirts 304	How to wash blankets ..304
Comforter shams.......312	Liquid bluing..........303
Glue for black dresses...306	Oxgall soap 305

THE LAUNDRY—Continued.

Patent washing soap ...302
To bleach 306-309
To clean laces 307
To make blue a fast color 308
To preserve wash tubs...309
To remove iron rust 307
To remove mildew..... 306
To remove grease spots.308
To renovate black silk..312
To renew black woolens.306
To wash calico 305
To wash lace mitts 307
To wash linen suits 308
Towels—colored borders 305

SICK ROOM AND NURSERY.

Blackberry cordial......356
Burns 317
Care of babies 322
Cough syrup...........320
Croup 315
Cuts or bruises.........313
Earache 314
Female weakness.......319
Hydrophobia 315
Lime water and milk ...318
Lemonade, egg 318
Milk for babies 321
Mothers, save yourselves 323
Mustard poultice 321
Neuralgia..............316
Nosebleed 321
Nursing bottles 314-322
On the care of the ear ..319
Piles 320
Poison antidote 321
Rheumatism 315
Sleeplessness 319
Small-pox—scarlet fever.318
Stimulating sponge bath 325
Sure cure for soft corns.325
Toothache 316
To cure frozen feet 317
To remove moles.......313
To thread a needle easily 314
To use hops in sickness.319
Warts 321
Whooping-cough cure ..320

DIET FOR THE SICK.

Arrow-root jelly........326
Baked milk 318
Beef tea...............327
Beaten egg 327
Chicken jelly...........325
Flaxseed lemonade 327
Indian meal gruel 326
Rennet whey 328
Rice jelly..............326
Sago jelly 326
Tamarind water 327
Tapioca jelly...........326
Mrs. Garfield's beef extr't 328

USEFUL HINTS.

A cement for rubber....332
Articles for housekeeping 342
A home-made carpet ...339
Camphor ice 338
Cologne water 341
Court plaster..........341
Fire kindlers..........341
Improved mutton tallow 340
Indelible ink 334
Invisible ink 335
Marking ink 335
Paint for kitchen floor ..339
Paste that keeps a year .332
Polished floors 339
Scent powder 338
Silver polish 334
To beautify teeth......338
To clean hair brushes...331
To clean paint brushes..331
To clean white fur......331

USEFUL HINTS--Continued.

To clean willow furniture 331	To remove glass stoppers 333
To cut rubber easily.... 333	To remove old putty.... 340
To get rid of ants...... 335	To remove ink stains... 330
To get rid of moths..... 335	To revive flowers....... 342
To gild a horse-shoe.... 336	To stop a bleeding tooth 341
To keep hair in crimp .. 337	To stop burning chimney 336
To keep lemons fresh... 341	To stop frothing of cream 336
To keep up windows.... 337	To stop honey candying . 333
To mend broken china.. 340	To soften chapped hands 337
To preserve shoe soles.. 328	To take grease from paper 330
To preserve stair carpets 340	Vermin exterminator... 335
To prevent incrustation. 334	Vermin in child's head.. 336
To prevent rusting of tin 333	Waterproof blacking.... 333
To purify water........ 329	Waxed floors 339

DYES.

Anatto 345	Orange 345
Black 345	Orange for cotton 343
Cochineal red.......... 342	Purple 343
Composition 345	Red 346
Green 344	Seal brown for woolens.. 346
Madder red............ 344	Yellow for cotton 343

BILLS OF FARE.

Entire for one week . 347-8-9   Dinners another week ..350
Breakfasts another week. 350

A CHILD'S PARTY.

Bill of fare 351	Pyramid paste 351
Hints 351	Whistles 351

AN OLD CITIZEN TO A YOUNG WIFE

A chapter of valuable suggestions 352

WEIGHTS AND MEASURES.

The relation of weights to measures................ 356

GAME.

SOUP.

Game soup 359
Green turtle soup 359
Brown rabbit soup 360
Rabbit soup............360

FOUR-FOOTED GAME.

Hare, jugged...........361
Opossum 361
Rabbit, broiled 361
Rabbit, fried 362
Rabbit pie 362
Rabbit, roasted........362
Rabbit stew 363
Raccoons 363
Squirrel pie...........363
Venison, roast 364
Venison sausage.......364
Venison steaks.........364
Venison stew 365
Woodchucks 365

WINGED GAME.

Cranes 366
Herons 366
Ducks, roasted 366
Ducks, stewed 367
Larks 367
Partridge, broiled 367
Partridge pie..........367
Pigeon pie 368
Pigeons, potted........368
Pilau of birds 368
Plover 369
Prairie chickens 369
Quail, broiled 369
Quail pie 369
Quail, steamed 370
Reed birds, rail birds and snipe 370
Woodcock 370-371

FROGS AND TERRAPIN.

Frogs 372
Terrapin or turtle 372

www.ingramcontent.com/pod-product-compliance
Lightning Source LLC
Chambersburg PA
CBHW032018220426
43664CB00006B/284